Spanish
Phrase Book
&
Dictionary

Berlitz Publishing
New York   Munich   Singapore

Contacting the Editors
Every effort has been made to provide accurate information in this publication, but changes are inevitable. The publisher cannot be responsible for any resulting loss, inconvenience or injury. We would appreciate it if readers would call our attention to any errors or outdated information. We also welcome your suggestions; if you come across a relevant expression not in our phrase book, please contact us: Berlitz Publishing, 193 Morris Avenue, Springfield, NJ 07081, USA. E-mail: comments@berlitzbooks.com

Second Printing: November 2007
Printed in Singapore

Publishing Director: Sheryl Olinsky Borg
Senior Editor/Project Manager: Lorraine Sova
Editors: Emily Bernath, Monica Bentley, Maria Amparo Pérez Poch
Translation: Publication Services, Inc., Laura F. Temes
Cover Design: Claudia Petrilli
Interior Design: Derrick Lim, Juergen Bartz
Production Manager: Elizabeth Gaynor
Cover Photo: © GoodShoot
Interior Photos: p. 14 © Royalty-Free/Corbis; p. 18 © Emin Kuliyev, 2006/Shutterstock, Inc.; p. 20 © European Central Bank; p. 23 © Wikipedia Commons/GNU Free Documentation License; p. 38 © Roman Krochuk, 2006/Shutterstock, Inc.; p. 42 © Chicadelatele/Flickr.com; p. 55 © Luca Vanzella; p. 60 © Alfredo Hisa; p. 63, 111, 123 © Miguel Raurich/Iberimage.com; p. 82 © Pilar Echevarria, 2006/Shutterstock, Inc.; p. 91 © felixfotografia.es, 2006/Shutterstock, Inc.; p. 93 © jhiker/Flickr.com; p. 109 © Allan Danahar/Digital Vision/Getty Images; p. 117 © Corbis/Fotosearch.com; p. 120, 155 © Stockbyte Platinum/Alamy; p. 126, 134, 144, 162, 183 © Heinz Hebeisen/Iberimage.com; p. 150 © Steve Yager, 2006/Shutterstock, Inc.; p. 153 © Royalty-Free/Corbis; p. 155 © Stockbyte/Fotosearch.com; p. 158 © 2006 JupiterImages Corporation; p. 161 © David McKee, 2006/Shutterstock, Inc.; p. 164 © Terry Harris/Alamy

Contents

Pronunciation 7
Consonants 7

Vowels 9
How to Use This Book 10

Survival

Arrival and Departure 13
ESSENTIAL 13
Passport Control and
    Customs 13

Money and Banking 15
ESSENTIAL 15
ATM, Bank and Currency
    Exchange 15

Transportation 19
ESSENTIAL 19
Ticketing 20
Plane 22
    Getting to the Airport . 22
    Check-in and Boarding 23
    Luggage 25
    Finding Your Way 25
Train 26
    Questions 27
    Departures 27
    Boarding 27
Bus 28
Subway [Underground] . . 29
Boat and Ferry 30
Bicycle and Motorcycle . . 31
Taxi 31
Car 33
    Car Rental [Hire] 33

Gas [Petrol] Station . . 34
Asking Directions . . . 35
Parking 36
Breakdown
    and Repairs 37
Accidents 37

Accommodations 38
ESSENTIAL 38
Finding Lodging 39
At the Hotel 40
    Price 42
    Questions 42
    Problems 44
    Check-out 45
Renting 46
    Household Items 47
Hostel 48
Camping 49

**Internet and
Communications** 50
ESSENTIAL 50
Computer, Internet
    and E-mail 51
Phone 54
    On the Phone 55
Fax 56
Post Office 57

Food

Eating Out 59
  ESSENTIAL 59
  Restaurant Types. 60
  Reservations and
    Questions. 60
  Ordering 62
  Cooking Methods 63
  Special Requirements . . . 64
  Dining with Kids 65
  Complaints 65
  Paying. 66
  Market 67
  Dishes, Utensils and
    Kitchen Tools 69

Meals. 70
  Breakfast. 70
  Appetizers [Starters]/
    Tapas. 72

Soup 73
Fish and Seafood. 74
Meat and Poultry. 76
Paella 79
Vegetables 80
Spices and Staples 82
Fruit 83
Cheese 84
Dessert 85

Drinks 87
  ESSENTIAL 87
  Non-alcoholic
    Drinks 88
  Aperitifs, Cocktails and
    Liqueurs. 89
  Beer 90
  Wine 90

Menu Reader. 91

People

Talking. 108
  ESSENTIAL 108
  Communication
    Difficulties 109
  Making Friends 110
  Travel Talk. 111
  Relationships. 112
  Work and School 113
  Weather 113

Romance 114
  ESSENTIAL 114
  Making Plans 115
  Pick-up [Chat-up]
    Lines 116
  Accepting and
    Rejecting 116
  Getting Physical. 117
  Sexual Preferences 117

Fun

Sightseeing 119
  ESSENTIAL 119
  Tourist Information
    Office 119
  Tours 120
  Sights 120
  Impressions 122
  Religion 122

Shopping 123
  ESSENTIAL 123
  Stores 124
  Services 125
    Spa 126
    Hair Salon 127
  Sales Help 128
  Preferences 129
  Decisions 129
  Bargaining 130
  Paying 130
  Complaints 131
  Souvenirs 131
  Antiques 134

Clothing 134
  Color 135
  Clothes and
    Accessories 136
  Fabric 137
  Shoes 137
  Sizes 138
Newsstand and
  Tobacconist 138
Photography 139

Sports and Leisure 139
  ESSENTIAL 139
  Spectator Sports 140
  Participating 141
  At the Beach/Pool 142
  Winter Sports 144
  In the Countryside 145

**Culture and
Nightlife** 147
  ESSENTIAL 147
  Entertainment 148
  Nightlife 149

Special Needs

Business Travel 152
  ESSENTIAL 152
  Business
    Communication 152

Travel with Children 155
  ESSENTIAL 155
  Fun with Kids 155

Basic Needs for Kids . . . 156
Babysitting 157
Health and
  Emergency 157

For the Disabled 158
  ESSENTIAL 158
  Getting Help 159

Resources

Emergencies 161
  ESSENTIAL 161

Police 161
  ESSENTIAL 161
  Lost Property and Theft . 163

Health 164
  ESSENTIAL 164
  Finding a Doctor 164
  Symptoms 165
  Health Conditions 166
  Hospital 167
  Dentist 167
  Gynecologist 168
  Optician 168
  Payment and
    Insurance 168
  Pharmacy [Chemist] . . . 169
    ESSENTIAL 169
    Dosage
      Instructions 170

  Health Problems . . . 171
  Basic Needs 171

Reference 172
  Grammar 172
  Numbers 178
    ESSENTIAL 178
    Ordinal Numbers . . . 179
  Time 180
    ESSENTIAL 180
  Days 181
    ESSENTIAL 181
  Dates 182
  Months 182
  Seasons 183
  Holidays 183
  Conversion Tables 184
    Mileage 184
    Measurement 184
    Temperature 185
    Oven Temperature . . 185
  Related Websites 185

Dictionary

**English-Spanish
Dictionary** 186

**Spanish-English
Dictionary** 206

Pronunciation

This section is designed to make you familiar with the sounds of Spanish using our simplified phonetic transcription. You'll find the pronunciation of the Spanish letters and sounds explained below, together with their "imitated" equivalents. This system is used throughout the phrase book; simply read the pronunciation as if it were English, noting any special rules below.

Underlined letters indicate that that syllable should be stressed. The acute accent ´ indicates stress, e.g. **río**, <u>ree</u>-oh. Some Spanish words have more than one meaning. In these instances, the accent mark is also used to distinguish between them, e.g.: **él** (he) and **el** (the); **sí** (yes) and **si** (if).

There are some differences in vocabulary and pronunciation between the Spanish spoken in Spain and that in the Americas—although each is easily understood by the other. This phrase book and dictionary is specifically geared to travelers in Spain.

Consonants

Letter	Approximate Pronunciation	Symbol	Example	Pronunciation
h	1. as in English	b	**bueno**	<u>bwen</u>·noh
	2. between vowels as in English, but softer	b	**bebida**	beh·<u>bee</u>·dah
c	1. before e and i like th in thin	th	**centro**	<u>thehn</u>·troh
	2. otherwise like k in kit	k	**como**	<u>koh</u>·moh
ch	as in English	ch	**mucho**	<u>moo</u>·choh

Letter	Approximate Pronunciation	Symbol	Example	Pronunciation
d	1. as in English	d	**donde**	<u>dohn</u>·deh
	2. between vowels and especially at the end of a word, like th in thin, but softer	th	**usted**	oos·<u>teth</u>
g	1. before e and i, like ch in Scottish loch	kh	**urgente**	oor·<u>khehn</u>·teh
	2. otherwise, like g in get	g	**ninguno**	neen·<u>goo</u>·noh
h	always silent		**hombre**	<u>ohm</u>·breh
j	like ch in Scottish loch	kh	**bajo**	<u>bah</u>·khoh
ll	like y in yellow	y	**lleno**	<u>yeh</u>·noh
ñ	like ni in onion	ny	**señor**	seh·<u>nyohr</u>
q	like k in kick	k	**quince**	<u>keen</u>·theh
r	trilled, especially at the beginning of a word	r	**río**	<u>ree</u>·oh
rr	strongly trilled	rr	**arriba**	ah·<u>rree</u>·bah
s	1. like s in same	s	**sus**	soos
	2. before b, d, g, l, m, n, like s in rose	z	**mismo**	<u>meez</u>·moh
v	like b in bad, but softer	b	**viejo**	<u>beeyeh</u>·khoh
z	like th in thin	th	**brazo**	<u>brah</u>·thoh

Letters f, k, l, m, n, p, t, w, x and y are pronounced as in English.

Vowels

Letter	Approximate Pronunciation	Symbol	Example	Pronunciation
a	like the a in father	ah	**gracias**	grah·theeyahs
e	like e in get	eh	**esta**	ehs·tah
i	like ee in meet	ee	**sí**	see
o	like o in rope	oh	**dos**	dohs
u	1. like oo in food	oo	**uno**	oo·noh
	2. silent after g and q		**que**	keh
	3. when marked ü, like we in well	w	**antigüedad**	ahn·tee·gweh·dahd
y	1. like y in yellow	y	**hoy**	oy
	2. when alone, like ee in meet	ee	**y**	ee
	3. when preceded by an a, sounds like y + ee, with ee faintly pronounced	aye	**hay**	aye

---

i With over 400 million Spanish speakers worldwide, Spanish is the third most widely spoken language in the world and the official language of 21 different nations. Over 17 million people in the United States speak Spanish as their native language, and it is one of the official languages of the United Nations. Spanish is the fourth most popular language on the internet, behind English, Japanese and German. Below are estimated numbers of Spanish speakers around the globe.

Central America: 55 million
North America: 112 million
South America: 190 million
Spain: 40 million

How to Use This Book

These essential phrases can also be heard on the audio CD.

Sometimes you see two alternatives in italics, separated by a slash. Choose the one that's right for your situation.

Essential

I'm on *vacation [holiday]/business*.

Estoy aquí *de vacaciones/en viaje de negocios*. ehs·<u>toy</u> ah·<u>kee</u> deh bah·kah·<u>theeyohn</u>·ehs/ehn <u>beeyah</u>·kheh deh neh·<u>goh</u>·theeyohs

I'm going to...

Voy a... boy ah...

I'm staying at the... Hotel.

Me alojo en el Hotel... meh ah·<u>loh</u>·khoh ehn ehl oh·<u>tehl</u>...

You May See...

ADUANAS	customs
ARTÍCULOS LIBRES DE IMPUESTOS	duty-free goods
ARTÍCULOS QUE DECLARAR	goods to declare

Bicycle and Motorcycle

I'd like to rent [hire]...

Quiero alquilar... <u>keeyeh</u>·roh ahl·kee·<u>lahr</u>...

– a bicycle

– una bicicleta <u>oo</u>·nah bee·thee·<u>kleh</u>·tah

– a moped

– un ciclomotor oon thee·kloh·moh·<u>tohr</u>

– a motorcycle

– una motocicleta <u>oo</u>·nah moh·toh·thee·<u>kleh</u>·tah

How much per *day/week*?

¿Cuánto cuesta por *día/semana*? <u>kwahn</u>·toh <u>kwehs</u>·tah pohr <u>dee</u>·ah/seh·<u>mah</u>·nah

Words you may see are shown in *You May See* boxes.

Any of the words or phrases preceded by dashes can be plugged into the sentence above.

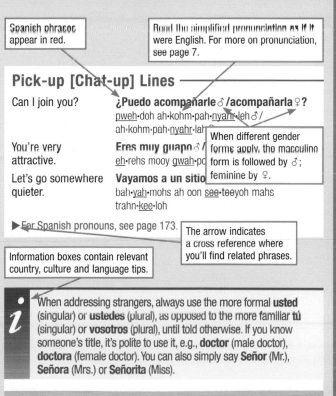

Spanish phrases appear in red.

Read the simplified pronunciation as if it were English. For more on pronunciation, see page 7.

Pick-up [Chat-up] Lines

Can I join you?
¿Puedo acompañarle ♂/acompañarla ♀?
pweh·doh ah·kohm·pah·nyahr·leh ♂ /
ah·kohm·pah·nyahr·lah ♀

When different gender forms apply, the masculine form is followed by ♂; feminine by ♀.

You're very attractive.
Eres muy guapo ♂ /
eh·rehs mooy gwah·po

Let's go somewhere quieter.
Vayamos a un sitio
bah·yah·mohs ah oon see·teeyoh mahs
trahn·kee·loh

▶ For Spanish pronouns, see page 173.

The arrow indicates a cross reference where you'll find related phrases.

Information boxes contain relevant country, culture and language tips.

i When addressing strangers, always use the more formal **usted** (singular) or **ustedes** (plural), as opposed to the more familiar **tú** (singular) or **vosotros** (plural), until told otherwise. If you know someone's title, it's polite to use it, e.g., **doctor** (male doctor), **doctora** (female doctor). You can also simply say **Señor** (Mr.), **Señora** (Mrs.) or **Señorita** (Miss).

You May Hear...

Hablo muy poco inglés.
ah·bloh mooy poh·koh een·glehs

I only speak a little English.

Color-coded side bars identify each section of the book.

Expressions you may hear are shown in *You May Hear* boxes.

▼ Survival

▶ **Arrival and Departure**   13
▶ **Money and Banking**   15
▶ **Transportation**   19
▶ **Accommodations**   38
▶ **Internet and Communications**   50

Arrival and Departure

Essential

I'm on *vacation* [holiday]/business.	**Estoy aquí *de vacaciones/en viaje de negocios.*** ehs·toy ah·kee deh bah·kah·theeyohn·ehs/ehn beeyah·kheh deh neh·goh·theeyohs
I'm going to…	**Voy a…** boy ah…
I'm staying at the… Hotel	**Me alojo en el Hotel…** meh ah·loh·khoh ehn ehl oh·tehl…

You May Hear…

Su pasaporte, por favor. soo pah·sah·pohr·teh pohr fah·bohr	Your passport, please.
¿Cuál es el propósito de su visita? kwahl ehs ehl proh·poh·see·toh deh soo bee·see·tah	What's the purpose of your visit?
¿Dónde se aloja? dohn·deh seh ah·loh·khah	Where are you staying?
¿Cuánto tiempo piensa quedarse? kwahn·toh teeyehm·poh peeyehn·sah keh·dar·seh	How long are you staying?
¿Con quién viaja? kohn keeyehn beeyah·khah	Who are you here with?

Passport Control and Customs

I'm just passing through.	**Estoy de paso.** chs·toy dch pah·soh
I'd like to declare…	**Quiero declarar…** kooych·roh dch·klah·rahr…
I have nothing to declare.	**No tengo nada que declarar.** noh tehn·goh nah·dah keh deh·klah·rahr

You May Hear…

¿Tiene algo que declarar?
teeyeh·neh ahl·goh keh deh·klah·rahr

Anything to declare?

Tiene que pagar impuestos por esto.
teeyeh·neh keh pah·gahr eem·pwehs·tohs
pohr ehs·toh

You must pay duty on this.

Abra esta maleta.
ah·brah ehs·tah mah·leh·tah

Open this bag.

You May See…

ADUANAS	customs
ARTÍCULOS LIBRES DE IMPUESTOS	duty-free goods
ARTÍCULOS QUE DECLARAR	goods to declare
NADA QUE DECLARAR	nothing to declare
CONTROL DE PASAPORTES	passport control
POLICÍA	police

Money and Banking

Essential

Where's…?	**¿Dónde está…?** <u>dohn</u>·deh ehs·<u>tah</u>…
– the ATM	**– el cajero automático** ehl kah·<u>kheh</u>·roh awtoh·<u>mah</u>·tee·koh
– the bank	**– el banco** ehl <u>bahn</u>·koh
– the currency exchange office	**– la casa de cambio** lah <u>kah</u>·sah deh <u>kahm</u>·beeyoh
When does the bank *open/close*?	**¿A qué hora *abre/cierra* el banco?** ah keh oh·rah *<u>ah</u>·breh/<u>theeyeh</u>·rrah* ehl <u>bahn</u>·koh
I'd like to change *dollars/pounds* into euros.	**Quiero cambiar *dólares/libras* a euros.** <u>keeyeh</u>·roh kahm·beeyahr *doh·<u>lah</u>·rehs/<u>lee</u>·brahs* ah <u>ew</u>·rohs
I'd like to cash traveler's checks [cheques].	**Quiero cobrar cheques de viaje.** <u>keeyeh</u>·roh koh·<u>brahr</u> <u>cheh</u>·kehs deh <u>beeyah</u>·kheh

ATM, Bank and Currency Exchange

I'd like to change money.	**Quiero cambiar dinero.** <u>keeyeh</u>·roh kahm·<u>beeyahr</u> dee·<u>neh</u>·roh
What's the exchange rate?	**¿Cuál es el tipo de cambio?** kwahl ehs ehl <u>tee</u>·poh dch <u>kahm</u>·bccyoh
How much is the fee?	**¿Cuánto es la tasa?** <u>kwahn</u>·toh ehs lah tah·sah

I lost my traveler's checks [cheques].	**He perdido los cheques de viaje.** eh pehr·<u>dee</u>·doh lohs <u>cheh</u>·kehs deh <u>beeyah</u>·kheh
My card was lost.	**Se me ha perdido la tarjeta.** seh meh ah pehr·<u>dee</u>·doh lah tahr·<u>kheh</u>·tah
My card was stolen.	**Me han robado la tarjeta.** meh ahn roh·<u>bah</u>·doh lah tahr·<u>kheh</u>·tah
My card doesn't work.	**Mi tarjeta no funciona.** mee tahr·<u>kheh</u>·tah noh foon·<u>theeyoh</u>·nah

▶For numbers, see page 178.

You May See...

INTRODUCIR TARJETA AQUÍ	insert card here
CANCELAR	cancel
BORRAR	clear
INTRODUCIR	enter
CLAVE	PIN
RETIRAR FONDOS	withdraw funds
DE CUENTA CORRIENTE	from checking [current account]
DE CUENTA DE AHORROS	from savings
RECIBO	receipt

i

ATMs arc located throughout Spain. Cash can be obtained from ATMs with Visa™, Eurocard™, American Express® and many other international cards. Instructions are often given in English. Debit cards are becoming a more accepted method of payment in Spain. Whether using a credit card or debit card, make sure you have your PIN (personal identification number) and that it is four digits. If you have an alphabetic PIN, be aware that Spanish ATMs do not have letters on the keypad.

The best rates for exchanging money will be found at banks and ATMs. You can change money at travel agencies and hotels, but the rate will not be as good. Remember your passport when you want to change money.

You May See…

Spanish currency is the **euro**, **€**, divided into 100 **céntimos** (cents).

Coins: 1, 2, 5, 10, 20, 50 **cts.**; **€**1, 2

Notes: **€**5, 10, 20, 50, 100, 200, 500

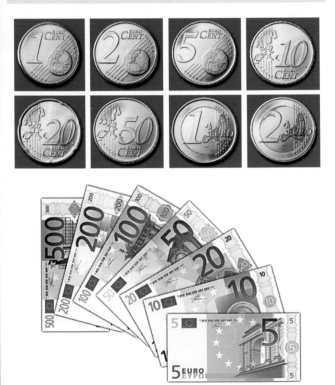

Transportation

Essential

How do I get to town?	**¿Cómo se llega a la ciudad?** <u>koh</u>·moh seh <u>yeh</u>·gah ah lah theew·<u>dahd</u>
Where's...?	**¿Dónde está...?** <u>dohn</u>·deh ehs·<u>tah</u>...
– the airport	– **el aeropuerto** ehl ah·eh·roh·<u>pwehr</u>·toh
– the train [railway] station	– **la estación de tren** lah ehs·tah·<u>theeyohn</u> deh trehn
– the bus station	– **la estación de autobuses** lah ehs·tah·<u>theeyohn</u> deh awtoh·<u>booses</u>
– the subway [underground] station	– **la estación de metro** lah ehs·tah·<u>theeyohn</u> deh <u>meh</u>·troh
How far is it?	**¿A qué distancia está?** ah keh dees·<u>tahn</u>·theeyah ehs·<u>tah</u>
Where do I buy a ticket?	**¿Dónde se compra el billete?** <u>dohn</u>·deh seh <u>kohm</u>·prah ehl bee·<u>yeh</u>·teh
A *one-way/round-trip [return]* ticket to...	**Un billete de *ida/ida y vuelta* a...** oon bee·<u>yeh</u>·teh deh <u>ee</u>·dah/<u>ee</u>·dah ee <u>bwehl</u>·tah ah...
How much?	**¿Cuánto es?** <u>kwahn</u>·toh ehs
Is there a discount?	**¿Hacen descuento?** <u>ah</u>·then dehs·<u>kwehn</u>·toh
Which...?	**¿De qué...?** deh keh...
– gate	– **puerta de embarque** <u>pwehr</u>·tah deh ehm·<u>bahr</u>·keh
– line	– **línea** <u>lee</u>·neh·ah
– platform	– **andén** ahn·<u>dehn</u>
Where can I get a taxi?	**¿Dónde puedo coger un taxi?** <u>dohn</u>·deh <u>pweh</u>·doh koh·<u>khehr</u> oon <u>tah</u>·xee

Take me to this address.	**Lléveme a esta dirección.** <u>yeh</u>·beh·meh ah <u>ehs</u>·tah dee·rek·<u>theeyohn</u>
Where's the car rental [hire]?	**¿Dónde está el alquiler de coches?** <u>dohn</u>·deh ehs·<u>tah</u> ehl ahl·kee·<u>lehr</u> deh <u>koh</u>·chehs
Can I have a map?	**¿Podría darme un mapa?** poh·<u>dree</u>·ah <u>dahr</u>·meh oon <u>mah</u>·pah

Ticketing

When's...to Madrid?	**¿Cuándo sale...a Madrid?** <u>kwahn</u>·doh <u>sah</u>·leh...ah mah·<u>dreeth</u>
– the (first) bus	**– el (primer) autobús** ehl (pree·<u>mehr</u>) awtoh·<u>boos</u>
– the (next) flight	**– el (próximo) vuelo** ehl (<u>proh</u>·xee·moh) <u>bweh</u>·loh
– the (last) train	**– el (último) tren** ehl (<u>ool</u>·tee·moh) trehn
Where do I buy a ticket?	**¿Dónde se compra el billete?** <u>dohn</u>·deh seh <u>kohm</u>·prah ehl bee·<u>yeh</u>·teh
One/Two ticket(s), please.	***Un/Dos** billete(s), por favor.* oon/dohs bee·<u>yeh</u>·teh(s) pohr fah·<u>bohr</u>
For *today/tomorrow*.	**Para *hoy/mañana.*** <u>pah</u>·rah *oy/mah·<u>nyah</u>·nah*

▶ For time, see page 180.

▶ For days, see page 181.

A...ticket.	**Un billete...** oon bee·<u>yeh</u>·teh...
– one-way	**– de ida** deh <u>ee</u>·dah
– round-trip [return]	**– de ida y vuelta** deh <u>ee</u>·dah ee <u>bwehl</u>·tah
– first class	**– de primera clase** deh pree·<u>meh</u>·rah <u>klah</u>·seh
– economy class	**– de clase económica** deh <u>klah</u>·seh eh·koh·<u>noh</u>·mee·kah

How much?	**¿Cuánto es?** <u>kwahn</u>·toh chs
Is there a... discount?	**¿Hacen descuento a...?** <u>ah</u>·thehn dehs·<u>kwehn</u>·toh ah...
– child	**– los niños** lohs <u>nee</u>·nyohs
– student	**– los estudiantes** lohs ehs·too·<u>deeyahn</u>·tehs
– senior citizen	**– los jubilados** lohs khoo·bee·<u>lah</u>·dohs
I have an e-ticket.	**Tengo un billete electrónico.** <u>tehn</u>·goh oon bee·<u>yeh</u>·teh eh·<u>lehk</u>·<u>troh</u>·nee·koh
Can I buy a ticket on the *bus/train*?	**¿Puedo comprar el billete a bordo del *autobús/tren*?** <u>pweh</u>·doh kohm·<u>prahr</u> ehl bee·<u>yeh</u>·teh ah <u>bohr</u>·doh dehl *awtoh·<u>boos</u>/trehn*
I'd like to...my reservation.	**Quiero...mi reserva.** <u>keeyeh</u>·roh...mee reh·<u>sehr</u>·bah
– cancel	**– cancelar** kahn·theh·<u>lahr</u>
– change	**– cambiar** kahm·<u>beeyahr</u>
– confirm	**– confirmar** kohn·feer·<u>mahr</u>

Plane

Getting to the Airport

How much is a taxi to the airport?
¿Cuánto cuesta el trayecto en taxi al aeropuerto? <u>kwahn</u>·toh <u>kwehs</u>·tah ehl trah·<u>yehk</u>·toh ehn <u>tah</u>·xee ahl ah·eh·roh·<u>pwehr</u>·toh

To…Airport, please.
Al aeropuerto de…, por favor. ahl ah·eh·roh·<u>pwehr</u>·toh deh…pohr fah·<u>bohr</u>

My airline is…
Mi compañía aérea es… mee kohm·pah·<u>nyee</u>·ah ah·<u>eh</u>·reh·ah ehs…

My flight leaves at…
Mi vuelo sale a la/las… mee <u>bweh</u>·loh <u>sah</u>·leh ah lah/lahs…

▶ For when to use **la** or **las**, see page 175.

▶ For time, see page 180.

I'm in a rush.
Tengo prisa. <u>tehn</u>·goh <u>pree</u>·sah

Can you take an alternate route?
¿Puede coger otro camino? <u>pweh</u>·deh koh·<u>khehr</u> oh·troh kah·<u>mee</u>·noh

Can you drive *faster/slower*?
¿Puede ir más *deprisa/despacio*? <u>pweh</u>·deh eer mahs deh·<u>pree</u>·sah/dehs·<u>pah</u>·theeyoh

You May Hear…

¿Con qué compañía aérea viaja? kohn keh kohm·pah·<u>nyee</u>·ah ah·<u>eh</u>·reh·ah <u>beeyah</u>·khah
What airline are you flying?

¿Nacional o internacional? nah·theeyoh·<u>nahl</u> oh een·tehr·nah·theeyoh·<u>nahl</u>
Domestic or international?

¿Qué terminal? keh tehr·mee·<u>nahl</u>
What terminal?

You May See...

LLEGADAS	arrivals
SALIDAS	departures
RECOGIDA DE EQUIPAJES	baggage claim
VUELOS NACIONALES	domestic flights
VUELOS INTERNACIONALES	international flights
MOSTRADOR DE FACTURACIÓN	check-in
FACTURACIÓN ELECTRÓNICA	e-ticket check-in
PUERTAS DE EMBARQUE	departure gates

Check-in and Boarding

Where's check-in?	**¿Dónde está el mostrador de facturación?** <u>dohn</u>·deh ehs·<u>tah</u> ehl mohs·trah·<u>dohr</u> deh fahk·too·rah·<u>theeyohn</u>
My name is...	**Me llamo...** meh <u>yah</u>·moh...
I'm going to...	**Voy a...** boy ah...
How much luggage is allowed?	**¿Cuánto equipaje está permitido?** <u>kwahn</u>·toh eh·kee·<u>pah</u>·kheh ehs·<u>tah</u> pehr·mee·<u>tee</u>·doh
Which *terminal/gate*?	**¿De qué *terminal/puerta de embarque*?** deh keh *tehr·mee·<u>nahl</u>/<u>pwehr</u>·tah deh ehm·<u>bahr</u>·keh*
I'd like *a window/an aisle* seat.	**Quiero un asiento de *ventana/pasillo*.** <u>keeyeh</u>·roh oon ah·<u>seeyehn</u>·toh deh *behn·<u>tah</u>·nah/pah·<u>see</u>·yoh*

When do we leave/arrive?	**¿A qué hora *salimos/llegamos*?** ah keh oh·rah *sah·lee·mohs/yeh·gah·mohs*
Is the flight delayed?	**¿Lleva retraso el vuelo?** yeh·bah reh·trah·soh ehl bweh·loh
How late?	**¿Cuánto retraso lleva?** kwahn·toh reh·trah·soh yeh·bah

You May Hear...

¡Siguiente! see·geeyehn·teh	Next!
Su *pasaporte/billete*, por favor. soo *pah·sah·pohr·teh/bee·yeh·teh* pohr fah·bohr	Your *passport/ticket*, please.
¿Va a facturar el equipaje? bah ah fahk·too·rahr ehl eh·kee·pah·kheh	Are you checking any luggage?
Lleva exceso de equipaje. yeh·bah ehx·theh·soh deh eh·kee·pah·kheh	You have excess luggage.
Eso es demasiado grande para equipaje de mano. eh·soh ehs deh·mah·seeyah·doh grahn·deh pah·rah eh·kee·pah·kheh deh mah·noh	That's too large for a carry-on [to carry on board].
¿Hizo las maletas usted? ee·thoh lahs mah·leh·tahs oos·teth	Did you pack these bags yourself?
¿Le entregó alguien algún paquete? leh ehn·treh·goh ahl·geeyehn ahl·goon pah·keh·teh	Did anyone give you anything to carry?
Vacíese los bolsillos. bah·thee·eh·seh lohs bohl·see·yohs	Empty your pockets.
Quítese los zapatos. kee·teh·seh lohs thah·pah·tohs	Take off your shoes.
Se está efectuando el embarque del vuelo... seh ehs·tah eh·fehk·too·ahn·doh ehl ehm·bahr·keh dehl bweh·loh...	Now boarding flight...

Luggage

Where *is/are*...?	**¿Dónde *está/están*...?** <u>dohn</u>·deh ehs·<u>tah</u>/ehs·<u>tahn</u>...
– the luggage carts [trolleys]	– **los carritos para el equipaje** lohs kah·<u>rree</u>·tohs <u>pah</u>·rah ehl eh·kee·<u>pah</u>·kheh
– the luggage lockers	– **las consignas automáticas** lahs kohn·<u>seeg</u>·nahs awtoh·<u>mah</u>·tee·kahs
– the baggage claim	– **la recogida de equipajes** lah reh·koh·<u>khee</u>·dah deh eh·kee·<u>pah</u>·khehs
My luggage has been lost.	**Han perdido mi equipaje.** ahn pehr·<u>dee</u>·doh mee eh·kee·<u>pah</u>·kheh
My luggage has been stolen.	**Me han robado el equipaje.** meh ahn roh·<u>bah</u>·doh ehl eh·kee·<u>pah</u>·kheh
My suitcase is damaged.	**Mi maleta ha sufrido daños.** mee mah·<u>leh</u>·tah ah soo·<u>free</u>·doh <u>dah</u>·nyohs

Finding Your Way

Where *is/are*...?	**¿Dónde *está/están*...?** <u>dohn</u>·deh ehs·<u>tah</u>/ehs·<u>tahn</u>...
– the currency exchange	– **la casa de cambio** lah <u>kah</u>·sah deh <u>kahm</u>·beeyoh
– the car rental [hire]	– **el alquiler de coches** ehl ahl·kee·<u>lehr</u> deh <u>koh</u>·chehs
– the exit	– **la salida** lah sah·<u>lee</u>·dah
– the taxis	– **los taxis** lohs <u>tah</u>·xees
Is there...into town?	**¿Hay...que vaya a la ciudad?** aye...keh <u>bah</u>·yah ah lah theew·<u>dahd</u>
– a bus	– **un autobús** oon awtoh·<u>boos</u>
– a train	– **un tren** oon trehn
– a subway [underground]	– **un metro** oon <u>meh</u>·troh

▶ For directions, see page 35.

Train

Where's the train [railway] station?	**¿Dónde está la estación de tren?** <u>dohn</u>·deh ehs·<u>tah</u> lah ehs·tah·<u>theeyohn</u> deh trehn
How far is it?	**¿A qué distancia está?** ah keh dees·<u>tahn</u>·theeyah ehs·<u>tah</u>
Where *is/are*…?	**¿Dónde *está/están*…?** <u>dohn</u>·deh ehs·<u>tah</u>/ehs·<u>tahn</u>…
– the ticket office	**– el despacho de billetes** ehl dehs·<u>pah</u>·choh deh bee·<u>yeh</u>·tehs
– the information desk	**– el mostrador de información** ehl mohs·trah·<u>dohr</u> deh een·fohr·mah·<u>theeyohn</u>
– the luggage lockers	**– las consignas automáticas** lahs kohn·<u>seeg</u>·nahs awtoh·<u>mah</u>·tee·kahs
– the platforms	**– los andenes** lohs ahn·<u>deh</u>·nehs

▶ For directions, see page 35.

▶ For ticketing, see page 20.

You May See…

ANDENES	platforms
INFORMACIÓN	information
RESERVAS	reservations
SALA DE ESPERA	waiting room
LLEGADAS	arrivals
SALIDAS	departures

Questions

Can I have a schedule [timetable]?	**¿Podría darme un horario?** poh·<u>dree</u>·ah <u>dahr</u>·meh oon oh·<u>rah</u>·reeyoh
How long is the trip?	**¿Cuánto dura el viaje?** <u>kwahn</u>·toh <u>doo</u>·rah ehl <u>veeyah</u>·kheh
Do I have to change trains?	**¿Tengo que cambiar de trenes?** <u>tehn</u>·goh keh kahm·<u>beeyahr</u> deh <u>treh</u>·nehs

Spain's major railway network is **RENFE, Red Nacional de Ferrocarriles Españoles**. RENFE offers a variety of train types, from express to local, national to international. You can purchase tickets or make reservations through the **RENFE** website or a travel agency, or at the station. It is sometimes necessary to purchase your tickets a day or two in advance for popular routes.

Departures

Which track [platform] for the train to…?	**¿De qué andén sale el tren a…?** deh keh ahn·<u>dehn</u> <u>sah</u>·leh ehl trehn ah…
Is this the *track [platform]/train* to…?	**¿Es éste el *andén/tren* a…?** ehs <u>ehs</u>·teh ehl *ahn·<u>dehn</u>/trehn* ah…
Where is track [platform]…?	**¿Dónde está el andén…?** <u>dohn</u>·deh ehs·<u>tah</u> ehl ahn·<u>dehn</u>…
Where do I change for…?	**¿Dónde tengo que cambiar para…?** <u>dohn</u>·deh <u>tehn</u>·goh keh kahm·<u>beeyahr</u> <u>pah</u>·rah…

Boarding

Can I sit here?	**¿Le importa si me siento aquí?** leh eem·<u>pohr</u>·tah see meh <u>seeyehn</u>·toh ah·<u>kee</u>
That's my seat.	**Ése es mi asiento.** <u>eh</u>·seh ehs mee ah·<u>seeyehn</u>·toh

¡Todos a bordo! toh·dohs ah bohr·doh — All aboard!

Billetes, por favor. bee·yeh·tehs pohr fah·bohr — Tickets, please.

Tiene que cambiar de tren en León. teeyeh·neh keh kahm·beeyahr deh trehn ehn leh·ohn — You have to change at Léon.

Próxima parada: Madrid. proh·xee·mah pah·rah· dah mah·dreeth — Next stop, Madrid.

Bus

Where's the bus station?	**¿Dónde está la estación de autobuses?** dohn·deh ehs·tah lah ehs·tah·theeyohn deh awtoh·boo·sehs
How far is it?	**¿A qué distancia está?** ah keh dees·tahn·theeyah ehs·tah
How do I get to…?	**¿Cómo se llega a…?** koh·moh seh yeh·gah ah…
Is this the bus to…?	**¿Es éste el autobús a…?** ehs ehs·teh ehl awtoh·boos ah…
Can you tell me when to get off?	**¿Podría decirme cuándo me tengo que bajar?** poh·dree·ah deh·theer·meh kwahn·doh meh tehn·goh keh bah·khahr
Do I have to change buses?	**¿Tengo que hacer transbordo?** tehn·goh keh ah·thehr trahns·bohr·doh
How many stops to…?	**¿Cuántas paradas hay hasta…?** kwahn·tahs pah·rah·dahs aye ahs·tah…
Stop here, please!	**¡Pare aquí, por favor!** pah·reh ah·kee pohr fah·bohr

► For ticketing, see page 20.

Bus service in Spain is extensive. For local service within a town, you usually pay as you board the bus. The fare is generally a fixed price. In larger cities, bus tickets are interchangeable with subway tickets. **Un bono** (**metrobús** in Madrid), a ten-trip ticket, is the cheapest way to go. These tickets are available at newsstands, banks, lottery-ticket shops and subway stations. When using the **bono** on a bus, make sure to validate your ticket by stamping it in the machine next to the driver as you board. Signal that you wish to get off by pushing a button, located throughout the bus; a sign will light up that says **parada solicitada** (stop requested).

You May See…

PARADA DE AUTOBUSES	bus stop
SUBIR/BAJAR	enter/exit
PICAR BILLETE	stamp your ticket

Subway [Underground]

Where's the subway [underground] station?	**¿Dónde está la estación de metro?** dohn·deh ehs·tah lah ehs·tah·theeyohn deh meh·troh
A map, please.	**Un plano, por favor.** oon plah·noh pohr fah·bohr
Which line for…?	**¿Qué línea tengo que coger para…?** keh lee·neh·ah tehn·goh keh koh·khehr pah·rah…
Do I have to transfer [change]?	**¿Tengo que hacer transbordo?** tehn·goh keh ah·thehr trahns·bohr·doh
Is this the subway [train] to…?	**¿Es éste el tren a…?** ehs ehs·teh ehl trehn ah…
Where are we?	**¿Dónde estamos?** dohn·deh ehs·tah·mohs

▶For ticketing, see page 20.

In Spain, there are **metro** (subway) systems in Madrid, Barcelona, Valencia and Bilbao. **Metro** systems are easy to use and reasonably priced. All three **metro** systems operate on a one-way, per-ride basis. You can save money by buying a 10-trip ticket or **un bono** (**metrobús** in Madrid), which can be purchased at **metro** stations, banks, newsstands and tobacco shops. In larger cities, **metro** and bus tickets are the same price and are interchangeable.

To enter the subway system, slip your ticket through the slot in the turnstile; remember to grab your ticket, which now has the date printed on it, so that you can pass through the turnstile.

Boat and Ferry

When is the ferry to…?	**¿Cuándo sale el ferry a…?** <u>kwahn</u>·doh <u>sah</u>·leh ehl feh·<u>rree</u> ah…
Can I take my car?	**¿Puedo llevar el coche?** <u>pweh</u>·doh yeh·<u>bahr</u> ehl <u>koh</u>·cheh

▶ For ticketing, see page 20.

You May See...	
BALSA SALVAVIDAS	life boat
CHALECO SALVAVIDAS	life jacket

In Spain, ferry and boat services run to and from the Balearic Islands (Mallorca, Menorca, Ibiza and Formentera), destinations in North Africa and the Canary Islands and ports in Genoa, Italy (from Barcelona) and southern England (from Bilbao and Santander).

Bicycle and Motorcycle

I'd like to rent [hire]…	**Quiero alquilar…** <u>keey</u>eh·roh ahl·kee·<u>lahr</u>…
– a bicycle	**– una bicicleta** <u>oo</u>·nah bee·thee·<u>kleh</u>·tah
– a moped	**– un ciclomotor** oon thee·kloh·moh·<u>tohr</u>
– a motorcycle	**– una motocicleta** <u>oo</u>·nah moh·toh·thee·<u>kleh</u>·tah
How much per *day/week*?	**¿Cuánto cuesta por *día/semana*?** <u>kwahn</u>·toh <u>kwehs</u>·tah pohr <u>dee</u>·ah/seh·<u>mah</u>·nah
Can I have a *helmet/lock*?	**¿Puede darme un *casco/candado*?** <u>pweh</u>·deh dahr·meh oon <u>kahs</u>·koh/kahn·<u>dah</u>·doh

Taxi

Where can I get a taxi?	**¿Dónde puedo coger un taxi?** <u>dohn</u>·deh <u>pweh</u>·doh koh·<u>khehr</u> oon tah·xee
Do you have the number for a taxi?	**¿Tiene el número de alguna empresa de taxi?** <u>teey</u>eh·neh ehl <u>noo</u>·meh·roh deh ahl·<u>goo</u>·nah ehm·<u>preh</u>·sah deh <u>tah</u>·xee
I'd like a taxi *now/ for tomorrow at…*	**Quiero un taxi *ahora/para mañana a la(s)…*** <u>keey</u>eh·roh oon <u>tah</u>·xee ah·<u>oh</u>·rah/ <u>pah</u>·rah mah·<u>nyah</u>·nah ah lah(s)…
Pick me up at (place/time)…	**Recójame *en/a la(s)…*** reh·<u>koh</u>·khah·meh *ehn/ah lah(s)…*

▶ For when to use **la** or **las**, see page 175.

In Spain, **coger** means to catch or get, as in: **¿Dónde puedo coger un taxi?** (Where can I catch a cab?). However, in Latin America, **coger** is a vulgarity for "to have sex". Use **tomar** (**¿Dónde puedo tomar un taxi?**) in Spanish-speaking Latin America.

I'm going to…	**Voy…** boy…
– this address	**– a esta dirección** ehs·tah dee·rehk·<u>theeyohn</u>
– the airport	**– al aeropuerto** ahl ah·eh·roh·<u>pwehr</u>·toh
– the train [railway] station	**– a la estación de trenes** ah lah ehs·tah·<u>theeyohn</u> deh <u>treh</u>·nehs
I'm late.	**Llego tarde.** <u>yeh</u>·goh <u>tahr</u>·deh
Can you drive *faster/slower*?	**¿Puede ir más *deprisa/despacio*?** <u>pweh</u>·deh eer mahs *deh·<u>pree</u>·sah/ dehs·<u>pah</u>·theeyoh*
Stop/Wait here.	***Pare/Espere* aquí.** *<u>pah</u>·reh/ehs·<u>peh</u>·reh* ah·<u>kee</u>
How much?	**¿Cuánto es?** <u>kwahn</u>·toh ehs
You said it would cost…	**Dijo que costaría…** <u>dee</u>·khoh keh kohs·tah·<u>ree</u>·ah…
Keep the change.	**Quédese con el cambio.** <u>keh</u>·deh·seh kohn ehl <u>kahm</u>·beeyoh

In major Spanish cities, taxis are reasonably priced. Extra fees are usually charged for trips to the airport, bus station and train station and also for extra luggage. When entering the taxi, make sure the meter is turned on; it should register a base fare when the trip begins. The fare is then increased by a set amount per kilometer traveled.

Car

Car Rental [Hire]

Where's the car rental [hire]?	**¿Dónde está el alquiler de coches?** <u>dohn</u>·deh ehs·<u>tah</u> ehl ahl·kee·<u>lehr</u> deh <u>koh</u>·chehs
I'd like	**Quiero...** <u>keeyeh</u>·roh...
– a *cheap/small* car	**– un coche *económico/pequeño*** oon <u>koh</u>·cheh eh·koh·<u>noh</u>·mee·koh/ peh·<u>keh</u>·nyoh
– an automatic/ a manual	**– un coche *automático/con transmisión manual*** oon koh·chch awtoh·<u>mah</u>·too koh/ kohn trahns·mee·<u>seeyohn</u> mah·noo·<u>ahl</u>
– air conditioning	**– un coche con aire acondicionado** oon <u>koh</u>·cheh kohn <u>ayee</u>·reh ah·kohn·dee·theeyoh·<u>nah</u>·doh
– a car seat	**– un asiento de niño** oon ah·<u>seeyehn</u>·toh deh <u>nee</u>·nyoh
How much...?	**¿Cuánto cobran...?** <u>kwahn</u>·toh <u>koh</u>·brahn...
– per *day/week*	**– por *día/semana*** pohr <u>dee</u>·ah/seh·<u>mah</u>·nah
– for...days	**– por...días** pohr...<u>dee</u>·ahs
– per kilometer	**– por kilómetro** pohr kcc·<u>loh</u>·meh·troh
– for unlimited mileage	**– por kilometraje ilimitado** pohr kee·loh·meh·<u>trah</u>·kheh ee·lee·mee·<u>tah</u>·doh
– with insurance	**– con el seguro** kohn ehl seh·<u>goo</u>·roh
Are there any discounts?	**¿Ofrecen algún descuento?** oh·<u>freh</u>·thehn ahl·<u>goon</u> dehs·<u>kwehn</u>·toh

You May Hear...

**¿Tiene permiso de conducir
internacional?** <u>teeyeh</u>·neh pehr·<u>mee</u>·soh deh
kohn·doo·<u>theer</u> een·tehr·nah·theeyoh·<u>nahl</u>

Do you have an
international driver's
license?

Su pasaporte, por favor.
soo pah·sah·<u>pohr</u>·teh pohr fah·<u>bohr</u>

Your passport,
please.

¿Quiere seguro?
<u>keeyeh</u>·reh seh·<u>goo</u>·roh

Do you want
insurance?

Tiene que dejar una fianza.
<u>teeyeh</u>·neh keh deh·<u>khahr</u> <u>oo</u>·nah fee·<u>ahn</u>·thah

I'll need a deposit.

Firme aquí. <u>feer</u>·meh ah·<u>kee</u>

Sign here.

Gas [Petrol] Station

Where's the gas
[petrol] station?

¿Dónde está la gasolinera? <u>dohn</u>·deh
ehs·<u>tah</u> lah gah·soh·lee·<u>neh</u>·rah

Fill it up.

Lleno. <u>yeh</u>·noh

...liters, please.

...litros, por favor. ...<u>lee</u>·trohs pohr fah·<u>bohr</u>

I'll pay *in cash/by
credit card*.

**Voy a pagar *en efectivo/con tarjeta de
crédito*.** boy ah pah·<u>gahr</u> *ehn eh·fehk·<u>tee</u>·boh/
kohn tahr·<u>kheh</u>·tah deh <u>kreh</u>·dee·toh*

You May See...

NORMAL	regular
SÚPER	super
DIESEL	diesel

Asking Directions

Is this the way to…?	**¿Es ésta la carretera a…?** ehs ehs·tah lah kah·rreh·tch·rah ah…
How far is it to…?	**¿A qué distancia está…?** ah keh dees·tahn·theeyah ehs·tah…
Where's…?	**¿Donde está…?** dohn·deh ehs·tah…
– …Street	**– la calle…** lah kah·yeh…
– this address	**– ésta dirección** ehs·tah dee·rek·theeyohn
– the highway [motorway]	**– la autopista** lah aw·toh·pees·tah
Can you show me on the map?	**¿Me lo puede indicar en el mapa?** meh loh pweh·dch een·dee·kalır ehn ehl mah·pah
I'm lost.	**Me he perdido.** meh eh pehr·dee·doh

You May Hear…

todo recto toh·doh rehk·toh	straight ahead
a la izquierda ah lah eeth·keeyehr·dah	left
a la derecha ah lah deh·reh·chah	right
en/doblando la esquina chn·doh·blahn·doh lah ehs·kee·nah	*on/around* the corner
frente a frehn·teh ah	opposite
detrás de deh·trahs deh	behind
al lado de ahl lah·doh deh	next to
después de dehs·pwehs dch	after
al *norte/sur* ahl nohr·teh/soor	north/south
al *este/oeste* ahl ehs·teh/oh·ehs·teh	east/west
en el semáforo en ehl seh·mah·foh·roh	at the traffic light
en el cruce en ehl kroo·theh	at the intersection

35

	ADELANTAMIENTO PROHIBIDO	no passing zone
	STOP	stop
	CALLE DE SENTIDO ÚNICO	one-way street
	CEDA EL PASO	yield [give way]
	ENTRADA PROHIBIDA	no entry
	ESTACIONAMIENTO PROHIBIDO	no parking
	FINAL DEL CARRIL LATERAL DERECHO	right lane ends (merge left)
	PROHIBICIÓN VELOCIDAD MÁXIMA	maximum speed limit

Parking

Can I park here?	**¿Puedo aparcar aquí?** <u>pweh</u>·doh ah·pahr·<u>kahr</u> ah·<u>kee</u>
Where's the *parking garage/parking lot [car park]*?	**¿Dónde está el *garaje/aparcamiento*?** <u>dohn</u>·deh ehs·<u>tah</u> ehl *gah·<u>rah</u>·kheh/ ah·pahr·kah·<u>meeyehn</u>·toh*

How much…?	¿Cuánto cobran…? <u>kwahn</u>·toh <u>koh</u>·brahn…
– per hour	– **por hora** pohr <u>oh</u>·rah
– per day	– **por día** pohr <u>dee</u>·ah
– for overnight	– **por la noche** pohr lah <u>noh</u>·cheh

---

i Public parking is noted by **P**. Many towns have **zonas azules** (blue zones), where parking is allowed; buy a ticket at the nearby parking machine. Larger cities have an **ora zona** (hourly parking). Purchase a ticket for 30, 60 or 90 minutes and display it in your windshield. Tickets for the **ora zona** can be purchased at tobacconists, hotels and other retailers—look for the **ora zona** signs in the window. Note: Spain's **Guardia Civil de Tráfico** (highway patrol) may enforce payment of fines for illegal parking on the spot for non-residents of Spain.

Breakdown and Repairs

My car *broke down/won't start*.	**El coche *se me ha averiado/no arranca.*** ehl <u>koh</u>·cheh *seh meh ah ah·beh·<u>reeyah</u>·doh/ noh ah·<u>rrahn</u>·kah*
Can you fix it (today)?	¿**Puede arreglarlo (hoy mismo)?** <u>pweh</u>·deh ah·rreh·<u>glahr</u>·loh (oy <u>meez</u>·moh)
When will it be ready?	¿**Cuándo estará listo?** <u>kwahn</u>·doh ehs·tah·<u>rah</u> <u>lees</u>·toh
How much?	¿**Cuánto es?** <u>kwahn</u>·toh ehs

Accidents

There was an accident.	**Ha habido un accidente.** ah ah·<u>bee</u>·doh oon ahk·thee·<u>dehn</u>·teh
Call *an ambulance/the police*.	**Llame a *una ambulancia/la policía.*** <u>yah</u>·meh ah *<u>oo</u>·nah ahm·boo·<u>lahn</u>·theeyah/ lah poh·lee·<u>thee</u>·ah*

37

Accommodations

Essential

Can you recommend a hotel?	**¿Puede recomendarme un hotel?** pweh·deh reh·koh·mehn·<u>dahr</u>·meh oon oh·<u>tehl</u>
I have a reservation.	**Tengo una reserva.** tehn·goh <u>oo</u>·nah reh·<u>sehr</u>·bah
My name is…	**Me llamo…** meh <u>yah</u>·moh…
Do you have a room…?	**¿Tienen habitaciones…?** <u>teeyeh</u>·nehn ah·bee·tah·<u>theeyoh</u>·nehs…
– for one/two	**– individuales/dobles** een·dee·bee·doo·<u>ah</u>·lehs/<u>doh</u>·blehs
– with a bathroom	**– con baño** kohn <u>bah</u>·nyoh
– with air conditioning	**– con aire acondicionado** kohn <u>ayee</u>·reh ah·kohn·dee·theeyoh·<u>nah</u>·doh
For…	**Para…** <u>pah</u>·rah…
– tonight	**– esta noche** ehs·tah <u>noh</u>·cheh
– two nights	**– dos noches** dohs <u>noh</u>·chehs
– one week	**– una semana** <u>oo</u>·nah seh·<u>mah</u>·nah
How much?	**¿Cuánto es?** <u>kwahn</u>·toh ehs
Is there anything cheaper?	**¿Hay alguna tarifa más barata?** aye ahl·<u>goo</u>·nah tah·<u>ree</u>·fah mahs bah·<u>rah</u>·tah
When's check-out?	**¿A qué hora hay que desocupar la habitación?** ah keh <u>oh</u>·rah aye keh deh·soh·koo·<u>pahr</u> lah ah·bee·tah·<u>theeyohn</u>
Can I leave this in the safe?	**¿Puedo dejar esto en la caja fuerte?** pweh·doh deh·<u>khahr</u> ehs·toh ehn lah <u>kah</u>·khah <u>fwehr</u>·teh

Can I leave my bags?	**¿Podría dejar mi equipaje?** poh-<u>dree</u>-ah deh- <u>khahr</u> mee eh-kee-<u>pah</u>-kheh
Can I have *the bill/ a receipt*?	**¿Me da *la factura/un recibo*?** meh dah *lah fahk-<u>too</u>-rah/oon reh-<u>thee</u>-boh*
I'll pay *in cash/by credit card*.	**Voy a pagar *en efectivo/con tarjeta de crédito*.** boy ah pah-<u>gahr</u> *ehn eh-fehk-<u>tee</u>-boh/kohn tahr-<u>kheh</u>-tah deh <u>kreh</u>-dee-toh*

If you didn't reserve accommodations before your trip, visit the local **Oficina de turismo** (Tourist Information Office) for recommendations on places to stay.

Finding Lodging

Can you recommend a hotel?	**¿Puede recomendarme un hotel?** <u>pweh</u>-deh reh-koh-mehn-<u>dahr</u>-meh oon oh-<u>tehl</u>
What is it near?	**¿Qué hay cerca?** kch aye <u>thehr</u>-kah
How do I get there?	**¿Cómo se llega allí?** <u>koh</u>-moh seh <u>yeh</u>-gah ah-<u>yee</u>

A variety of accommodations are available in Spain. Hotels are rated from one to five stars, with five stars being the most expensive and having the most amenities. **Paradores** are government-run inns located throughout the country. These inns are usually castles, monasteries, palaces and other landmark buildings that have been restored and converted into hotels. Reservations are recommended far in advance for **paradores**, as they are very popular, especially in the summer months. Other unique accommodations in Spain include spas, resorts, farm house rentals, apartment rentals, villas and camping.

At the Hotel

I have a reservation.	**Tengo una reserva.** <u>tehn</u>·goh <u>oo</u>·nah reh·<u>sehr</u>·bah
My name is…	**Me llamo…** meh <u>yah</u>·moh…
Do you have a room…?	**¿Tiene una habitación…?** <u>teeyeh</u>·neh <u>oo</u>·nah ah·bee·tah·<u>theeyohn</u>…
– for *one/two*	– **individuales/dobles** een·dee·bee·<u>dwahl</u>·ehs/<u>doh</u>·blehs
– with a *bathroom [toilet]/shower*	– **con *un baño/una ducha*** kohn *oon* <u>bah</u>·nyoh/<u>oo</u>·nah <u>doo</u>·chah
– with air conditioning	– **con aire acondicionado** kohn <u>ayee</u>·reh ah·kohn·dee·theeyoh·<u>nah</u>·doh
– with a *single/double* bed	– **con una *cama/cama de matrimonio*** kohn una <u>kah</u>·mah/<u>kah</u>·mah mah·tree·<u>moh</u>·neeyoh
– that's *smoking/non-smoking*	– **para *fumadores/no fumadores*** <u>pah</u>·rah foo·mah·<u>doh</u>·rehs/noh foo·mah·<u>doh</u>·rehs

For...	**Para...** pah·rah...
– tonight	– **esta noche** ehs·tah noh·cheh
– two nights	– **dos noches** dohs noh·chehs
– a week	– **una semana** oo·nah seh·mah·nah

▶For numbers, see page 178.

Does the hotel have...?	**¿Tiene el hotel...?** teeyeh·neh ehl oh·tehl...
– a computer	– **un ordenador** oon ohr·deh·nah·dohr
– an elevator [a lift]	– **un ascensor** oon ah·thehn·sohr
– (wireless) internet service	– **acceso (inalámbrico) a Internet** ahk·theh·soh (een·ah·lahm·bree·koh) ah een·tehr·neht
– room service	– **servicio de habitaciones** sehr·bee·theeyoh deh ah·bee·tah·theeyoh·nehs
– a pool	– **una piscina** oo·nah pees·thee·nah
– a gym	– **un gimnasio** oon kheem·nah·seeyoh
I need...	**Necesito...** neh·theh·see·toh...
– an extra bed	– **otra cama** oh·trah kah·mah
– a cot	– **un catre** oon kah·treh
– a crib	– **una cuna** oo·nah koo·nah

You May Hear...

Su *pasaporte/tarjeta de crédito*, por favor. soo pah·sah·pohr·teh/tahr·kheh·tah deh kreh·dee·toh pohr fah·bohr	Your *passport/credit card*, please.
Rellene este formulario. reh·yeh·neh ehs·teh fohr·moo·lah·reeyoh	Fill out this form.
Firme aquí. feer·meh ah·kee	Sign here.

Price

How much per *night/week*?

¿Cuánto cuesta por *noche/semana*? kwahn·toh kwehs·tah pohr *noh·cheh/seh·mah·nah*

Does that include *breakfast/sales tax [VAT]*?

¿Incluye el precio el *desayuno/IVA*? een·kloo·yeh ehl preh·theeyoh ehl *deh·sah·yoo·noh/eh·beh·ah*

Questions

Can I see the room?

¿Puedo ver la habitación? pweh·doh behr lah ah·bee·tah·theeyohn

Where's…?

¿Dónde está…? dohn·deh ehs·tah…

– the bar

– el bar ehl bahr

– the bathroom [toilet]

– el baño ehl bah·nyoh

– the elevator [lift]

– el ascensor ehl ahs·thehn·sohr

Can I have…?

¿Puede darme…? pweh·deh dahr·meh…

– a blanket

– una manta oo·nah mahn·tah

– an iron

– una plancha oo·nah plahn·chah

– a pillow

– una almohada oo·nah ahl·moh·ah·dah

– soap

– jabón khah·bohn

– toilet paper

– papel higiénico pah·pehl ee·kheeyeh·nee·koh

– a towel

– una toalla oo·nah toh·ah·yah

Do you have an adapter for this?

¿Tiene un adaptador para esto? teeyeh·neh oon ah·dahp·tah·dohr pah·rah ehs·toh

How do I turn on the lights?

¿Cómo enciendo las luces? koh·moh ehn·theeyehn·doh lahs loo·thehs

Can you wake me at…?

¿Podría despertarme a la/las…? poh·dree·ah dehs·pehr·tahr·meh ah lah/lahs…

▶ For when to use **la** or **las**, see page 175.

Can I leave this in the safe?	**¿Puedo dejar esto en la caja fuerte?** <u>pweh</u>·doh deh·<u>khahr</u> <u>ehs</u>·toh chn lah <u>kah</u>·khah <u>fwchr</u>·teh
Can I have my things from the safe?	**¿Podría darme mis cosas de la caja fuerte?** poh·<u>dree</u>·ah <u>dahr</u>·meh mees <u>koh</u> oahs deh lah <u>kah</u>·khah <u>fwehr</u>·teh
Is there *mail [post]/ a message* for me?	**¿Hay *correo/algún mensaje* para mí?** aye koh·<u>rreh</u>·oh/ahl·<u>goon</u> mehn·<u>sah</u>·kheh <u>pah</u>·rah mee

When asking for a public restroom, it's more common and polite to use the term **servicio**. The term **baño** tends to be used when asking for a private bathroom such as in a home or a hotel room. Native speakers sometimes use both words interchangeably, but you will almost always see **servicio** on a sign.

You May See…

EMPUJAR/TIRAR	push/pull
BAÑO/SERVICIO	bathroom/restroom [toilet]
DUCHA	shower
ASCENSOR	elevator [lift]
ESCALERAS	stairs
LAVANDERÍA	laundry
NO MOLESTAR	do not disturb
PUERTA DE INCENDIOS	fire door
SALIDA (DE EMERGENCIA)	(emergency) exit
LLAMADA DESPERTADOR	wake-up call

Problems

There's a problem.	**Hay un problema.** aye oon proh-<u>bleh</u>-mah
I lost my *key/ key card.*	**He perdido la *llave/llave electrónica.*** eh pehr-<u>dee</u>-doh lah <u>yah</u>-beh/<u>yah</u>-beh eh-lehk-<u>troh</u>-nee-kah
I'm locked out of the room.	**He dejado la llave dentro de la habitación.** eh deh-<u>khah</u>-doh lah <u>yah</u>-beh <u>dehn</u>-troh deh lah ah-bee-tah-<u>theeyohn</u>
There's no *hot water/toilet paper.*	**No hay *agua caliente/papel higiénico.*** no aye <u>ah</u>-gwah kah-<u>leeyehn</u>-teh/pah-<u>pehl</u> ee-<u>kheeyeh</u>-nee-koh
The room is dirty.	**La habitación está sucia.** lah ah-bee-tah-<u>theeyohn</u> ehs-<u>tah</u> <u>soo</u>-theeyah
There are bugs in the room.	**Hay insectos en la habitación.** aye een-<u>sehk</u>-tohs ehn lah ah-bee-tah-<u>theeyohn</u>
…doesn't work.	**…no funciona.** …no foon-<u>theeyoh</u>-nah
Can you fix…?	**¿Pueden arreglar…?** <u>pweh</u>-dehn ah-rreh-<u>glahr</u>…
– the air conditioning	**– el aire acondicionado** ehl <u>ayee</u>-reh ah-kohn-dee-theeyoh-<u>nah</u>-doh
– the fan	**– el ventilador** ehl behn-tee-lah-<u>dohr</u>
– the heat [heating]	**– la calefacción** lah kah-leh-fahk-<u>theeyohn</u>
– the light	**– la luz** lah looth
– the TV	**– la televisión** lah teh-leh-bee-<u>seeyohn</u>
– the toilet	**– el retrete** ehl reh-<u>treh</u>-teh
I'd like another room.	**Quiero otra habitación.** <u>keeyeh</u>-roh <u>oh</u>-trah ah-bee-tah-<u>theeyohn</u>

Spain's electricity is 220 volts. You may need a converter and/or an adapter for your appliances.

Check-out

When's check-out?	**¿A qué hora hay que desocupar la habitación?** ah keh <u>oh</u>·rah aye keh deh·soh·koo·<u>pahr</u> lah ah·bee·tah·<u>theeyohn</u>
Can I leave my bags here until…?	**¿Puedo dejar mi equipaje aquí hasta…?** <u>pweh</u>·doh deh·<u>khahr</u> mee eh·kee·<u>pah</u>·kheh ah·<u>kee</u> <u>ahs</u>·tah…
Can I have an itemized bill/a receipt?	**¿Puede darme una factura detallada/un recibo?** <u>pweh</u>·deh <u>dahr</u>·meh <u>oo</u>·nah fahk·<u>loo</u>·rah deh·tah·<u>yah</u>·dah/oon reh·<u>thee</u>·boh
I think there's a mistake.	**Creo que hay un error.** <u>kreh</u>·oh keh aye oon eh·<u>rrohr</u>
I made… phone calls.	**He hecho…llamadas.** eh <u>eh</u>·choh… yah·<u>mah</u>·dahs
I took…from the mini-bar.	**He tomado…del minibar.** eh toh·<u>mah</u>·doh… dehl <u>mee</u>·nee·bar
I'll pay in cash/by credit card.	**Voy a pagar en efectivo/con tarjeta de crédito.** boy ah pah·<u>gahr</u> ehn eh·fehk·<u>tee</u>·boh/ kohn tahr·<u>kheh</u>·tah deh <u>kreh</u>·dee·toh

Tipping in hotels, restaurants and bars isn't customary in Spain. However, if you wish to leave a tip for good service, it will be appreciated; just round up a bill to the nearest euro or two.

Renting

I reserved *an apartment/a room*.	**He reservado *un apartamento/una habitación.*** eh reh·sehr·<u>bah</u>·doh *oon ah·pahr·tah·<u>mehn</u>·toh/<u>oo</u>·nah ah·bee·tah·<u>theeyohn</u>*
My name is…	**Me llamo…** meh <u>yah</u>·moh…
Can I have the *key/key card*?	**¿Puede darme la *llave/llave electrónica*?** <u>pweh</u>·deh <u>dahr</u>·meh lah <u>yah</u>·beh/<u>yah</u>·beh eh·lehk·<u>troh</u>·nee·kah
Are there…?	**¿Hay…?** aye…
– dishes	**– platos** <u>plah</u>·tohs
– pillows	**– almohadas** ahl·moh·<u>ah</u>·dahs
– sheets	**– sábanas** <u>sah</u>·bah·nahs
– towels	**– toallas** toh·<u>ah</u>·yahs
– utensils	**– cubiertos** koo·<u>beeyehr</u>·tohs
When do I put out the *trash [rubbish]/ recycling*?	**¿Cuándo saco *la basura/el reciclado*?** <u>kwahn</u>·doh <u>sah</u>·koh *lah bah·<u>soo</u>·rah/ehl reh·thee·<u>klah</u>·doh*
…is broken.	**…está estropeado♂/estropeada♀.** …ehs·<u>tah</u> ehs·troh·peh·<u>ah</u>·doh♂/ ehs·troh·peh·<u>ah</u>·dah♀
How does… work?	**¿Cómo funciona…?** <u>koh</u>·moh foon·<u>theeyoh</u>·nah…
– the air conditioner	**– el aire acondicionado** ehl <u>ayee</u>·reh ah·kohn·dee·theeyoh·<u>nah</u>·doh
– the dishwasher	**– el lavavajillas** ehl lah·bah·bah·<u>khee</u>·yahs
– the freezer	**– el congelador** ehl kohn·kheh·lah·<u>dohr</u>
– the heater	**– la calefacción** lah kah·leh·fahk·<u>theeyohn</u>
– the microwave	**– el microondas** ehl mee·kroh·<u>ohn</u>·dahs
– the refrigerator	**– la nevera** lah neh·<u>beh</u>·rah
– the stove	**– el horno** ehl <u>ohr</u>·noh
– the washing machine	**– la lavadora** lah lah·bah·<u>doh</u>·rah

Household Items

I need...	**Necesito...** neh·theh·<u>see</u>·toh...
– an adapter	– **un adaptador** oon ah·dahp·tah·<u>dohr</u>
– aluminum [kitchen] foil	– **papel de aluminio** pah·<u>pehl</u> deh ah·loo·<u>mee</u>·neeyoh
– a bottle opener	– **un abrebotellas** oon ah·breh·boh·<u>teh</u>·yahs
– a broom	– **una escoba** <u>oo</u>·nah ehs·<u>koh</u>·bah
– a can opener	– **un abrelatas** oon ah·breh·<u>lah</u>·tahs
– cleaning supplies	– **productos de limpieza** proh·<u>dook</u>·tohs deh leem·<u>peeyeh</u>·thah
– a corkscrew	– **un sacacorchos** oon sah·kah·<u>kohr</u>·chohs
– detergent	– **detergente** deh·tehr·<u>khehn</u>·teh
– dishwashing liquid	– **líquido lavavajillas** <u>lee</u>·kee·doh lah·bah·bah·<u>khee</u>·yahs
– garbage [rubbish] bags	– **bolsas de basura** <u>bohl</u>·sahs deh bah·<u>soo</u>·rah
– a lightbulb	– **una bombilla** <u>oo</u>·nah bohm·<u>bee</u>·yah
– matches	– **cerillas** theh·<u>ree</u>·yahs
– a mop	– **una fregona** <u>oo</u>·nah freh·<u>goh</u>·nah
– napkins	– **servilletas** sehr·bee·<u>yeh</u>·tahs
– paper towels	– **papel de cocina** pah·<u>pehl</u> deh koh·<u>thee</u>·nah
– plastic wrap [cling film]	– **film transparente** feelm trahns·pah·<u>rehn</u>·teh
– a plunger	– **un desatascador** oon deh·sah·tahs·kah·<u>dohr</u>
– scissors	– **tijeras** tee·<u>kheh</u>·rahs
– a vacuum cleaner	– **una aspiradora** <u>oo</u>·nah ahs·pee·rah·<u>doh</u>·rah

▶ For dishes and utensils, see page 69.

▶ For oven temperatures, see page 185.

Hostel

Is there a bed available?	**¿Hay camas disponibles?** aye <u>kah</u>·mahs dees·poh·<u>nee</u>·blehs
Can I have…?	**¿Me puede dar…?** meh <u>pweh</u>·deh dahr…
– a *single/double* room	**– una habitación *individual/doble*** <u>oo</u>·nah ah·bee·tah·<u>theeyohn</u> *een·dee·bee·doo·<u>ahl</u>/<u>doh</u>·bleh*
– a blanket	**– una manta** <u>oo</u>·nah <u>mahn</u>·tah
– a pillow	**– una almohada** <u>oo</u>·nah ahl·moh·<u>ah</u>·dah
– sheets	**– sábanas** <u>sah</u>·bah·nahs
– a towel	**– una toalla** <u>oo</u>·nah toh·<u>ah</u>·yah
When do you lock up?	**¿A qué hora cierran las puertas?** ah keh <u>oh</u>·rah <u>theeyeh</u>·rrahn lahs <u>pwehr</u>·tahs
Do I need a membership card?	**¿Necesito una tarjeta de socio?** neh·theh·<u>see</u>·toh <u>oo</u>·nah tahr·<u>kheh</u>·tah de <u>soh</u>·theeyoh
Here's my International Student Card.	**Aquí tiene mi carnet internacional de estudiante.** ah·<u>kee</u> <u>teeyeh</u>·neh mee kahr·<u>neht</u> een·tehr·nah·theeyoh·<u>nahl</u> deh ehs·too·<u>deeyahn</u>·teh

i

With more than 100 hostels around Spain, finding an inexpensive place to stay should be easy. Hostels are inexpensive accommodations that have dormitory-style rooms and, sometimes, private or semi-private rooms. Some offer private bathrooms, though most have shared facilities. There is usually a self-service kitchen on site. Reservations are recommended in advance in larger cities and popular destinations during the tourist season.

Camping

Can I camp here?	**¿Puedo acampar aquí?** <u>pweh</u>·doh ah·kahm·<u>pahr</u> ah·<u>kee</u>
Where's the campsite?	**¿Dónde está el cámping?** <u>dohn</u>·deh ehs·<u>tah</u> ehl <u>kahm</u>·peeng
What is the charge per *day/week*?	**¿Cuánto cobran por *día/semana*?** <u>kwahn</u>·toh <u>koh</u>·brahn pohr *<u>dee</u>·ah/seh·<u>mah</u>·nah*
Are there…?	**¿Hay…?** aye…
– cooking facilities	– **Instalaciones para cocinar** eens·tah·lah·<u>theeyoh</u>·nohs <u>pah</u>·rah koh·thee·<u>nahr</u>
– electric outlets	– **enchufes eléctricos** ehn·<u>choo</u>·fehs eh·<u>lehk</u>·tree·kohs
– laundry facilities	– **servicio de lavandería** sehr·<u>bee</u>·theeyoh deh lah·bahn·deh·<u>ree</u>·ah
– showers	– **duchas** <u>doo</u>·chahs
– tents for rent [hire]	– **tiendas de alquiler** <u>teeychn</u>·dahs deh ahl·kee·<u>lehr</u>
Where can I empty the chemical toilet?	**¿Dónde puedo vaciar el váter químico?** <u>dohn</u>·deh <u>pweh</u>·doh bah·thee·<u>ahr</u> ehl <u>bah</u>·tehr <u>kee</u>·mee·koh

You May See…

AGUA POTABLE	drinking water
PROHIBIDO ACAMPAR	no camping
PROHIBIDO HACER *HOGUERAS/BARBACOAS*	no *fires/barbecues*

▶ For household items, see page 47.
▶ For dishes and utensils, see page 69.

Internet and Communications

Essential

Where's an internet cafe?	**¿Dónde hay un cibercafé?** <u>dohn</u>·deh aye oon thee·behr·kah·<u>feh</u>
Can I *access the internet/check e-mail*?	**¿Puedo *acceder a Internet/revisar el correo electrónico*?** <u>pweh</u>·doh *ahk·theh·<u>dehr</u> ah een·tehr·<u>neht</u>/reh·bee·<u>sahr</u> ehl koh·<u>rreh</u>·oh eh·lehk·<u>troh</u>·nee·koh*
How much per (half) hour?	**¿Cuánto cuesta por (media) hora?** <u>kwahn</u>·toh <u>kwehs</u>·tah pohr (<u>meh</u>·deeyah) <u>oh</u>·rah
How do I *connect/log on*?	**¿Cómo *entro al sistema/inicio la sesión*?** <u>koh</u>·moh *<u>ehn</u>·troh ahl sees·<u>teh</u>·mah/ ee·nee·<u>theeyoh</u> lah seh·<u>seeyohn</u>*
A phone card, please.	**Una tarjeta telefónica, por favor.** <u>oo</u>·nah tahr·<u>kheh</u>·tah teh·leh·<u>foh</u>·nee·kah pohr fah·<u>bohr</u>
Can I have your phone number?	**¿Me puede dar su número de teléfono?** meh <u>pweh</u>·deh dahr soo <u>noo</u>·meh·roh deh teh·<u>leh</u>·foh·noh
Here's my *number/e-mail address*.	**Aquí tiene mi *número/dirección de correo electrónico*.** ah·<u>kee</u> <u>teeyeh</u>·neh mee *<u>noo</u>·meh·roh/dee·rehk·<u>theeyohn</u> deh koh·<u>rreh</u>·oh eh·lehk·<u>troh</u>·nee·koh*
Call me.	**Llámeme.** <u>yah</u>·meh·meh
E-mail me.	**Envíeme un correo.** ehn·<u>bee</u>·eh·meh oon koh·<u>rreh</u>·oh
Hello. This is…	**Hola. Soy…** <u>oh</u>·lah soy…
Can I speak to…?	**¿Puedo hablar con…?** <u>pweh</u>·doh ah·<u>blahr</u> kohn…

Can you repeat that?	**¿Puede repetir eso?** pweh·deh reh·peh·teer eh·soh
I'll call back later.	**Llamaré más tarde.** yah·mah·reh mahs tahr·deh
Bye.	**Adiós.** ah·deeyohs
Where's the post office?	**¿Dónde está la oficina de correos?** dohn·deh ehs·tah lah oh·fee·thee·nah deh koh·rreh·ohs
I'd like to send this to...	**Quiero mandar esto a...** keeyeh·roh mahn·dahr ehs·toh ah...

Computer, Internet and E-mail

Where's an internet cafe?	**¿Dónde hay un cibercafé?** dohn·deh aye oon thee·behr·kah·feh
Does it have wireless internet?	**¿Tiene Internet inalámbrico?** teeyeh·neh een·tehr·neht een·ah·lahm·bree·koh
How do I turn the computer *on/off*?	**¿Cómo *enciendo/apago* el ordenador?** koh·moh ehn·theeyen·doh/ah·pah·goh ehl ohr·deh·nah·dohr
Can I...?	**¿Puedo...?** pweh·doh...
– access the internet	**– acceder a Internet** ahk·theh·dehr ah een·tehr·neht
– check e-mail	**– revisar el correo electrónico** reh·bee·sahr ehl koh·rreh·oh eh·lehk·troh·nee·koh
– print	**– imprimir** eem·pree·meer
How much per (half) hour?	**¿Cuánto cuesta por (media) hora?** kwahn·toh kwehs·tah pohr (meh·deeyah) oh·rah

How do I...?	¿Cómo...? koh·moh...
– connect/ disconnect	– **me conecto/me desconecto** meh koh·<u>nehk</u>·toh/meh dehs·koh·<u>nehk</u>·toh
– log *on/off*	– *inicio/cierro* **la sesión** ee·<u>nee</u>·theeyoh/ <u>theeyeh</u>·rroh lah seh·<u>seeyohn</u>
– type this symbol	– **escribo este símbolo** ehs·<u>kree</u>·boh ehs·teh <u>seem</u>·boh·loh
What's your e-mail?	**¿Cuál es su dirección de correo electrónico?** kwahl ehs soo dee·rehk·<u>theeyohn</u> deh koh·<u>rreh</u>·oh eh·lehk·<u>troh</u>·nee·koh
My e-mail is...	**Mi dirección de correo electrónico es...** mee dee·rehk·<u>theeyohn</u> deh koh·<u>rreh</u>·oh eh·lehk·<u>troh</u>·nee·koh ehs...

You May See...

CERRAR	close
BORRAR	delete
CORREO ELECTRÓNICO	e-mail
SALIR	exit
AYUDA	help
MENSAJERO INSTANTÁNEO	instant messenger
INTERNET	internet
INICIO DE SESIÓN	login
NUEVO (MENSAJE)	new (message)
ENCENDER/APAGAR	on/off
ABRIR	open
IMPRIMIR	print
GUARDAR	save
ENVIAR	send
NOMBRE DE USUARIO/CONTRASEÑA	username/password
INTERNET INALÁMBRICO	wireless internet

Phone

A *phone card/ prepaid phone*, please.	***Una tarjeta telefónica/Un teléfono prepago*, por favor.** *oo*-nah tahr-*kheh*-tah teh-leh-*foh*-nee-kah/oon teh-*leh*-foh-noh preh-*pah*-goh pohr fah-*bohr*
How much?	**¿Cuánto es?** <u>kwahn</u>-toh ehs
My phone doesn't work here.	**Mi teléfono no funciona aquí.** mee teh-leh-foh-noh no foon-<u>theeyoh</u>-nah ah-<u>kee</u>
What's the *area code/country code* for…?	**¿Cuál es el *prefijo/código de país* para…?** kwahl ehs ehl preh-*fee*-khoh/ <u>koh</u>-dee-goh deh pah-<u>ees</u> <u>pah</u>-rah…
What's the number for Information?	**¿Cuál es el número de información?** kwahl ehs ehl <u>noo</u>-meh-roh deh een-fohr-mah-<u>theeyohn</u>
I'd like the number for…	**Quiero que me dé el número de teléfono de…** <u>keeyeh</u>-roh keh meh deh ehl <u>noo</u>-meh-roh deh teh-<u>leh</u>-foh-noh deh…
Can I have your number?	**¿Me puede dar su número de teléfono?** meh <u>pweh</u>-deh dahr soo <u>noo</u>-meh-roh deh teh-<u>leh</u>-foh-noh
Here's my number.	**Aquí tiene mi número.** ah-<u>kee</u> <u>teeyeh</u>-neh mee <u>noo</u>-meh-roh

▶For numbers, see page 178.

Please call me.	**Llámame, por favor.** <u>yah</u>-mah-meh pohr fah-<u>bohr</u>
Please text me.	**Envíame un mensaje de texto, por favor.** ehn-<u>beeyah</u>-meh oon mehn-<u>sah</u>-kheh deh <u>tehx</u>-toh pohr fah-<u>bohr</u>
I'll call you.	**Le♂/La♀ llamaré.** leh♂/lah♀ yah-mah-<u>reh</u>
I'll text you.	**Te enviaré un mensaje de texto.** teh ehn-beeyah-<u>reh</u> oon mehn-<u>sah</u>-kheh deh <u>tehx</u>-toh

On the Phone

Hello. This is…	**Hola. Soy…** <u>oh</u>·lah soy…
Can I speak to…?	**¿Puedo hablar con…?** pweh·doh ah·<u>blahr</u> kohn…
Extension…	**Extensión…** ehks·tehn·<u>seeyohn</u>…
Speak *louder/more slowly,* please.	**Hable más *alto/despacio*, por favor.** <u>ah</u>·bleh mahs *<u>ahl</u>·toh/dehs·<u>pah</u>·theeyoh* pohr fah·<u>bohr</u>
Can you repeat that?	**¿Puede repetir eso?** <u>pweh</u>·deh reh·peh·<u>teer</u> <u>eh</u>·soh
I'll call back later.	**Llamaré más tarde.** yah·mah·<u>roh</u> mahs <u>tahr</u>·deh
Bye.	**Adiós.** ah·<u>deeyohs</u>

▶For business travel, see page 152.

You May Hear…

¿Quién llama? keeyehn <u>yah</u>·mah	Who's calling?
Espere. ehs·<u>peh</u>·reh	Hold on.
Le paso. leh <u>pah</u>·soh	I'll put you through.
No está. noh ehs·<u>tah</u>	He/She is not here.
No puede atenderle en este momento. noh <u>pweh</u>·deh ah·tehn·<u>dehr</u>·leh ehn <u>ehs</u>·teh moh·<u>mehn</u>·toh	He/She can't come to the phone.
¿Quiere dejarle un mensaje? <u>keeyeh</u>·reh deh·<u>khahr</u>·leh oon mehn·sah·kheh	Would you like to leave a message?
Vuelva a llamar *más tarde/en diez minutos.* <u>bwehl</u>·bah ah yah·<u>mahr</u> *mahs <u>tahr</u>·deh/ehn <u>deeyeth</u> mee·<u>noo</u>·tohs*	Call back *later/in 10 minutes.*
¿Le puede llamar él♂/ella♀ a usted? leh <u>pweh</u>·deh yah·<u>mahr</u> ehl♂/<u>eh</u>·yah♀ ah oos·<u>tehth</u>	Can he/she call you back?
¿Me da su número? meh dah soo <u>noo</u>·meh·roh	What's your number?

i Public phones are either coin- or card-operated, though coin-operated phones are becoming less common. Phone cards can be purchased in post offices, newsstands and tobacconists. For international calls, calling cards are the most economical. You can also make your long-distance calls at **locutorios** (call centers); these additionally offer internet, fax and wireless phone-charging services at reasonable prices. Calling internationally from your hotel may be convenient, but the rates can be very expensive.

Important telephone numbers:
  emergencies, 112
  information, 010
  operator assistance, 025

To call the U.S. or Canada from Spain, dial 00 + 1 + area code + phone number. To call the U.K. from Spain, dial 00 + 44 + area code (minus the first 0) + phone number.

Fax

Can I *send/receive* a fax here?	**¿Puedo *enviar/recibir* un fax aquí?** pweh·doh *ehn·bee·ahr/reh·thee·beer* oon fahx ah·kee
What's the fax number?	**¿Cuál es el número de fax?** kwahl ehs ehl noo·meh·roh deh fahx
Please fax this to…	**Por favor envíe este fax a…** pohr fah·bohr ehn·bee·eh ehs·teh fahx ah…

Post Office

Where's the *post office/mailbox [postbox]*?

¿Dónde está *la oficina/el buzón* de correos? <u>dohn</u>·deh ehs·<u>tah</u> lah oh·fee·<u>thee</u>·nah/ ehl boo·<u>thohn</u> deh koh·<u>rreh</u>·ohs

A stamp for this *postcard/letter* to…

Un sello para esta *postal/carta* a… oon <u>seh</u>·yoh pah·rah ehs·tah pohs·<u>tahl</u>/<u>kahr</u>·tah ah…

How much?

¿Cuánto es? <u>kwahn</u>·toh ehs

I want to send this package *by airmail/ express*.

Quiero mandar este paquete por correo *aéreo/urgente*. <u>keeyeh</u>·roh mahn·<u>dahr</u> ehs·teh pah·<u>keh</u>·teh pohr koh·<u>rreh</u>·oh uh·<u>eh</u>·reh·oh/oor·<u>khen</u>·teh

A receipt, please.

Un recibo, por favor. oon reh·<u>thee</u>·boh pohr fah·<u>bohr</u>

You May Hear…

Rellene la declaración para la aduana. reh·<u>yeh</u>·neh lah deh·klah·rah·<u>theeyohn</u> pah·rah lah ah·doo·<u>ah</u>·nah

Fill out the customs declaration form.

¿Qué valor tiene? keh bah·<u>lohr</u> teeyeh·neh

What's the value?

¿Qué hay dentro? keh aye <u>dehn</u>·troh

What's inside?

Oficinas de Correos (post offices) in Spain offer more than just standard postal services. You may be able to fax, scan and e-mail documents and send money orders from the local post office. Services available vary by location.

▼ Food

▶ **Eating Out**   59

▶ **Meals**   70

▶ **Drinks**   87

▶ **Menu Reader**   91

Eating Out

Essential

Can you recommend a good *restaurant/bar*?	**¿Puede recomendarme un buen restaurante/bar?** pweh·deh reh·koh·mehn·<u>dahr</u>·meh oon bwehn *rehs·taw·<u>rahn</u>·teh/bahr*
Is there a *traditional Spanish/inexpensive* restaurant nearby?	**¿Hay un restaurante *típico español/barato* cerca de aquí?** aye oon rehs·taw·<u>rahn</u>·teh *<u>tee</u>·poo·koh oho pah <u>nyohl</u>/bah·<u>rah</u>·toh* <u>thehr</u>·kah deh ah·<u>kee</u>
A table for…, please.	**Una mesa para…, por favor.** <u>oo</u>·nah <u>meh</u>·sah <u>pah</u>·rah…pohr fah·<u>bohr</u>
Can we sit…?	**¿Podemos sentarnos…?** poh·<u>deh</u>·mohs sehn·<u>tahr</u>·nohs…
– here/there	**– aquí/allí** ah·<u>kee</u>/ah·<u>yee</u>
– outside	**– fuera** <u>fweh</u>·rah
– in a non-smoking area	**– en una zona de no fumadores** ehn <u>oo</u>·nah <u>thoh</u>·nah deh noh foo·mah·<u>doh</u>·rehs
I'm waiting for someone.	**Estoy esperando a alguien.** ohs·<u>toy</u> ehs·peh·<u>rahn</u>·doh ah <u>ahl</u>·geeyehn
Where's the restroom [toilet]?	**¿Dónde están los servicios?** <u>dohn</u>·deh ehs·<u>tahn</u> lohs sehr·<u>bee</u>·theeyohs
A menu, please.	**Una carta, por favor.** <u>oo</u>·nah <u>kahr</u>·tah pohr fah·<u>bohr</u>
What do you recommend?	**¿Qué me recomienda?** keh meh reh·koh·<u>meeyehn</u>·dah
I'd like…	**Quiero…** <u>keeyeh</u>·roh…
Some more…, please.	**Quiero más…, por favor.** <u>keeyeh</u>·roh mahs…pohr fah·<u>bohr</u>

Enjoy your meal!	**¡Que aproveche!** keh ah·proh·<u>beh</u>·cheh
The check [bill], please.	**La cuenta, por favor.** lah <u>kwen</u>·tah pohr fah·<u>bohr</u>
Is service included?	**¿Está incluido el servicio?** ehs·<u>tah</u> een·kloo·<u>ee</u>·doh ehl sehr·<u>bee</u>·theeyoh
Can I pay by credit card?	**¿Puedo pagar con tarjeta de crédito?** <u>pweh</u>·doh pah·<u>gahr</u> kohn tahr·<u>kheh</u>·tah deh <u>kreh</u>·dee·toh
Can I have a receipt?	**¿Podría darme un recibo?** poh·<u>dree</u>·ah <u>dahr</u>·meh oon reh·<u>thee</u>·boh
Thank you!	**¡Gracias!** <u>grah</u>·theeyahs

Restaurant Types

Can you recommend...?	**¿Puede recomendarme...?** <u>pweh</u>·deh reh·koh·mehn·<u>dahr</u>·meh...
– a restaurant	**– un restaurante** oon rehs·taw·<u>rahn</u>·teh
– a bar	**– un bar** oon bahr
– a cafe	**– un café** oon kah·<u>feh</u>
– a fast-food place	**– un restaurante de comida rápida** oon rehs·taw·<u>rahn</u>·teh deh koh·<u>mee</u>·dah <u>rah</u>·pee·dah
– a tapas bar	**– un bar de tapas** oon bahr deh <u>tah</u>·pahs

Reservations and Questions

I'd like to reserve a table...	**Quiero reservar una mesa...** <u>keeyeh</u>·roh reh·sehr·<u>bahr</u> <u>oo</u>·nah <u>meh</u>·sah...
– for 2	**– para dos** <u>pah</u>·rah dohs
– for this evening	**– para esta noche** <u>pah</u>·rah ehs·tah <u>noh</u>·cheh
– for tomorrow at...	**– para mañana a la/las...** <u>pah</u>·rah mah·<u>nyah</u>·nah ah lah/lahs...

▶ For when to use **la** or **las**, see page 175.

A table for 2, please.	**Una mesa para dos, por favor.** <u>oo</u>·nah <u>meh</u>·sah <u>pah</u>·rah dohs pohr fah·<u>bohr</u>
We have a reservation.	**Tenemos una reserva.** teh·<u>neh</u>·mohs <u>oo</u>·nah reh·<u>sehr</u>·bah
My name is…	**Me llamo…** meh <u>yah</u>·moh…
Can we sit…?	**¿Podríamos sentarnos…?** poh·<u>dree</u>·ah·mohs sehn·<u>tahr</u>·nohs…
– here/there	**– aquí/allí** ah·<u>kee</u>/ah·<u>yee</u>
– outside	**– fuera** <u>fweh</u>·rah
– in a non-smoking area	**– en una zona de no fumadores** ehn <u>oo</u>·nah <u>thoh</u>·nah deh noh foo·mah·<u>doh</u>·rehs
– by the window	**– al lado de la ventana** ahl <u>lah</u>·doh de lah behn·<u>tah</u>·nah
Where's the restroom [toilet]?	**¿Dónde están los servicios?** <u>dohn</u>·deh ehs·<u>tahn</u> lohs sehr·<u>bee</u>·theeyohs

You May Hear...

¿Tiene reserva?
teeyeh·neh reh·sehr·bah

Do you have
a reservation?

¿Cuántos son? kwahn·tohs sohn

How many?

¿Fumador o no fumador?
foo·mah·dohr oh noh foo·mah·dohr

Smoking or
non-smoking?

¿Está listo♂/lista♀ para pedir?
ehs·tah lees·toh♂/lees·tah♀ pah·rah
peh·deer

Are you ready to order?

¿Qué va a tomar? keh bah ah toh·mahr

What would you like?

Le recomiendo...
leh reh·koh·meeyehn·doh...

I recommend...

Que aproveche. keh ah·proh·beh·cheh

Enjoy your meal.

Ordering

Waiter/Waitress!	**¡Camarero♂/Camarera♀!** kah·mah·reh·roh♂/kah·mah·reh·rah♀
We're ready to order.	**Estamos listos para pedir.** ehs·tah·mohs lees·tohs pah·rah peh·deer
The wine list, please.	**La carta de vinos, por favor.** lah kahr·tah deh bee·nohs pohr fah·bohr
I'd like...	**Quiero...** keeyeh·roh...
– a bottle of...	**– una botella de...** oo·nah boh·teh·yah deh...
– a carafe of...	**– una garrafa de...** oo·nah gah·rrah·fah deh...
– a glass of...	**– un vaso de...** oon bah·soh deh...

▶For alcoholic and non-alcoholic drinks, see page 87.

The menu, please.	**La carta, por favor.** lah <u>kahr</u>·tah pohr fah·<u>bohr</u>
Do you have…?	**¿Tiene…?** <u>teeyeh</u>·neh…
– a menu in English	**– una carta en inglés** <u>oo</u>·nah <u>kahr</u>·tah ehn een·<u>glehs</u>
– a fixed-price menu	**– el menú del día** ehl meh·<u>noo</u> dehl <u>dee</u>·ah
– a children's menu	**– una carta para niños** <u>oo</u>·nah <u>kahr</u>·tah <u>pah</u>·rah <u>nee</u>·nyohs
What do you recommend?	**¿Qué me recomienda?** keh meh reh·koh·<u>meeyehn</u>·dah
What's this?	**¿Qué es esto?** keh ehs <u>ehs</u>·toh
What's in it?	**¿Que lleva?** keh <u>yeh</u>·bah
Is it spicy?	**¿Es picante?** ehs pee·<u>kahn</u>·teh
Without…, please.	**Sin…, por favor.** seen…pohr fah·<u>bohr</u>
It's to go [take away].	**Es para llevar.** ehs <u>pah</u>·rah yeh·<u>bahr</u>

You May See…

CARTA	menu
MENÚ DEL DÍA	menu of the day
SERVICIO (NO) INCLUIDO	service (not) included
ESPECIALIDADES DE LA CASA	specials

Cooking Methods

baked	**al horno** ahl <u>ohr</u>·noh
boiled	**hervido** ♂ **/hervida** ♀ ehr·bee·doh ♂ / ehr·<u>bee</u>·dah ♀

braised	**a fuego lento** ah fweh·goh lehn·toh
breaded	**empanado♂/empanada♀** ehm·pah·nah·doh♂/ehm·pah·nah·dah♀
creamed	**con nata** kohn nah·tah
diced	**cortado en taquitos** kohr·tah·doh ehn tah·kee·tohs
fileted	**cortado en filetes** kohr·tah·doh ehn fee·leh·tehs
fried	**frito♂/frita♀** free·toh♂/free·tah♀
grilled	**a la plancha** ah lah plahn·chah
poached	**escalfado♂/escalfada♀** ehs·kahl·fah·doh♂/ehs·kahl·fah·dah♀
roasted	**asado♂/asada♀** ah·sah·doh♂/ah·sah·dah♀
sautéed	**salteado♂/salteada♀** sahl·teh·ah·doh♂/sahl·teh·ah·dah♀
smoked	**ahumado♂/ahumada♀** ah·oo·mah·doh♂/ah·oo·mah·dah♀
steamed	**al vapor** ahl bah·pohr
stewed	**guisado♂/guisada♀** gee·sah·doh♂/gee·sah·dah♀
stuffed	**relleno♂/rellena♀** reh·yeh·noh♂/reh·yeh·nah♀

Special Requirements

I'm...	**Soy...** soy...
– diabetic	– **diabético♂/diabética♀** dee·ah·beh·tee·koh♂/dee·ah·beh·tee·kah♀
– lactose intolerant	– **alérgico♂/alérgica♀ a la lactosa** ah·lehr·khee·koh♂/ah·lehr·khee·kah♀ ah lah lahk·toh·sah
– vegetarian	– **vegetariano♂/vegetariana♀** beh·kheh·tah·reeyah·noh♂/beh·kheh·tah·reeyah·nah♀

I'm allergic to…	**Soy alérgico** ♂ **/alérgica** ♀ **a…** soy ah·<u>lehr</u>·khee·koh ♂ /ah·<u>lehr</u>·khee·kah ♀ ah…
I can't eat…	**No puedo comer…** noh <u>pweh</u>·doh koh·<u>mehr</u>…
– dairy	– **productos lácteos** proh·<u>dook</u>·tohs <u>lahk</u>·teh·ohs
– gluten	– **gluten** <u>gloo</u>·tehn
– nuts	– **frutos secos** <u>froo</u>·tohs <u>seh</u>·kohs
– pork	– **carne de cerdo** <u>kahr</u>·neh deh <u>thehr</u>·doh
– shellfish	– **marisco** mah·<u>rees</u>·koh
– spicy foods	– **comidas picantes** koh·<u>mee</u>·dahs pee·<u>kahn</u>·tehs
– wheat	– **trigo** <u>tree</u>·goh
Is it *halal/kosher*?	**¿Es *halal/kosher*?** ehs *ah·lahl/koh·<u>sehr</u>*

Dining with Kids

Do you have children's portions?	**¿Sirven raciones para niños?** <u>seer</u>·behn rah·<u>theeyoh</u>·nehs <u>pah</u>·rah <u>nee</u>·nyohs
A *highchair/child's seat,* please.	**Una *trona/silla para niños*, por favor.** <u>oo</u>·nah <u>troh</u>·nah/<u>see</u>·yah <u>pah</u>·rah <u>nee</u>·nyohs pohr fah·<u>bohr</u>
Where can I *feed/change* the baby?	**¿Dónde puedo *darle de comer/cambiar* al niño?** <u>dohn</u>·deh <u>pweh</u>·doh *<u>dahr</u>·leh deh koh·<u>mehr</u>/kahm·<u>beeyahr</u>* ahl <u>nee</u>·nyoh
Can you warm this?	**¿Puede calentar esto?** <u>pweh</u>·deh kah·lehn·<u>tahr</u> <u>ohs</u>·toh

▶ For travel with children, see page 155.

Complaints

| How much longer will our food be? | **¿Cuánto más tardará la comida?** <u>kwahn</u>·toh mahs tahr·dah·<u>rah</u> lah koh·<u>mee</u>·dah |
| We can't wait any longer. | **No podemos esperar más.** noh poh·<u>deh</u>·mohs ehs·peh·<u>rahr</u> mahs |

We're leaving.	**Nos vamos.** nohs bah·mohs
I didn't order this.	**Esto no es lo que pedí.** ehs·toh noh ehs loh keh peh·dee
I ordered…	**Pedí…** peh·dee…
I can't eat this.	**No puedo comerme esto.** noh pweh·doh koh·mehr·meh ehs·toh
This is too…	**Esto está demasiado…** ehs·toh ehs·tah deh·mah·seeyah·doh…
– cold/hot	**– frío/caliente** free·oh/kah·leeyehn·teh
– salty/spicy	**– salado/picante** sah·lah·doh/pee·kahn·teh
– tough/bland	**– duro/soso** doo·roh/soh·soh
This isn't *clean/fresh.*	**Esto no está *limpio/fresco.*** ehs·toh noh ehs·tah *leem·peeyoh/frehs·koh*

Paying

The check [bill], please.	**La cuenta, por favor.** lah kwehn·tah pohr fah·bohr
Separate checks [bills], please.	**Cuentas separadas, por favor.** kwehn·tahs seh·pah·rah·dahs pohr fah·bohr
It's all together.	**Póngalo todo junto.** pohn·gah·loh toh·doh khoon·toh
Is service included?	**¿Está incluido el servicio?** ehs·tah een·kloo·ee·doh ehl sehr·bee·theeyoh
What's this amount for?	**¿De qué es esta cantidad?** deh keh ehs ehs·tah kahn·tee·dahth
I didn't have that. I had…	**Yo no tomé eso. Tomé…** yoh noh toh·meh eh·soh toh·meh…
Can I pay by credit card?	**¿Puedo pagar con tarjeta de crédito?** pweh·doh pah·gahr kohn tahr·kheh·tah deh kreh·dee·toh

Can I have *a receipt/ an itemized bill*?	**¿Podría darme *un recibo/una cuenta detallada*?** poh-dree-ah dahr-meh *oon reh-thee-boh/oo-nah kwehn-tah dch-tah-yah-dah*
That was delicious!	**¡Estuvo delicioso!** ehs-too-boh deh-lee-theeyoh-soh

> Restaurants are generally required to include service charges as part of the bill and, so, tipping isn't customary. If you wish to leave a tip for good service, though, just round up the bill to the nearest euro or two.

Market

Where are the *carts [trolleys]/baskets*?	**¿Dónde están *los carritos/las cestas*?** dohn-deh ehs-tahn *lohs kah-rree-tohs/lahs thehs-tahs*
Where is ...?	**¿Donde está...?** dohn-deh ehs-tah...

▶ For food items, see page 91.

I'd like some of *that/this.*	**Quiero un poco de *eso/esto*.** keeyeh-roh oon poh-koh deh *eh-soh/ehs-toh*
Can I taste it?	**¿Puedo probarlo?** pweh-doh proh-bahr-loh
I'd like...	**Quiero...** keeyeh-roh...
– a *kilo/half-kilo* of...	**– un *kilo/medio kilo* de...** oon *kee-loh/ mch-deeyoh kee-loh* deh...
– a liter of...	**– un litro de...** oon lee-troh deh...
– a piece of...	**– un trozo de...** oon troh-thoh deh...
– a slice of...	**– una rodaja de...** oo-nah roh-dah-khah deh...
More./Less.	**Más./Menos.** mahs/meh-nohs
How much?	**¿Cuánto es?** kwahn-toh ehs

Where do I pay?	**¿Dónde se paga?** <u>dohn</u>·deh seh <u>pah</u>·gah
A bag, please.	**Una bolsa, por favor.** <u>oo</u>·nah <u>bohl</u>·sah pohr fah·<u>bohr</u>
I'm being helped.	**Ya me atienden.** yah meh ah·<u>teeyehn</u>·dehn

▶For conversion tables, see page 184.

You May Hear...

¿Necesita ayuda? neh·theh·<u>see</u>·tah ah·<u>yoo</u>·dah	Can I help you?
¿Qué desea? keh deh·<u>seh</u>·ah	What would you like?
¿Algo más? <u>ahl</u>·goh mahs	Anything else?
Son…euros. sohn…<u>ew</u>·rohs	That's…euros.

i In Spain, food is often purchased at local family-run markets. These are excellent places for regional and specialty foods, fresh fruit and vegetables, meat and baked goods. **Hipermercados** (large grocery store chains) are also common, but these are usually found on the outskirts of town or in the suburbs. These stores have a larger selection than regular supermarkets, and are often less expensive. **Alcampo**, **Carrefour** and **Hipercor** are common chains. **El Corte Inglés** is a popular department store chain that has a supermarket on the ground floor in some locations, but it tends to have higher prices than regular supermarkets.

You May See...

CONSUMIR PREFERENTEMENTE ANTES DE…	best if used by…
CALORÍAS	calories
SIN GRASA	fat free
CONSERVAR EN FRIGORÍFICO	keep refrigerated

PUEDE CONTENER TRAZAS DE…	may contain traces of…
FECHA LÍMITE DE VENTA…	sell by…
APTO PARA VEGETARIANOS	suitable for vegetarians

Dishes, Utensils and Kitchen Tools

bottle opener	**el abrebotellas** ehl ah·breh·boh·<u>teh</u>·yahs
bowl	**el cuenco** ehl <u>kwehn</u>·koh
can opener	**el abrelatas** ehl ah·breh·<u>lah</u>·tahs
corkscrew	**el sacacorchos** ehl sah·kah·<u>kohr</u>·chohs
cup	**la taza** lah <u>tah</u>·thah
fork	**el tenedor** ehl teh·nch·<u>dohr</u>
frying pan	**la sartén** lah sahr·<u>tehn</u>
glass	**el vaso** ehl <u>bah</u>·soh
(steak) knife	**el cuchillo (de carne)** ehl koo·<u>chee</u>·yoh (deh <u>kahr</u>·neh)
measuring cup/spoon	*la taza/la cuchara medidora* lah <u>tah</u>·thah/ lah koo·<u>chah</u>·rah meh·dee·<u>doh</u>·rah
napkin	**la servilleta** lah sehr·bee·<u>yeh</u>·tah
plate	**el plato** ehl <u>plah</u>·toh
pot	**la olla** lah <u>oh</u>·yah
saucepan	**el cazo** ehl <u>kah</u>·thoh
spatula	**la espátula** lah ehs·<u>pah</u>·too·lah
spoon	**la cuchara** lah koo·<u>chah</u>·rah

Meals

El desayuno (breakfast) is usually served from 8:00 a.m. to 10:00 a.m. **La comida** (lunch), generally the largest meal of the day, is served from 2–4 p.m. **La cena** (dinner) is typically smaller and lighter than in the U.S. or U.K., and is usually served after 9 p.m. For a snack between meals, you can get **tapas** in smaller restaurants and some bars.

Breakfast

el agua ehl <u>ah</u>·gwah	water
el café/el té… ehl kah·<u>feh</u>/ehl teh…	coffee/tea…
– con azúcar kohn ah·<u>thoo</u>·kahr	– with sugar
– con edulcorante artificial kohn eh·dool·koh·<u>rahn</u>·teh ahr·tee·fee·<u>theeyahl</u>	– with artificial sweetener
– con leche kohn <u>leh</u>·cheh	– with milk
– descafeinado dehs·kah·feyee·<u>nah</u>·doh	– decaf
– solo <u>soh</u>·loh	– black
los cereales (calientes/fríos) lohs theh·reh·<u>ah</u>·lehs (kah·<u>leeyehn</u>·tehs/<u>free</u>·ohs)	(cold/hot) cereal
los fiambres lohs fee·<u>ahm</u>·brehs	cold cuts [charcuterie]
la harina de avena lah ah·<u>ree</u>·nah deh ah·<u>beh</u>·nah	oatmeal
el huevo… ehl <u>weh</u>·boh…	egg…
– *duro/pasado* por agua <u>doo</u>·roh/pah·<u>sah</u>·doh pohr <u>ah</u>·gwah	– *hard-/soft*-boiled

I'd like…	**Quiero…** <u>keeyeh</u>·roh…
More…, please.	**Más…, por favor.** mahs…pohr fah·<u>bohr</u>

– frito <u>free</u>·toh	– fried
– revuelto reh·<u>bwehl</u>·toh	– scrambled
los huevos a la flamenca lohs <u>weh</u>·bohs ah lah flah·<u>mehn</u>·kah	baked eggs with tomato, onion and ham
la leche lah <u>leh</u>·cheh	milk
la magdalena lah mahg·dah·<u>leh</u>·nah	muffin
la mantequilla lah mahn·teh·<u>kee</u>·yah	butter
la mermelada/la jalea lah mehr·meh·<u>lah</u>·dah/khah·<u>leh</u>·ah	jam/jelly
el muesli ehl <u>mwehs</u>·lee	granola [muesli]
el pan ehl pahn	bread
el panecillo ehl pah·neh·<u>thee</u>·yoh	roll
el queso ohl <u>keh</u>·soh	cheese
la salchicha lah sahl·<u>chee</u>·chah	sausage
el tocino ehl toh·<u>thee</u>·noh	bacon
la tortilla... lah tohr·<u>tee</u>·yah...	omelet...
– de patatas deh pah·<u>tah</u>·tahs	– with potato (and sometimes onion)
– de jamón deh khah·<u>mohn</u>	– with ham
– paisana payee·<u>sah</u>·nah	– with potatoes, peas and shrimp or ham
– de queso deh <u>keh</u>·soh	– with cheese
– de setas deh <u>seh</u>·tahs	– with mushrooms
la tostada lah tohs·<u>tah</u>·dah	toast

With/Without...	**Con/Sin...** kohn/seen...
I can't have...	**No puedo tomar...** noh <u>pweh</u>·doh toh·<u>mahr</u>...

el yogur ehl yoh·<u>goor</u>	yogurt
el zumo de... ehl <u>thoo</u>·moh deh...	...juice
– manzana mahn·<u>thah</u>·nah	– apple
– pomelo poh·<u>meh</u>·loh	– grapefruit
– naranja nah·<u>rahn</u>·khah	– orange

Appetizers [Starters]/Tapas

las aceitunas (rellenas) lahs ah·theyey·<u>too</u>·nahs (reh·<u>yeh</u>·nahs)	(stuffed) olives
las albóndigas lahs ahl·<u>bohn</u>·dee·gahs	meatballs
el bacalao ehl bah·kah·<u>laoh</u>	dried salt cod
los boquerones en vinagre lohs boh·keh·<u>roh</u>·nehs ehn bee·<u>nah</u>·greh	anchovies marinated in garlic and olive oil
los callos lohs <u>kah</u>·yohs	tripe in hot paprika sauce
los caracoles lohs kah·rah·<u>koh</u>·lehs	snails
los champiñones al ajillo lohs chahm·pee·<u>nyoh</u>·nehs ahl ah·<u>khee</u>·yoh	mushrooms fried in olive oil with garlic
las croquetas lahs kroh·<u>keh</u>·tahs	croquettes with various fillings
las gambas al ajillo lahs <u>gahm</u>·bahs ahl ah·<u>khee</u>·yoh	broiled shrimp in garlic
el pan con tomate ehl pahn kohn toh·<u>mah</u>·teh	toasted bread with garlic, tomato and olive oil
los pescados fritos lohs pehs·<u>kah</u>·dohs <u>free</u>·tohs	fried fish

I'd like...	**Quiero...** <u>keeyeh</u>·roh...
More..., please.	**Más..., por favor.** mahs...pohr fah·<u>bohr</u>

los pimientos lohs pee·<u>mecychn</u>·tohs	peppers
los pinchos lohs <u>peen</u>·chohs	grilled, skewered meat
los quesos lohs <u>keh</u>·sohs	cheese platter
la tortilla española lah tohr·<u>tee</u>·yah chs·pah·<u>nyoh</u>·lah	potato omelet

> *i* **Tapas** are snacks, similar to appetizers, served in cafés and bars. Many bars have their own specialties. When ordering, **una tapa** is a mouthful, **una ración** is half a plateful and **una porción** is a generous amount.

Soup

el caldo gallego chl <u>kahl</u>·doh gah·<u>yeh</u>·goh	stew of cabbage, potatoes, beans and meat, from Galicia region
el cocido ehl koh·<u>thee</u>·doh	chickpea stew with potatoes, cabbage, turnips, beef, bacon, chorizo and black pudding
el consomé al jerez ehl kohn·soh·<u>meh</u> ahl kheh·<u>rehth</u>	chicken broth with sherry
la fabada asturiana lah fah·<u>bah</u>·dah ahs·too·<u>reeyah</u>·nah	white bean stew
el gazpacho ehl gahth·<u>pah</u>·choh	cold tomato soup
el marmitako ehl mahr·mee·<u>tah</u>·koh	tuna fish and potato stew, from the Basque region

With/Without…	**Con/Sin…** kohn/seen…
I can't have…	**No puedo tomar…** noh <u>pweh</u>·doh toh·<u>mahr</u>…

la sopa... lah <u>soh</u>·pah...	...soup
– **castellana** kahs·teh·<u>yah</u>·nah	– with garlic, chunks of ham and a poached egg
– **de ajo blanco** deh <u>ah</u>·khoh <u>blahn</u>·koh	– with garlic and almond, served cold, popular in Andalucia
– **de habas** deh <u>ah</u>·bahs	– bean
– **de mariscos** deh mah·<u>rees</u>·kohs	– seafood
– **de pollo** deh <u>poh</u>·yoh	– chicken
– **de tomate** deh toh·<u>mah</u>·teh	– tomato
– **de verduras** deh behr·<u>doo</u>·rahs	– vegetable

Fish and Seafood

la almeja lah ahl·<u>meh</u>·khah	clam
el arenque ehl ah·<u>rehn</u>·keh ·	herring
el atún ehl ah·<u>toon</u>	tuna
el bacalao a la vizcaína ehl bah·kah·<u>laoh</u> ah lah beeth·<u>kayee</u>·nah	cod with dried peppers and onions
el bacalao ehl bah·kah·<u>laoh</u>	cod
el besugo ehl beh·<u>soo</u>·goh	sea bream
el boquerón ehl boh·keh·<u>rohn</u>	fresh baby anchovy
la caballa lah kah·<u>bah</u>·yah	mackerel
el calamar ehl kah·lah·<u>mahr</u>	squid
los calamares a la romana lohs kah·lah·<u>mahr</u>·ehs ah lah roh·<u>mah</u>·nah	deep-fried battered squid

| I'd like... | **Quiero...** <u>keeyeh</u>·roh... |
| More..., please. | **Más..., por favor.** mahs...pohr fah·<u>bohr</u> |

el cangrejo ehl kahn·<u>greh</u>·khoh	crab
el chipirón ehl chee·pee·<u>rohn</u>	small whole squid
las cigalas lahs thee·<u>gah</u>·lahs	crayfish
las cigalas cocidas lahs thee·<u>gah</u>·lahs koh·<u>thee</u>·dahs	boiled crayfish
el fletán ehl fleh·<u>tahn</u>	halibut
la gamba lah <u>gahm</u>·bah	shrimp
las gambas en cerveza lahs <u>gahm</u>·bahs ehn thehr·<u>beh</u>·thah	shrimp in beer
la langosta lah lahn·<u>goh</u>·tah	lobster
el lenguado ehl lehn·<u>gwah</u>·doh	sole
la lubina lah loo·<u>bee</u>·nah	sea bass
la mariscada lah mah·rees·<u>kah</u>·dah	cold mixed shellfish
los mejillones lohs meh·khee·<u>yoh</u>·nehs	mussels
los mejillones en escabeche lohs meh·khee·<u>yohn</u>·ehs ehn ehs·kah·<u>beh</u>·cheh	mussels in a marinade
la merluza lah mehr·<u>loo</u>·thah	hake
la merluza a la sidra lah mehr·<u>loo</u>·thah ah lah <u>see</u>·drah	hake in cider
el mero ehl <u>meh</u>·roh	grouper
la ostra lah <u>ohs</u>·trah	oyster
el pez espada ehl pehth ehs·<u>pah</u>·dah	swordfish
el pulpo ehl <u>pool</u>·poh	octopus
el pulpo a la gallega ehl <u>pool</u>·poh ah lah gah·<u>yeh</u>·gah	octopus with olive oil and paprika

With/Without...	**Con/Sin...** kohn/seen...
I can't have...	**No puedo tomar...** noh <u>pweh</u>·doh toh·<u>mahr</u>...

el salmón ehl sahl·<u>mohn</u> — salmon

el tiburón ehl tee·boo·<u>rohn</u> — shark

la trucha lah <u>troo</u>·chah — trout

la trucha a la navarra lah <u>troo</u>·chah ah lah nah·<u>bah</u>·rrah — grilled trout stuffed with ham

la zarzuela de pescado lah thahr·<u>thweh</u>·lah deh pehs·<u>kah</u>·doh — mixed fish and seafood cooked in broth, served over bread

Meat and Poultry

la asadurilla de cordero lah ah·sah·doo·<u>rree</u>·yah deh kohr·<u>deh</u>·roh — lamb's liver

la butifarra lah boo·tee·<u>fah</u>·rrah — spiced pork sausage, popular in Cataluña and Valencia

los callos a la madrileña lohs <u>kah</u>·yohs ah lah mah·dree·<u>leh</u>·nyah — tripe stew, a Madrid specialty

la carne lah <u>kahr</u>·neh — meat

la carne de cerdo lah <u>kahr</u>·neh deh <u>thehr</u>·doh — pork

la carne picada lah <u>kahr</u>·neh pee·<u>kah</u>·dah — ground beef

la carne de vaca lah <u>kahr</u>·neh deh <u>bah</u>·kah — beef

el chorizo ehl choh·<u>ree</u>·thoh — highly-seasoned pork sausage

la chuleta lah choo·<u>leh</u>·tah — chop

el cochifrito navarro ehl koh·chee·<u>free</u>·toh nah·<u>bah</u>·rroh — deep-fried lamb pieces

el conejo ehl koh·<u>neh</u>·khoh — rabbit

I'd like…	**Quiero…** <u>keeyeh</u>·roh…
More…, please.	**Más…, por favor.** mahs…pohr fah·<u>bohr</u>

el cordero ehl kohr·<u>deh</u>·roh	lamb
la cordorniz lah kohr·dohr·<u>neeth</u>	quail
las costillas de cerdo lahs kohs·<u>tee</u>·yahs deh <u>thehr</u>·doh	pork ribs
las empanadas lahs ehm·pah·<u>nah</u>·dahs	pastry filled with meat, chicken or tuna, a specialty of Galicia
los espárragos montañeses lohs ehs·pah·rrah·gohs mohn·tah·<u>nyeh</u>·sehs	calves's tails
la falda de buey lah <u>fahl</u>·dah deh bwehy	beef flank steak
el filete ehl fee·<u>leh</u>·teh	steak
las gallinejas lahs gah·yee·<u>neh</u>·khahs	fried lamb intestine
el guisado de riñones ehl gee·<u>sah</u>·doh deh ree·<u>nyoh</u>·nehs	kidney stew
el hígado ehl <u>ee</u>·gah·doh	liver
el jamón ehl khah·<u>mohn</u>	ham
el jamón ibérico ehl khah·<u>mohn</u> ee·<u>beh</u>·ree·koh	aged Iberian ham
el jamón serrano ehl khah·<u>mohn</u> seh·<u>rrah</u>·noh	dry-cured serrano ham
el lacón con grelos ehl lah·kohn kohn <u>greh</u>·lohs	salted ham with turnip greens, typical of Galicia
las magras con tomate lahs <u>mah</u>·grahs kohn toh·<u>mah</u>·teh	lightly fried ham dipped in tomato sauce
las manos de cerdo lahs <u>mah</u>·nohs deh <u>thehr</u>·doh	pig's feet [trotters]

With/Without...	**Con/Sin...** kohn/seen...
I can't have...	**No puedo tomar...** noh <u>pweh</u>·doh toh·<u>mahr</u>...

las mollejas de ternera lahs moh·<u>yeh</u>·khahs deh tehr·<u>neh</u>·rah	veal sweetbread
la morcilla lah mohr·<u>thee</u>·yah	blood sausage
las patatas con chorizo lahs pah·<u>tah</u>·tahs kohn choh·<u>ree</u>·thoh	potatoes with chorizo sausage
el pato ehl <u>pah</u>·toh	duck
el pavo ehl <u>pah</u>·boh	turkey
el pollo ehl <u>poh</u>·yoh	chicken
el pollo frito ehl <u>poh</u>·yoh <u>free</u>·toh	fried chicken
el riñón ehl ree·<u>nyohn</u>	kidney
la salchicha lah sahl·<u>chee</u>·chah	sausage
el salchichón ehl sahl·chee·<u>chohn</u>	salami-type sausage
el solomillo ehl soh·loh·<u>mee</u>·yoh	filet mignon
la ternera lah tehr·<u>neh</u>·rah	veal
el tocino ehl toh·<u>thee</u>·noh	bacon
la trucha a la navarra lah <u>troo</u>·chah ah lah nah·<u>bah</u>·rrah	trout fried with a piece of ham
el venado ehl beh·<u>nah</u>·doh	venison

rare	**muy poco hecho** ♂ **/hecha** ♀ mooy <u>poh</u>·koh <u>eh</u>·choh ♂ /<u>eh</u>·chah ♀
medium	**medio hecho** ♂ **/hecha** ♀ meh·deeyoh <u>eh</u>·choh ♂ /<u>eh</u>·chah ♀
well-done	**bien hecho** ♂ **/hecha** ♀ beeyehn <u>eh</u>·choh ♂ /<u>eh</u>·chah ♀

I'd like…	**Quiero…** <u>keeyeh</u>·roh…
More…, please.	**Más…, por favor.** mahs…pohr fah·<u>bohr</u>

Paella

la paella... lah pah·<u>eh</u>·yah...

paella...

– de carne deh <u>kahr</u>·neh

– with chicken and sausage, may be made with beef

– de marisco deh mah·<u>rees</u>·koh

– with seafood

– de verduras deh behr·<u>doo</u>·rahs

– with vegetables

– valenciana bah·lehn·<u>theeyah</u>·nah

– with chicken, shrimp, mussels, squid, peas, tomato, garlic, olive oil, paprika; from the Valencia region

– zamorana thah·moh·<u>rah</u>·nah

– with ham, pork loin, pig's feet; popular in the Zamora region

---

Paella is a specialty dish of Spain. Traditional **paella**, which originated in Valencia, includes rice, saffron, vegetables, rabbit and chicken. **Paella de marisco** (seafood **paella**) is a very popular version of this dish, especially along the coast. Other delicious versions are noted above.

| With/Without... | **Con/Sin...** kohn/seen... |
| I can't have... | **No puedo tomar...** noh <u>pweh</u>·doh toh·<u>mahr</u>... |

Vegetables

la aceituna lah ah·theyee·<u>too</u>·nah	olive
la acelga lah ah·<u>thehl</u>·gah	chard
el aguacate ehl ah·gwah·<u>khah</u>·teh	avocado
el ajo ehl <u>ah</u>·khoh	garlic
la alcachofa (salteada) lah ahl·kah·<u>choh</u>·fah (sahl·teh·<u>ah</u>·dah)	(sauteed) artichoke
el apio ehl <u>ah</u>·peeyoh	celery
los bajoques farcides lohs bah·<u>khoh</u>·kwehs fahr·<u>thee</u>·dehs	red peppers stuffed with rice, pork and tomatoes; from Catalonia
la batata lah bah·<u>tah</u>·tah	yam
la berenjena lah beh·rehn·<u>kheh</u>·nah	eggplant [aubergine]

I'd like…	**Quiero…** <u>keeyeh</u>·roh…
More…, please.	**Más…, por favor.** mahs…pohr fah·<u>bohr</u>

el brécol ehl <u>breh</u>·kohl	broccoli
los brotes de soja lohs <u>broh</u>·tehs deh <u>soh</u>·khah	bean sprouts
el calabacín ehl kah·lah·bah·<u>theen</u>	zucchini [courgette]
la cebolla lah theh·<u>boh</u>·yah	onion
el champiñon (a la plancha/salteado) ehl chahm·pee·<u>nyohn</u> (ah lah <u>plahn</u>·chah/sahl·teh·<u>ah</u>·doh)	(grilled/sautéed) mushroom
la coliflor lah koh·lee·<u>flohr</u>	cauliflower
el espárrago ehl ehs·<u>pah</u>·rrah·goh	asparagus
la espinaca lah ehs·pee·<u>nah</u>·kah	spinach
la faba lah <u>fah</u>·bah	white bean
el guisante ehl gee·<u>sahn</u>·teh	pea
las habas a la catalana lahs <u>ah</u>·bahs a lah kah·tah·<u>lah</u>·nah	broad bean
la judía lah khoo·<u>dee</u>·ah	bean
la judía verde lah khoo·<u>dee</u>·ah <u>behr</u>·deh	green bean
la lechuga lah leh·<u>choo</u>·gah	lettuce
la lenteja lah lehn·<u>teh</u>·khah	lentil
el maíz ehl mah·<u>eeth</u>	corn
la menestra lah meh·<u>nehs</u>·trah	vegetable stew
la patata lah pah·<u>tah</u>·tah	potato
el pepino ehl peh·<u>pee</u>·noh	cucumber
el pimiento relleno ehl pee·<u>meeyehn</u>·toh reh·<u>yeh</u>·noh	stuffed pepper

With/Without…	**Con/Sin…** kohn/seen…
I can't have…	**No puedo tomar…** noh <u>pweh</u>·doh toh·<u>mahr</u>…

el pimiento *rojo/verde* ehl
pee·<u>meeyehn</u>·toh <u>*roh*</u>·*khoh*/*behr*·*deh*

red/green pepper

el repollo ehl reh·<u>poh</u>·yoh

cabbage

la seta lah <u>seh</u>·tah

mushroom

el tomate ehl toh·<u>mah</u>·teh

tomato

la verdura lah behr·<u>doo</u>·rah

vegetable

la zanahoria lah thah·nah·<u>oh</u>·reeyah

carrot

Spices and Staples

la albahaca lah ahl·bah·<u>ah</u>·kah

basil

la alcaparra lah ahl·kah·<u>pah</u>·rrah

caper

la almendra lah ahl·<u>mehn</u>·drah

almond

el anís ehl ah·<u>nees</u>

aniseed

el arroz... ehl ah·<u>rrohth</u>...

rice...

– con habas y nabos
kohn <u>ah</u>·bahs ee <u>nah</u>·bohs

– with beans
and turnips

– a la cubana ah lah koo·<u>bah</u>·nah

– with fried eggs
and banana fritters

– empedrado ehm·peh·<u>drah</u>·doh

– with tomatoes
and cod and a top
layer of white beans

– santanderino sahn·tahn·deh·<u>ree</u>·noh

– with salmon
and milk

el azafrán ehl ah·thah·<u>frahn</u>

saffron

el azúcar ehl ah·<u>thoo</u>·kahr

sugar

I'd like...   **Quiero...** <u>keeyeh</u>·roh...

More..., please.   **Más..., por favor.** mahs...pohr fah·<u>bohr</u>

la cassolada lah kahs·soh·<u>lah</u>·dah	rice casserole with thrushes (a type of bird) and ribs, from Catalonia
la harina lah ah·<u>ree</u>·nah	flour
la mantequilla lah mahn·teh·<u>kee</u>·yah	butter
las migas de pastor lahs <u>mee</u>·gahs deh pahs·<u>tohr</u>	bread soaked in water then fried with pieces of bacon and dried peppers
el pan ehl pahn	bread
la pasta lah <u>pahs</u>·tah	pasta
el perejil ehl peh·reh·<u>kheel</u>	parsley
la pimienta negra lah pee·<u>meeyehn</u>·tah <u>neh</u>·grah	black pepper
la sal lah sahl	salt

Fruit

el albaricoque ehl ahl·bah·ree·<u>koh</u>·keh	apricot
el arándano ehl ah·<u>rahn</u>·dah·noh	blueberry
el arándano rojo ehl ah·<u>rahn</u>·dah·noh <u>roh</u>·khoh	cranberry
la cereza lah theh·<u>reh</u>·thah	cherry
la ciruela lah thee·<u>rweh</u>·lah	plum
el coco ehl <u>koh</u>·koh	coconut
la frambuesa lah frahm·<u>bweh</u>·sah	raspberry
la fresa lah <u>freh</u>·sah	strawberry
la fruta lah <u>froo</u>·tah	fruit

With/Without…	**Con/Sin…** kohn/seen…
I can't have…	**No puedo tomar…** noh <u>pweh</u>·doh toh·<u>mahr</u>…

la guayaba lah gwah·<u>yah</u>·bah	guava
el kiwi ehl <u>kee</u>·wee	kiwi
la lima lah <u>lee</u>·mah	lime
el limón ehl lee·<u>mohn</u>	lemon
el mango ehl <u>mahn</u>·goh	mango
la mandarina lah mahn·dah·<u>ree</u>·nah	tangerine
la manzana lah mahn·<u>thah</u>·nah	apple
el melocotón ehl meh·loh·koh·<u>tohn</u>	peach
el melón ehl meh·<u>lohn</u>	melon
la naranja lah nah·<u>rahn</u>·khah	orange
la papaya lah pah·<u>pah</u>·yah	papaya
la pera lah <u>peh</u>·rah	pear
la piña lah <u>pee</u>·nyah	pineapple
el plátano ehl <u>plah</u>·tah·noh	banana
el pomelo ehl poh·<u>meh</u>·loh	grapefruit
la sandía lah sahn·<u>dee</u>·ah	watermelon
la uva lah <u>oo</u>·bah	grape

Cheese

el queso... ehl <u>keh</u>·soh...	...cheese
– blando <u>blahn</u>·doh	– soft, mild-flavored
– de Burgos deh <u>boor</u>·gohs	– soft, creamy regional variety
– Cabrales kah·<u>brah</u>·lehs	– tangy, blue-veined regional variety

I'd like...	**Quiero...** <u>keeyeh</u>·roh...
More..., please.	**Más..., por favor.** mahs...pohr fah·<u>bohr</u>

– **cremoso** kreh·<u>moh</u>·soh	– cream
– **curado** koo·<u>rah</u>·doh	– ripe
– **de leche de cabra** deh <u>leh</u>·cheh deh <u>kah</u>·brah	– from goat's milk
– **duro** <u>doo</u>·roh	– hard
– **fuerte** <u>fwehr</u>·teh	– strong
– **Manchego** mahn·<u>cheh</u>·goh	– hard cheese from Manchego sheep's milk
– **Perilla** peh·<u>ree</u>·yah	– firm, bland regional variety
– **rallado** rah·<u>yah</u>·doh	– grated
– **requesón** reh·keh·<u>sohn</u>	– cottage
– **Roncal** rohn·kahl	– sharp goat cheese, salted and smoked, regional variety
– **suave** <u>swah</u>·beh	– mild
– **tipo roquefort** <u>tee</u>·poh roh·qeh·<u>fohrt</u>	– blue

Dessert

el arroz con leche ehl ah·<u>rroth</u> kohn <u>leh</u>·cheh	rice pudding
el buñuelo ehl boo·<u>nyweh</u>·loh	thin, deep-fried fritter, covered in sugar
el brazo de gitano ehl <u>brah</u>·thoh deh khee·<u>tah</u>·noh	sponge cake roll with cream filling

With/Without…	**Con/Sin…** kohn/seen…
I can't have…	**No puedo tomar…** noh <u>pweh</u>·doh toh·<u>mahr</u>…

el canutillo ehl kah·noo·<u>tee</u>·yoh	custard pastry horn with cinnamon
el churro ehl <u>choo</u>·rroh	deep-fried fritter sprinkled with sugar
la filloa lah fee·<u>yoh</u>·ah	crepe (used in sweet or savory dishes), typical of Galicia region
el flan ehl flahn	caramel custard
la galleta lah gah·<u>yeh</u>·tah	cookie [biscuit]
el helado ehl eh·<u>lah</u>·doh	ice cream
la leche frita lah <u>leh</u>·cheh <u>free</u>·tah	fried milk custard
la mantecada lah mahn·teh·<u>kah</u>·dah	small sponge cake
la manzana asada lah mahn·<u>thah</u>·nah ah·<u>sah</u>·dah	baked apple
el pastel de queso ehl pahs·<u>tehl</u> deh <u>keh</u>·soh	cheesecake
el sorbete ehl sohr·<u>beh</u>·teh	sorbet
la tarta de Santiago lah <u>tahr</u>·tah deh sahn·<u>teeyah</u>·goh	dense almond cake topped with powdered sugar
el tocino de cielo ehl toh·<u>thee</u>·noh deh <u>theeyeh</u>·loh	egg yolk custard

I'd like…	**Quiero…** <u>keeyeh</u>·roh…
More…, please.	**Más…, por favor.** mahs…pohr fah·<u>bohr</u>
With/Without…	**Con/Sin…** kohn/seen…
I can't have…	**No puedo tomar…** noh <u>pweh</u>·doh toh·<u>mahr</u>…

Essential

The *wine list/drink menu*, please.	**La carta de *vinos/bebidas*, por favor.** lah <u>kahr</u>·tah deh *<u>bee</u>·nohs/beh·<u>bee</u>·dahs* pohr fah·<u>bohr</u>
What do you recommend?	**¿Qué me recomienda?** keh meh reh·koh·<u>meeyehn</u>·dah
I'd like a *bottle/glass* of *red/white* wine.	**Quiero *una botella/un vaso* de vino *tinto/blanco*.** <u>keeyeh</u>·roh *<u>oo</u>·nah boh·<u>teh</u>·yah/ oon <u>bah</u>·soh* deh bee·noh *teen·toh/<u>blahn</u>·koh*
The house wine, please.	**El vino de la casa, por favor.** ehl <u>bee</u>·noh deh lah <u>kah</u>·sah pohr fah·<u>bohr</u>
Another *bottle/glass*, please.	***Otra botella/Otro vaso*, por favor.** <u>oh</u>·trah boh·<u>teh</u>·yah/<u>oh</u>·troh <u>bah</u>·soh pohr fah·<u>bohr</u>
I'd like a local beer.	**Quiero una cerveza española.** <u>keeyeh</u>·roh <u>oo</u>·nah thehr·<u>beh</u>·thah ehs·pah·<u>nyoh</u>·lah
Can I buy you a drink?	**¿Puedo invitarle♂/invitarla♀ a una copa?** <u>pweh</u>·doh een·bee·<u>tahr</u>·leh♂/ een·bee·<u>tahr</u>·lah♀ ah <u>oo</u>·nah <u>koh</u>·pah
Cheers!	**¡Salud!** sah·<u>looth</u>
A *coffee/tea*, please.	**Un *café/té*, por favor.** oon kah·<u>feh</u>/teh pohr fah·<u>bohr</u>
Black.	**Solo.** <u>soh</u>·loh
With...	**Con...** kohn...
– milk	**– leche** <u>lch</u>·cheh
– sugar	**– azúcar** ah·<u>thoo</u>·kahr
– artificial sweetener	**– edulcorante artificial** eh·dool·koh·<u>rahn</u>·teh ahr·tee·fee·<u>theeyahl</u>

A..., please.	**Un..., por favor.** oon...pohr fah·<u>bohr</u>
– juice	**– zumo** <u>thoo</u>·moh
– soda	**– refresco** reh·<u>frehs</u>·koh
– (sparkling/still) water	**– agua (*con/sin* gas)** <u>ah</u>·gwah (*kohn/seen* gahs)
Is the tap water safe to drink?	**¿Se puede beber el agua del grifo?** seh <u>pweh</u>·deh beh·<u>behr</u> ehl <u>ah</u>·gwah dehl <u>gree</u>·foh

Non-alcoholic Drinks

el agua (*con/sin* gas) ehl <u>ah</u>·gwah (*kohn/seen* gahs)	(sparkling/still) water
el café ehl kah·<u>feh</u>	coffee
el chocolate caliente ehl choh·koh·<u>lah</u>·teh kah·<u>leeyehn</u>·teh	hot chocolate
el granizado ehl grah·nee·<u>thah</u>·doh	iced drink
la horchata lah ohr·<u>chah</u>·tah	sweet drink made from tiger nuts and sugar
la leche lah <u>leh</u>·cheh	milk
la limonada lah lee·moh·<u>nah</u>·dah	lemonade
el refresco ehl reh·<u>frehs</u>·koh	soda
el té (con hielo) ehl teh (kohn <u>eeyeh</u>·loh)	(iced) tea
el zumo ehl <u>thoo</u>·moh	juice

> *i* Many Spaniards love coffee and drink it throughout the day. Bottled water is available, though tap water is used in the home and is generally safe to drink. Restaurants will almost always serve bottled water with meals, unless you specifically request **agua del grifo** (tap water). Juice is usually served with breakfast, but it's not common at lunch or dinner.

You May Hear...

¿Qué desea beber?
keh deh·<u>seh</u>·ah beh·<u>behr</u>

Can I get you
a drink?

¿Con leche o azúcar?
kohn <u>leh</u>·cheh oh ah·<u>thoo</u>·kahr

With milk or sugar?

¿Agua con gas o sin gas?
<u>ah</u>·gwah kohn gahs oh seen gahs

Sparkling or still
water?

Aperitifs, Cocktails and Liqueurs ─────

el coñac ehl koh·<u>nyahk</u>	brandy
la ginebra lah khee·<u>neh</u>·brah	gin
el jerez fino ehl kheh·rehth <u>fee</u>·noh	pale, dry sherry
el jerez oloroso ehl kheh·<u>rehth</u> oh·loh·<u>roh</u>·soh	dark, heavy sherry
el licor ehl lee·<u>kohr</u>	liqueur
el oporto ehl oh·<u>pohr</u>·toh	port
el ron ehl rohn	rum
la sangría lah sahn·<u>gree</u>·ah	wine punch
el tequila ehl teh·<u>kee</u>·lah	tequila
el vodka ehl <u>bohd</u>·kah	vodka

el whisky ehl <u>wees</u>·kee   whisky

el whisky escocés ehl <u>wees</u>·kee   scotch
ehs·koh·<u>thehs</u>

Beer

la cerveza... lah thehr·<u>beh</u>·thah...   ...beer

– **en botella/de barril** ehn boh·<u>teh</u>·yah/deh   – bottled/draft
bah·<u>rreel</u>

– **española/extranjera** ehs·pah·<u>nyoh</u>·lah/   – local/imported
ehx·trahn·<u>kheh</u>·rah

– **negra/ligera** <u>neh</u>·grah/lee·<u>kheh</u>·rah   – dark/light

– **rubia/pilsner** <u>roo</u>·beeyah/peels·<u>nehr</u>   – lager/pilsner

– **sin alcohol** seen ahl·koh·<u>ohl</u>   – non-alcoholic

---

i
There are many popular brands of beer in Spain, including **San
Miguel®**, **Cruzcampo®**, **Alhambra®**, **Mahou®**, **Estrella Damm®**
and **Zaragozana®**. Each brand usually has several classes and
types of beer available, though most will be a lager-type beer.
The classes of beer include **clásica**, a light, pale, pilsner-type
lager; **especial**, a heavier pilsner-type lager; **negra**, a dark,
malty lager; and **extra**, a heavy, high-alcohol lager.

Wine

el cava ehl <u>kah</u>·bah   sparkling wine

el champán ehl chahm·<u>pahn</u>   champagne

el vino... ehl <u>bee</u>·noh...   ...wine

– **de la casa/de mesa** deh lah <u>kah</u>·sah/deh   – house/table
<u>meh</u>·sah

– **espumoso** ehs·poo·<u>moh</u>·soh   – sparkling

– **tinto/blanco** <u>teen</u>·toh/<u>blahn</u>·koh   – red/white

– **seco/dulce** <u>seh</u>·koh/<u>dool</u>·theh   – dry/sweet

With 40 recognized wine regions, Spain has the largest land area under vine in the world and is the third largest producer and exporter of wine. The most well-known types of wine include red wine from Rioja and Ribera del Duero, sherries from Jerez, white wine from Rueda and red wine and white wine from Penedés. Another popular wine, especially in the summer time, is the sparkling white known as **cava**. Spanish wineries are known as **bodegas**; the winemaker is known as a **bodeguero**.

Menu Reader

el aceite ehl ah·<u>they</u>ee·teh	oil
el aceite de oliva ehl ah·<u>they</u>ee·teh deh oh·<u>lee</u>·bah	olive oil
la aceituna lah ah·they<u>ee</u>·<u>too</u>·nah	olive
la acelga lah ah·<u>thehl</u>·gah	chard

la achicoria lah ah·chee·<u>koh</u>·reeyah	chicory
el agua ehl <u>ah</u>·gwah	water
el aguacate ehl ah·gwah·<u>kah</u>·teh	avocado
el ajo ehl <u>ah</u>·khoh	garlic
el ajo chalote ehl <u>ah</u>·khoh chah·<u>loh</u>·teh	shallot
la albahaca lah ahl·bah·<u>ah</u>·kah	basil
el albaricoque ehl ahl·bah·ree·<u>koh</u>·keh	apricot
la albóndiga lah ahl·<u>bohn</u>·dee·gah	meatball
la alcachofa lah ahl·kah·<u>choh</u>·fah	artichoke
la alcaparra lah ahl·kah·<u>pah</u>·rrah	caper
la alcaravea lah ahl·kah·rah·<u>beh</u>·ah	caraway
la almeja lah ahl·<u>meh</u>·khah	clam
la almendra lah ahl·<u>mehn</u>·drah	almond
el almíbar ehl ahl·<u>mee</u>·bahr	syrup
el anacardo ehl ah·nah·<u>kahr</u>·doh	cashew
las ancas de rana lahs <u>ahn</u>·kahs deh <u>rah</u>·nah	frog's legs
la anchoa lah ahn·<u>choh</u>·ah	anchovy
la anguila lah ahn·<u>gee</u>·lah	eel
la angula lah ahn·<u>goo</u>·lah	baby eel
el anís ehl ah·<u>nees</u>	aniseed
el aperitivo ehl ah·peh·ree·<u>tee</u>·boh	aperitif
el apio ehl <u>ah</u>·peeyoh	celery
el arándano ehl ah·<u>rahn</u>·dah·noh	blueberry
el arándano rojo ehl ah·<u>rahn</u>·dah·noh <u>roh</u>·khoh	cranberry
el arenque ehl ah·<u>rehn</u>·keh	herring
el arroz ehl ah·<u>rrohth</u>	rice
el arroz integral ehl ah·<u>rrohth</u> een·teh·<u>grahl</u>	whole grain rice

el arroz salvaje ehl ah·<u>rrohth</u> sahl·<u>bah</u>·kheh	wild rice
el asado ehl ah·<u>sah</u>·doh	roast
las asaduras lahs ah·sah·<u>doo</u>·rahs	organ meat [offal]
el atún ehl ah·<u>toon</u>	tuna
la avellana lah ah·beh·<u>yah</u>·nah	hazelnut
la avena lah ah·<u>beh</u>·nah	oat
las aves lahs <u>ah</u>·behs	poultry
el azafrán ehl ah·thah·<u>frahn</u>	saffron
el azúcar ehl ah·<u>thoo</u>·kahr	sugar
el bacalao bah·kah·<u>lao</u>	cod
los barquillos lohs bahr·<u>kee</u>·yohs	wafers/ice cream cones
la batata lah bah·<u>tah</u>·tah	sweet potato
el batido ehl bah·<u>tee</u>·doh	milk shake
la bebida lah beh·<u>bee</u>·dah	drink
la berenjena lah beh·rehn·<u>khch</u>·nah	eggplant [aubergine]
la berraza lah beh·<u>rrah</u>·thah	parsnip
el berro chl <u>beh</u>·rroh	watercress
la borza lah <u>behr</u>·thah	kale
el besugo ehl beh·<u>soo</u>·goh	sea bream
blando blahn·doh	soft
el bollo ehl <u>boh</u>·yoh	pastry
el brandy ehl <u>brahn</u>·dee	brandy
el brécol ehl <u>breh</u>·kohl	broccoli
los brotes de soja lohs <u>broh</u>·tehs deh <u>soh</u>·khah	bean sprouts
el buey ehl bwehy	ox
el buñuelo ehl boo·<u>nyweh</u>·loh	fritter

la caballa lah kah·<u>bah</u>·yah	mackerel
la cabra lah <u>kah</u>·brah	goat
el cabrito ehl kah·<u>bree</u>·toh	young goat
el cacahuete ehl kah·kah·<u>weh</u>·teh	peanut
el café ehl kah·<u>feh</u>	coffee
el café solo ehl kah·<u>feh</u> <u>soh</u>·loh	espresso
el calabacín ehl kah·lah·bah·<u>theen</u>	zucchini [courgette]
la calabaza lah kah·lah·<u>bah</u>·thah	pumpkin
el calamar ehl kah·lah·<u>mahr</u>	squid
el caldo ehl <u>kahl</u>·doh	broth
los callos lohs <u>kah</u>·yohs	tripe
la canela lah kah·<u>neh</u>·lah	cinnamon
el cangrejo ehl kahn·<u>greh</u>·khoh	crab
el capuchino ehl kah·poo·<u>chee</u>·noh	cappuccino
el caracol ehl kah·rah·<u>kohl</u>	snail
el caramelo ehl kah·rah·<u>meh</u>·loh	candy [sweet]
la carne lah <u>kahr</u>·neh	meat
la carne de cangrejo lah <u>kahr</u>·neh deh kahn·<u>greh</u>·khoh	crabmeat
la carne de cerdo lah <u>kahr</u>·neh deh <u>thehr</u>·doh	pork
la carne picada lah <u>kahr</u>·neh pee·<u>kah</u>·dah	ground beef
la carne de vaca lah <u>kahr</u>·neh deh <u>bah</u>·kah	beef
el carnero ehl kahr·<u>neh</u>·roh	mutton
las carrilladas lahs kah·rree·<u>yah</u>·dahs	cow's cheeks
casero kah·<u>seh</u>·roh	homemade
la castaña lah kahs·<u>tah</u>·nyah	chestnut
el cava ehl <u>kah</u>·bah	sparkling wine

la caza lah <u>kah</u>·thah	game
la cebolla lah theh·<u>boh</u>·yah	onion
la cebolleta lah theh·boh·<u>yeh</u>·tah	scallion [spring onion]
los cebollinos lohs theh·boh·<u>yee</u>·nohs	chives
la cecina de bovino lah theh·<u>thee</u>·nah deh boh·<u>bee</u>·noh	corned beef
el centeno ehl thehn·<u>teh</u>·noh	rye
el centollo ehl thehn·<u>toh</u>·yoh	spider crab
el cereal ehl theh·reh·<u>ahl</u>	cereal
la cereza lah theh·<u>reh</u>·thah	cherry
la cerveza lah thehr·<u>beh</u>·thah	beer
el champiñón ehl chahm·pee·<u>nyohn</u>	mushroom
el champán ehl chahm·<u>pahn</u>	champagne
la chirivia lah chee·ree·<u>bee</u>·ah	parsnip
el chipirón ehl chee·pee·<u>rohn</u>	small whole squid
el chocolate ehl choh·koh·<u>lah</u>·teh	chocolate
el chocolate caliente ehl choh·koh·<u>lah</u>·teh kah·<u>leeyehn</u>·teh	hot chocolate
el chorizo ehl choh·<u>ree</u>·thoh	highly-seasoned pork sausage
la chuleta lah choo·<u>leh</u>·tah	chop
el chuletón ehl choo·leh·<u>tohn</u>	T-bone steak
el ciervo ehl <u>theeyehr</u>·boh	deer
la cigala lah thee·<u>gah</u>·lah	crayfish
el cilantro ehl thee·<u>lahn</u>·troh	cilantro [coriander]
la ciruela lah thee·<u>rweh</u>·lah	plum
la ciruela pasa lah thee·<u>rweh</u>·lah pah·sah	prune
el clavo ehl <u>klah</u>·boh	clove

el cochinillo ehl koh·chee·<u>nee</u>·yoh	suckling pig
el coco ehl <u>koh</u>·koh	coconut
la codorniz lah koh·dohr·<u>neeth</u>	quail
la col lah kohl	cabbage
las coles de Bruselas lahs <u>koh</u>·lehs deh broo·<u>seh</u>·lahs	Brussels sprouts
la coliflor lah koh·lee·<u>flohr</u>	cauliflower
el comino ehl koh·<u>mee</u>·noh	cumin
la compota lah kohm·<u>poh</u>·tah	stewed fruit
con alcohol kohn ahl·koh·<u>ohl</u>	with alcohol
con nata kohn <u>nah</u>·tah	with cream
el condimento ehl kohn·dee·<u>mehn</u>·toh	relish
el conejo ehl koh·<u>neh</u>·khoh	rabbit
el congrio ehl <u>kohn</u>·greeyoh	conger eel
el consomé ehl kohn·soh·<u>meh</u>	consommé
el coñac ehl koh·<u>nyahk</u>	brandy
el corazón ehl koh·rah·<u>thohn</u>	heart
el cordero ehl kohr·<u>deh</u>·roh	lamb
la cordorniz lah kohr·dohr·<u>neeth</u>	quail
el coriandro ehl koh·<u>reeyahn</u>·droh	coriander
la croqueta lah kroh·<u>keh</u>·tah	croquette
el cruasán ehl krwah·<u>sahn</u>	croissant
crudo <u>kroo</u>·doh	raw
los dátiles lohs <u>dah</u>·tee·lehs	dates
descafeinado dehs·kah·feyee·<u>nah</u>·doh	decaffeinated
el edulcorante artificial ehl eh·dool·koh·<u>rahn</u>·teh ahr·tee·fee·<u>theeyahl</u>	artificial sweetener

la empanada lah ehm·pah·<u>nah</u>·dah	pastry filled with meat, chicken, tuna or vegetabloo
el encurtido ehl ehn·koor·<u>tee</u>·doh	pickled
la endibia lah ehn·<u>dee</u>·beeyah	endive
el eneldo ehl eh·<u>nehl</u>·doh	dill
la ensalada lah ehn·sah·<u>lah</u>·dah	salad
la escarola lah ehs·kah·<u>roh</u>·lah	escarole [chicory]
el espagueti ehl ehs·pah·<u>geh</u>·tee	spaghetti
la espaldilla lah ehs·pahl·<u>dee</u>·ynh	shoulder
el espárrago ehl ehs·<u>pah</u>·rrah·goh	asparagus
las especias lahs ehs·<u>peh</u>·theeyahs	spices
la espinaca lah ehs·pee·<u>nah</u>·kah	spinach
el estragón ehl ehs·trah·<u>gohn</u>	tarragon
el faisán ehl fayee·<u>sahn</u>	pheasant
la falda de ternera lah <u>fahl</u>·dah deh tehr·<u>neh</u>·rah	beef brisket
los fiambres lohs <u>feeyahm</u>·brehs	cold cuts [charcuterie]
el fideo ehl fee·<u>deh</u>·oh	noodle
el filete ehl fee·<u>leh</u>·teh	steak
el flan ehl flahn	caramel custard
el fletán ehl fleh·<u>tahn</u>	halibut
la frambuesa lah frahm·<u>bweh</u>·sah	raspberry
la fresa lah <u>freh</u>·sah	strawberry
la fruta lah <u>froo</u>·tah	fruit
los frutos secos lohs <u>froo</u>·tohs seh·kohs	nuts

la galleta lah gah·<u>yeh</u>·tah	cookie [biscuit]
la galleta salada lah gah·<u>yeh</u>·tah sah·<u>lah</u>·dah	cracker
la gamba lah <u>gahm</u>·bah	shrimp
el ganso ehl <u>gahn</u>·soh	wild goose
el garbanzo ehl gahr·<u>bahn</u>·thoh	chickpea
el gazpacho ehl gahth·<u>pah</u>·choh	cold tomato-based soup
la ginebra lah khee·<u>neh</u>·brah	gin
el gofre ehl <u>goh</u>·freh	waffle
la granada lah grah·<u>nah</u>·dah	pomegranate
el granizado ehl grah·nee·<u>thah</u>·doh	iced drink
la grosella espinosa lah groh·<u>seh</u>·yah ehs·pee·<u>noh</u>·sah	gooseberry
la grosella negra lah groh·<u>seh</u>·yah <u>neh</u>·grah	black currant
la grosella roja lah groh·<u>seh</u>·yah <u>roh</u>·khah	red currant
la guayaba lah gwah·<u>yah</u>·bah	guava
la guinda lah <u>geen</u>·dah	sour cherry
la guindilla en polvo lah geen·<u>dee</u>·yah ehn <u>pohl</u>·boh	chili pepper
el guirlache ehl geer·<u>lah</u>·cheh	nougat
el guisante ehl gee·<u>sahn</u>·teh	pea
la hamburguesa lah ahm·boor·<u>geh</u>·sah	hamburger
la harina lah ah·<u>ree</u>·nah	flour
la harina de avena lah ah·<u>ree</u>·nah deh ah·<u>beh</u>·nah	oatmeal
la harina de maíz lah ah·<u>ree</u>·nah deh mah·<u>eeth</u>	cornmeal
el helado ehl eh·<u>lah</u>·doh	ice cream
el (cubito de) hielo ehl (kooh·<u>bee</u>·toh deh) <u>eeyeh</u>·loh	ice (cube)

el hígado ehl <u>ee</u>·gah·doh	liver
el higo ehl <u>ee</u>·goh	fig
el hinojo ehl ee·<u>noh</u>·khoh	fennel
la hoja de laurel lah <u>oh</u>·khah deh lawoo·<u>rehl</u>	bay leaf
el hueso ehl <u>weh</u>·soh	bone
el huevo ehl <u>weh</u>·boh	egg
el jabalí ehl khah·bah·lee	wild boar
la jalea lah khah·<u>leh</u>·ah	jelly
el jamón ehl khah·<u>mohn</u>	ham
el jengibre ehl khehn·<u>khee</u>·breh	ginger
el jerez ehl kheh·<u>rehth</u>	sherry
la judía lah khoo·<u>dee</u>·ah	bean
la judía verde lah khoo·<u>dee</u>·ah hehr·deh	green bean
el ketchup ehl keht·<u>choop</u>	ketchup
el kiwi ehl <u>kee</u>·wee	kiwi
el lacón ehl lah·<u>kohn</u>	pork shoulder
la langosta lah lahn·<u>gohs</u>·tah	lobster
el lavanco ehl lah·<u>bahn</u>·koh	wild duck
la leche lah <u>leh</u>·cheh	milk
la leche de soja lah <u>leh</u>·cheh deh <u>soh</u>·khah	soymilk [soya milk]
la lechuga lah leh·<u>choo</u>·gah	lettuce
la lengua lah <u>lehn</u>·gwah	tongue
el lenguado ehl lehn·<u>gwah</u>·doh	sole
la lenteja lah lehn·<u>teh</u>·khah	lentil
el licor ehl lee·<u>kohr</u>	liqueur
el licor de naranja ehl lee·<u>kohr</u> deh nah·<u>rahn</u>·khah	orange liqueur
los licores lohs lee·<u>kohr</u>·ehs	spirits

la liebre lah <u>leyee</u>·breh		hare
la lima lah <u>lee</u>·mah		lime
el limón ehl lee·<u>mohn</u>		lemon
la limonada lah leeh·moh·<u>nah</u>·dah		lemonade
la lombarda lah lohm·<u>bahr</u>·dah		red cabbage
el lomo ehl <u>loh</u>·moh		loin
la lubina lah loo·<u>bee</u>·nah		(sea) bass
los macarrones lohs mah·kah·<u>rrohn</u>·ehs		macaroni
la magdalena lah mahg·dah·<u>leh</u>·nah		muffin
la maicena lah mayee·<u>theh</u>·nah		cornmeal
el maíz ehl mah·<u>eeth</u>		sweet corn
la mandarina lah mahn·dah·<u>ree</u>·nah		tangerine
el mango ehl <u>mahn</u>·goh		mango
las manos de cerdo lahs <u>mah</u>·nohs deh <u>thehr</u>·doh		pig's feet [trotters]
la mantequilla lah mahn·teh·<u>kee</u>·yah		butter
la manzana lah mahn·<u>thah</u>·nah		apple
la margarina lah mahr·gah·<u>ree</u>·nah		margarine
el marisco ehl mah·<u>rees</u>·koh		shellfish
la mayonesa lah mah·yoh·<u>neh</u>·sah		mayonnaise
el mazapán ehl mah·thah·<u>pahn</u>		marzipan
el mejillón ehl meh·khee·<u>yohn</u>		mussel
la mejorana lah meh·khoh·<u>rah</u>·nah		marjoram
la melaza lah meh·<u>lah</u>·thah		molasses
el melocotón ehl meh·loh·koh·<u>tohn</u>		peach
el melón ehl meh·<u>lohn</u>		melon
la menta lah <u>mehn</u>·tah		mint
el menudillo ehl meh·noo·<u>dee</u>·yoh		giblet

el merengue ehl meh·<u>rehn</u>·geh		meringue
la merluza lah mehr·<u>loo</u>·thah		hake
la mermelada lah mehr·meh·<u>lah</u>·dah		marmalade/jam
el mero ehl <u>meh</u>·roh		grouper
la miel lah <u>meeyehl</u>		honey
la molleja lah moh·<u>yeh</u>·khah		sweetbread
la morcilla lah mohr·<u>thee</u>·yah		black pudding
la mostaza lah mohs·<u>tah</u>·thah		mustard
el muesli ehl <u>mwehs</u>·lee		granola [muesli]
el nabo ehl <u>nah</u>·boh		turnip
la naranja lah nah·<u>rahn</u>·khah		orange
la nata lah <u>nah</u>·tah		cream
la nata agria lah <u>nah</u>·tah <u>ah</u>·greeyah		sour cream
la nata montada lah <u>nah</u>·tah mohn·<u>tah</u>·dah		whipped cream
las natillas lahs nah·<u>tee</u>·yahs		custard
la nuez lah nwehth		walnut
la nuez moscada lah nwehth mohs·<u>kah</u>·dah		nutmeg
el oporto ehl oh·<u>pohr</u>·toh		port
el orégano ehl oh·<u>reh</u>·gah·noh		oregano
la ostra lah <u>ohs</u>·trah		oyster
la pacana lah pah·<u>kah</u>·nah		pecan
la paella lah pah·<u>eh</u>·yah		rice dish
la paletilla lah pah·leh·<u>tee</u>·yah		shank
el palmito ehl pahl·<u>mee</u>·toh		palm heart
el pan ehl pahn		bread
el panecillo ehl pah·neh·<u>thee</u>·yoh		roll
la papaya lah pah·<u>pah</u>·yah		papaya
la paprika lah pah·<u>pree</u>·kah		paprika

la pasa lah pah·sah	raisin
la pasta lah pahs·tah	pasta
el pastel ehl pahs·tehl	pie
el pastel de queso ehl pahs·tehl deh keh·soh	cheesecake
la pata lah pah·tah	leg
la patata lah pah·tah·tah	potato
las patatas fritas lahs pah·tah·tahs free·tahs	French fries
las patatas fritas lahs pah·tah·tahs free·tahs	potato chips [crisps]
el paté ehl pah·teh	pâté
el pato ehl pah·toh	duck
el pavo ehl pah·boh	turkey
la pechuga (de pollo) lah peh·choo·gah (deh poh·yoh)	breast (of chicken)
el pepinillo ehl peh·pee·nee·yoh	pickle
el pepino ehl peh·pee·noh	cucumber
la pera lah peh·rah	pear
la perca lah pehr·kah	sea perch
la perdiz lah pehr·deeth	partridge
el perejil ehl peh·reh·kheel	parsley
el perrito caliente ehl peh·rree·toh kah·leeyehn·teh	hot dog
el pescadito ehl pehs·kah·dee·toh	small fish
el pescado ehl pehs·kah·doh	fish
el pescado frito ehl pehs·kah·doh free·toh	fried fish
pescado y marisco pehs·kah·doh ee mah·rees·koh	seafood
el pez espada ehl peth ehs·pah·dah	swordfish
el pichón ehl pee·chohn	young pigeon

pilsner peels·<u>nehr</u>	pilsner (beer)
el pimentón ehl pee·mehn·<u>tohn</u>	paprika
la pimienta lah pee·<u>meeyehn</u>·tah	pepper (seasoning)
la pimienta negra lah pee·<u>meeyehn</u>·tah <u>neh</u>·grah	black pepper
la pimienta inglesa lah pee·<u>meeyehn</u>·tah een·<u>gleh</u>·sah	allspice
el pimiento ehl pee·<u>meeyehn</u>·toh	pepper (vegetable)
la piña lah <u>pee</u>·nyah	pineapple
los piñones lohn pee·<u>nyohn</u>·ehs	pine nuts
la pintada lah peen·<u>tah</u>·dah	guinea fowl
la pizza lah <u>peeth</u>·thah	pizza
el plátano ehl <u>plah</u>·tah·noh	banana
el pollo ehl <u>poh</u>·yoh	chicken
el pollo frito ehl <u>poh</u>·yoh <u>free</u>·toh	fried chicken
el pomelo ehl poh·<u>meh</u>·loh	grapefruit
el puerro ehl <u>pweh</u>·rroh	leek
el pulpo ehl <u>pool</u>·poh	octopus
el queso ehl <u>keh</u>·soh	cheese
el queso de cabra ehl <u>keh</u>·soh deh <u>kah</u>·brah	goat cheese
el queso crema ehl <u>keh</u>·soh <u>kreh</u>·mah	cream cheese
el queso roquefort ehl <u>keh</u>·soh roh·keh·<u>fohrt</u>	blue cheese
el rábano ehl <u>rah</u>·bah·noh	radish
el rabo de buey ehl <u>rah</u>·boh deh bwehy	oxtail
el rape ehl <u>rah</u>·peh	monkfish
el ravioli ehl rah·<u>beeyoh</u>·lee	ravioli
la raya lah <u>rah</u>·yah	skate
el refresco ehl reh·<u>frehs</u>·koh	soda

relleno reh·yeh·noh	stuffed/stuffing
la remolacha lah reh·moh·lah·chah	beet
el repollo ehl reh·poh·yoh	cabbage
el requesón ehl reh·keh·sohn	cottage cheese
el requesón de soja ehl reh·keh·sohn deh soh·khah	tofu
los retoños de bambú lohs reh·toh·nyohs deh bahm·boo	bamboo shoots
el riñón ehl ree·nyohn	kidney
el róbalo ehl roh·bah·loh	haddock
el romero ehl roh·meh·roh	rosemary
el ron ehl rohn	rum
el rosbif ehl rohs·beef	roast beef
la rosquilla lah rohs·kee·yah	doughnut
rubia roo·beeyah	lager (beer)
el ruibarbo ehl rwee·bahr·boh	rhubarb
la sal lah sahl	salt
el salami ehl sah·lah·mee	salami
la salchicha lah sahl·chee·chah	sausage
el salmón ehl sahl·mohn	salmon
el salmonete ehl sahl·moh·neh·teh	red mullet
la salsa lah sahl·sah	sauce
la salsa agridulce lah sahl·sah ah·gree·dool·theh	sweet and sour sauce
la salsa alioli lah sahl·sah ah·yee·oh·lee	garlic sauce
la salsa picante lah sahl·sah pee·kahn·teh	hot pepper sauce
la salsa de soja lah sahl·sah deh soh·khah	soy sauce
la salvia lah sahl·beeyah	sage

la sandía lah sahn·<u>dee</u>·ah	watermelon
el sándwich ehl <u>sahnd</u>·weech	sandwich
la sangría lah sahn·<u>gree</u>·ah	wine punch
la sardina lah sahr·<u>dee</u>·nah	sardine
la semilla lah seh·<u>mee</u>·yah	seed
la semilla de soja lah seh·<u>mee</u>·yah deh <u>soh</u>·khah	soybean [soya bean]
el sésamo ehl <u>seh</u>·sah·moh	sesame
los sesos lohs <u>seh</u>·sohs	brains
la seta lah <u>seh</u>·tah	mushroom
la sidra lah <u>see</u>·drah	cider
el sifón ehl see·<u>fohn</u>	seltzer water
el sirope ehl see·<u>roh</u>·peh	syrup
la soja lah <u>soh</u>·khah	soy [soya]
el solomillo ehl soh·loh·<u>mee</u>·yoh	sirloin
la sopa lah <u>soh</u>·pah	soup
el sorbete ehl sohr·<u>beh</u>·teh	sorbet
el suero de leche ehl <u>sweh</u>·roh deh <u>leh</u>·cheh	buttermilk
la tarta lah <u>tahr</u>·tah	cake
el té ehl teh	tea
la ternera lah tehr·<u>neh</u>·rah	veal
el tequila ehl teh·<u>kee</u>·lah	tequila
el tiburón ehl tee·boo·<u>rohn</u>	shark
tinto <u>teen</u>·toh	red (wine)
el tocino ehl toh·<u>thee</u>·noh	bacon
el tofu ehl <u>toh</u>·foo	tofu
el tomate ehl toh·<u>mah</u>·teh	tomato
el tomillo ehl toh·<u>mee</u>·yoh	thyme

la tónica lah <u>toh</u>·nee·kah	tonic water
la tortilla lah tohr·<u>tee</u>·yah	omelet
la tortita lah tohr·<u>tee</u>·tah	large pancake served as an afternoon snack
la tostada lah tohs·<u>tah</u>·dah	toast
el trigo ehl <u>tree</u>·goh	wheat
la trucha lah <u>troo</u>·chah	trout
las trufas lahs <u>troo</u>·fahs	truffles
la uva lah <u>oo</u>·bah	grape
la vainilla lah bayee·<u>nee</u>·yah	vanilla
el venado ehl beh·<u>nah</u>·doh	venison
la verdura lah behr·<u>doo</u>·rah	vegetable
el vermut ehl behr·<u>moot</u>	vermouth
las vieiras lahs bee·<u>eyee</u>·rahs	scallop
el vinagre ehl bee·<u>nah</u>·greh	vinegar
el vino ehl <u>beeh</u>·noh	wine
el vino dulce ehl <u>bee</u>·noh <u>dool</u>·theh	dessert wine
el vodka ehl <u>bohd</u>·kah	vodka
el whisky ehl <u>wees</u>·kee	whisky
el whisky escocés ehl <u>wees</u>·kee ehs·koh·<u>thehs</u>	scotch
la *yema/clara* de huevo lah *<u>yeh</u>·mah/<u>klah</u>·rah* deh <u>weh</u>·boh	egg *yolk/white*
el yogur ehl yoh·<u>goor</u>	yogurt
la zanahoria lah thah·nah·<u>oh</u>·reeyah	carrot
la zarzamora lah thahr·thah·<u>moh</u>·rah	blackberry
el zumo ehl <u>thoo</u>·moh	juice

▼ *People*

▶ *Talking*   *108*
▶ *Romance*   *114*

Talking

Essential

Hello!	**¡Hola!** oh·lah
How are you?	**¿Cómo está?** koh·moh ehs·tah
Fine, thanks.	**Bien, gracias.** beeyehn grah·theeyahs
Excuse me! (to get attention)	**¡Perdón!** pehr·dohn
Do you speak English?	**¿Habla inglés?** ah·blah een·glehs
What's your name?	**¿Cómo se llama?** koh·moh seh yah·mah
My name is…	**Me llamo…** meh yah·moh…
Nice to meet you.	**Encantado♂/Encantada♀.** ehn·kahn·tah·doh ♂/ehn·kahn·tah·dah ♀
Where are you from?	**¿De dónde es usted?** deh dohn·deh ehs oos·teth
I'm from the U.S./U.K.	**Soy de Estados Unidos/del Reino Unido.** soy deh ehs·tah·dohs oo·nee·dohs/dehl reyee·noh oo·nee·doh
What do you do?	**¿A qué se dedica?** ah keh seh deh·dee·kah
I work for…	**Trabajo para…** trah·bah·khoh pah·rah…
I'm a student.	**Soy estudiante.** soy ehs·too·deeyahn·teh
I'm retired.	**Estoy jubilado♂/jubilada♀.** ehs·toy khoo·bee·lah·doh ♂/khoo·bee·lah·dah ♀
Do you like…?	**¿Le gusta…?** leh goos·tah…
Goodbye.	**Adiós.** ah·deeyohs
See you later.	**Hasta luego.** ah·stah lweh·goh

When addressing strangers, always use the more formal **usted** (singular) or **ustedes** (plural), as opposed to the more familiar **tú** (singular) or **vosotros** (plural), until told otherwise. If you know someone's title, it's polite to use it, e.g., **doctor** (male doctor), **doctora** (female doctor). You can also simply say **Señor** (Mr.), **Señora** (Mrs.) or **Señorita** (Miss).

▶ For Spanish pronouns, see page 173.

Communication Difficulties

Do you speak English?	**¿Habla Inglés?** ah-blah cen-glehs
Does anyone here speak English?	**¿Hay alguien que hable inglés?** aye ahl-geeyenh keh ah-bleh een-glehs
I don't speak (much) Spanish.	**No hablo (mucho) español.** noh ah-bloh (moo-choh) ehs-pah-nyol
Can you speak more slowly?	**¿Puede hablar más despacio?** pweh-deh ah-blahr mahs dehs-pah-theeyoh
Can you repeat that?	**¿Podría repetir eso?** poh-dree-ah reh-peh-teer eh-soh
Excuse me?	**¿Cómo?** koh-moh

109

What was that?	**¿Qué ha dicho?** keh ah <u>dee</u>·choh
Can you spell it?	**¿Podría deletrearlo?** poh·<u>dree</u>·ah deh·leh·treh·<u>ahr</u>·loh
Please write it down.	**Escríbamelo, por favor.** ehs·<u>kree</u>·bah·meh·loh pohr fah·<u>bohr</u>
Can you translate this into English for me?	**¿Podría traducirme esto al inglés?** poh·<u>dree</u>·ah trah·doo·<u>theer</u>·meh ehs·toh ahl een·<u>glehs</u>
What does *this/that* mean?	**¿Qué significa *esto/eso*?** keh seeg·nee·<u>fee</u>·kah *ehs·toh/eh·soh*
I understand.	**Entiendo.** ehn·<u>teeyehn</u>·doh
I don't understand.	**No entiendo.** noh ehn·<u>teeyehn</u>·doh
Do you understand?	**¿Entiende?** ehn·<u>teeyehn</u>·deh

You May Hear...

| **Hablo muy poco inglés.** <u>ah</u>·bloh mooy <u>poh</u>·koh een·<u>glehs</u> | I only speak a little English. |
| **No hablo inglés.** noh <u>ah</u>·bloh een·<u>glehs</u> | I don't speak English. |

Making Friends

Hello!	**¡Hola!** <u>oh</u>·lah
Good morning.	**Buenos días.** <u>bweh</u>·nohs <u>dee</u>·ahs
Good afternoon.	**Buenas tardes.** <u>bweh</u>·nahs <u>tahr</u>·dehs
Good evening.	**Buenas noches.** <u>bweh</u>·nahs <u>noh</u>·chehs
My name is...	**Me llamo...** meh <u>yah</u>·moh...
What's your name?	**¿Cómo se llama?** <u>koh</u>·moh seh <u>yah</u>·mah
I'd like to introduce you to...	**Quiero presentarle a...** <u>keeyeh</u>·roh preh·sehn·<u>tahr</u>·leh ah...

Pleased to meet you.	**Encantado♂/Encantada♀.** ehn·kahn·<u>tah</u>·doh♂/ehn·kahn·<u>tah</u>·dah♀
How are you?	**¿Cómo está?** <u>koh</u>·moh ehs·<u>tah</u>
Fine, thanks. And you?	**Bien gracias. ¿Y usted?** beeyehn <u>grah</u>·theeyahs ee oos·<u>tehth</u>

When first meeting someone in Spain always greet him or her with **hola** (hello), **buenos días** (good morning) or **buenas tardes** (good afternoon). Spaniards even extend this general greeting to strangers when in elevators, waiting rooms and other small public spaces. A general acknowledgment or reply is expected from all. When leaving, say **adiós** (goodbye).

Travel Talk

I'm here...	**Estoy aquí...** ehs·<u>toy</u> ah·<u>kee</u>...
– on business	**– en viaje de negocios** ehn <u>beeyah</u>·kheh deh neh·<u>goh</u>·theeyohs
– on vacation [holiday]	**– de vacaciones** deh bah·kah·<u>theeyoh</u>·nehs
– studying	**– estudiando** ehs·too·<u>deeyahn</u>·doh
I'm staying for...	**Voy a quedarme...** boy ah keh·<u>dahr</u>·meh...
I've been here...	**Llevo aquí...** <u>yeh</u>·boh <u>ah</u>·kee...
– a day	**– un día** oon <u>dee</u>·ah
– a week	**– una semana** <u>oo</u>·nah seh·<u>mah</u>·nah
– a month	**– un mes** oon mehs

▶For numbers, see page 178.

Where are you from?	**¿De dónde es usted?** deh <u>dohn</u>·deh ehs oos·<u>tehth</u>
I'm from...	**Soy de...** soy deh...

111

Relationships

Who are you with?	**¿Con quién ha venido?** kohn keeyehn ah beh·<u>nee</u>·doh
I'm here alone.	**He venido solo♂/sola♀.** eh beh·<u>nee</u>·doh <u>soh</u>·loh ♂/<u>soh</u>·lah ♀
I'm with my…	**He venido con mi…** eh beh·<u>nee</u>·doh kohn mee…
– husband/wife	**– marido/mujer** mah·<u>ree</u>·doh/moo·<u>khehr</u>
– boyfriend/girlfriend	**– novio/novia** <u>noh</u>·beeyoh/<u>noh</u>·beeyah
– friend(s)/ colleague(s)	**– amigo(s)/colega(s)** ah·<u>mee</u>·goh(s)/koh·<u>leh</u>·gah(s)
When's your birthday?	**¿Cuándo es su cumpleaños?** <u>kwahn</u>·doh ehs soo koom·pleh·<u>ah</u>·nyohs
How old are you?	**¿Qué edad tiene usted?** keh eh·<u>dahth</u> <u>teeyeh</u>·neh oos·<u>tehth</u>
I'm…	**Tengo…años.** <u>tehn</u>·goh…<u>ah</u>·nyohs

▶For numbers, see page 178.

Are you married?	**¿Está casado♂/casada♀?** ehs·<u>tah</u> kah·<u>sah</u>·doh ♂/kah·<u>sah</u>·dah ♀
I'm…	**Estoy…** ehs·<u>toy</u>…
– single	**– soltero♂/soltera♀** sohl·<u>teh</u>·roh ♂/sohl·<u>teh</u>·rah ♀
– in a relationship	**– en una relación** ehn <u>oo</u>·nah reh·lah·<u>theeyohn</u>
– married	**– casado♂/casada♀** kah·<u>sah</u>·doh ♂/kah·<u>sah</u>·dah ♀
– divorced	**– divorciado♂/divorciada♀** dee·bohr·<u>theeyah</u>·doh ♂/dee·bohr·<u>theeyah</u>·dah ♀
– separated	**– separado♂/separada♀** seh·pah·<u>rah</u>·doh ♂/seh·pah·<u>rah</u>·dah ♀

I'm widowed.	**Soy viudo** ♂/**viuda** ♀. soy <u>beeyoo</u>·doh ♂/ <u>beeyoo</u>·dah ♀
Do you have *children/ grandchildren*?	**¿Tiene *hijos/nietos*?** <u>teeyeh</u>·neh <u>ee</u>·khohs/<u>neeyeh</u>·tohs

Work and School

What do you do?	**¿A qué se dedica?** ah keh seh deh·<u>dee</u>·kah
What are you studying?	**¿Qué estudia?** keh ehs·<u>too</u>·deeyah
I'm studying Spanish.	**Estudio español.** ehs·<u>too</u>·deeyoh ehs·pah·<u>nyohl</u>
I...	**Yo...** yoh...
work *full-time/ part-time*	**– trabajo a tiempo *completo/parcial*** trah·<u>bah</u>·khoh ah teeyehm·poh kohm·<u>pleh</u>·toh/pahr·<u>theeyahl</u>
– am unemployed	**– estoy en el paro** ehs·<u>toy</u> ehn ehl <u>pah</u>·roh
– work at home	**– trabajo desde casa** trah·<u>bah</u>·khoh <u>dehs</u>·deh <u>kah</u>·sah
Who do you work for?	**¿Para quién trabaja?** <u>pah</u>·rah keeyehn trah·bah·khah
I work for...	**Trabajo para...** trah·<u>bah</u>·khoh <u>pah</u>·rah...
Here's my business card.	**Aquí tiene mi tarjeta.** ah·<u>kee</u> <u>teeyeh</u>·neh mee tahr·<u>kheh</u>·tah

▶ For business travel, see page 152.

Weather

What's the forecast?	**¿Cuál es el pronóstico del tiempo?** kwahl ehs ehl proh·<u>nohs</u>·tee·koh dehl <u>teeyehm</u>·poh
What *beautiful/ terrible* weather!	**¡Qué tiempo *más bonito/feo* hace!** keh <u>teeyehm</u>·poh mahs boh·<u>nee</u>·toh/<u>feh</u>·oh ah·theh

It's *cool/warm*.	**Hace *frío/calor*.** ah·theh *free*·oh/kah·*lohr*
It's *rainy/sunny*.	**Está *lluvioso/soleado*.** ehs·*tah* yoo·*beeyoh*·soh/soh·lee·*ah*·doh
It's *snowy/icy*.	**Hay *nieve/hielo*.** aye *neeyeh*·beh/*eeyeh*·loh
Do I need a *jacket/an umbrella*?	**¿Necesito *una chaqueta/un paraguas*?** neh·theh·*see*·toh *oo*·nah chah·*keh*·tah/oon pah·*rah*·gwahs

▶ For temperature, see page 185.

Romance

Essential

Would you like to go out for a *drink/dinner*?	**¿Le gustaría salir a *tomar una copa/cenar*?** leh goos·tah·*ree*·ah sah·*leer* ah toh·*mahr* *oo*·nah *koh*·pah/theh·*nahr*
What are your plans for *tonight/tomorrow*?	**¿Qué planes tiene para *esta noche/ mañana*?** keh *plah*·nehs *teeyeh*·nehs pah·rah *ehs*·tah *noh*·cheh/mah·*nyah*·nah
Can I have your number?	**¿Puede darme su número?** *pweh*·deh *dahr*·meh soo *noo*·meh·roh
Can I join you?	**¿Puedo acompañarle♂/ acompañarla♀?** *pweh*·doh ah·kohm·pah·*nyahr*·leh♂/ ah·kohm·pah·*nyahr*·lah♀
Can I get you a drink?	**¿Puedo invitarle♂/invitarla♀ a una copa?** *pweh*·doh een·bee·*tahr*·leh♂/ een·bee·*tahr*·lah♀ ah *oo*·nah *koh*·pah
I like you.	**Me gustas.** meh *goos*·tahs
I love you.	**Te quiero.** teh *keeyeh*·roh

Making Plans

Would you like to go out for…?
¿**Le gustaría ir…?** Ieh goos·tah·ree·ah eer…

– coffee
– **a tomar un café** ah toh·mahr oon kah·feh

– a drink
– **a tomar un copa** ah toh·mahr oo·nah koh·pah

– dinner
– **a cenar** ah theh·nahr

What are your plans for…?
¿**Qué planes tiene para…?** keh plahn·ehs teeyeh·neh pah·rah

– tonight
– **esta noche** ehs·tah noh·cheh

– tomorrow
– **mañana** mah·nyah·nah

– this weekend
– **este fin de semana** ehs·teh feen deh seh·mah·nah

Where would you like to go?
¿**Adónde le gustaría ir?** ah dohn·deh leh goos·tah·ree·ah eer

I'd like to go to…	**Me gustaría ir a…** meh goos·tah·<u>ree</u>·ah eer ah…
Do you like…?	**¿Le gusta…?** leh <u>goos</u>·tah…
Can I have your *number/e-mail*?	**¿Puede darme su *número/dirección de correo electrónico*?** pweh·deh dahr·meh soo <u>noo</u>·meh·roh/dee·rehk·<u>theeyohn</u> deh koh·<u>rreh</u>·oh eh·lehk·<u>troh</u>·nee·koh

▶ For e-mail and phone, see page 50.

Pick-up [Chat-up] Lines

Can I join you?	**¿Puedo acompañarle♂/acompañarla♀?** <u>pweh</u>·doh ah·kohm·pah·<u>nyahr</u>·leh♂/ ah·kohm·pah·<u>nyahr</u>·lah♀
You're very attractive.	**Eres muy guapo♂/guapa♀.** <u>eh</u>·rehs mooy <u>gwah</u>·poh♂/<u>gwah</u>·pah♀
Let's go somewhere quieter.	**Vayamos a un sitio más tranquilo.** bah·<u>yah</u>·mohs ah oon <u>see</u>·teeyoh mahs trahn·<u>kee</u>·loh

Accepting and Rejecting

I'd love to.	**Me encantaría.** meh ehn·kahn·tah·<u>ree</u>·yah
Where should we meet?	**¿Dónde quedamos?** <u>dohn</u>·deh keh·<u>dah</u>·mohs
I'll meet you at *the bar/your hotel*.	**Quedamos en *el bar/su hotel*.** keh·<u>dah</u>·mohs ehn *ehl bahr/soo oh·<u>tehl</u>*
I'll come by at…	**Pasaré a recogerle♂/recogerla♀ a las…** pah·sah·<u>reh</u> ah reh·koh·<u>khehr</u>·leh♂/ reh·koh·<u>khehr</u>·lah♀ ah lahs…

▶ For time, see page 180.

What is your address?	**¿Cuál es su dirección?** kwahl ehs soo dee-rehk-<u>theeyohn</u>
I'm busy.	**Estoy ocupado♂/ocupada♀.** ehs-<u>toy</u> oh-koo-<u>pah</u>-doh♂/oh-koo-<u>pah</u>-dah♀
I'm not interested.	**No me interesa.** noh meh een-teh-<u>reh</u>-sah
Leave me alone.	**Déjeme en paz.** <u>deh</u>-kheh-meh ehn pahth
Stop bothering me!	**¡Deje de molestarme!** <u>deh</u>-kheh deh moh-lehs-<u>tahr</u>-meh

Getting Physical

Can I *hug/kiss* you?	**¿Puedo *abrazarte/besarte*?** <u>pweh</u>-doh ah-brah-<u>thahr</u>-teh/beh-<u>sahr</u>-teh
Yes.	**Sí.** see
No.	**No.** noh
Stop!	**¡Para!** <u>pah</u>-rah

Sexual Preferences

Are you gay?	**¿Eres gay?** <u>eh</u>-rehs gay
I'm...	**Soy...** soy...
– heterosexual	– **heterosexual** eh-teh-roh-sehks-<u>wahl</u>
– homosexual	– **homosexual** oh-moh-sehks-<u>wahl</u>
– bisexual	– **bisexual** bee-sehks-<u>wahl</u>
Do you like *men/women*?	**¿Te gustan *los hombres/las mujeres*?** teh <u>goos</u>-tahn *lohs <u>ohm</u>-brehs/lahs moo-<u>kheh</u>-rehs*

▶ For informal and formal "you," see page 172.

▼ Fun

▶ *Sightseeing*   *119*
▶ *Shopping*   *123*
▶ *Sports and Leisure*   *139*
▶ *Culture and Nightlife*   *147*

Sightseeing

Essential

Where's the tourist information office?	**¿Dónde está la oficina de turismo?** <u>dohn</u>·deh ehs·<u>tah</u> lah oh·fee·<u>thee</u>·nah deh too·<u>rees</u>·moh
What are the main attractions?	**¿Dónde están los principales sitios de interés?** <u>dohn</u>·deh ehs·<u>tahn</u> lohs preen·thee·<u>pah</u>·lehs <u>see</u>·teeyohs deh een·teh·<u>rehs</u>
Do you have tours in English?	**¿Hay visitas en inglés?** aye bee·<u>see</u>·tahs ehn een·<u>glehs</u>
Can I have a *map/guide*?	**¿Puede darme *un mapa/una guía*?** <u>pweh</u>·deh <u>dahr</u>·meh *oon <u>mah</u>·pah/<u>oo</u>·nah <u>gee</u>·ah*

Tourist Information Office

Do you have information on...?	**¿Tiene información sobre...?** <u>teeyeh</u>·neh een·fohr·mah·<u>theeyohn</u> soh·breh...
Can you recommend...?	**¿Puede recomendarme...?** <u>pweh</u>·deh reh·koh·mehn·<u>dahr</u>·meh...
– a bus tour	**– un recorrido en autobús** oon reh·koh·<u>rree</u>·doh ehn awtoh·<u>boos</u>
– an excursion to...	**– una excursión a...** <u>oo</u>·nah ehx·koor·<u>seeyohn</u> ah...
– a sightseeing tour	**– un recorrido turístico** oon reh·koh·<u>rree</u>·doh too·<u>rees</u>·tee·koh

Tourist offices are located in major Spanish cities and in many of the smaller towns that are popular tourist attractions. Ask at your hotel or check online to find the nearest office.

Tours

I'd like to go on the tour to…	**Quiero ir a la visita de…** keeyeh·roh eer ah lah bee·see·tah deh…
When's the next tour?	**¿Cuándo es la próxima visita?** kwahn·doh ehs lah proh·xee·mah bee·see·tah
Are there tours in English?	**¿Hay visitas en inglés?** aye bee·see·tahs ehn een·glehs
Is there an English *guide book/audio guide*?	**¿Hay una *guía/audioguía* en inglés?** aye oo·nah *gee·ah/awoo·deeyoh·gee·ah* ehn een·glehs
What time do we *leave/return*?	**¿A qué hora *salimos/volvemos*?** ah keh oh·rah *sah·lee·mohs/bohl·beh·mohs*
We'd like to see…	**Queremos ver…** keh·reh·mohs behr…
Can we stop here…?	**¿Podemos parar aquí…?** poh·deh·mohs pah·rahr ah·kee…
– to take photos	**– para tomar fotos** pah·rah toh·mahr foh·tohs
– for souvenirs	**– para comprar recuerdos** pah·rah kohm·prahr reh·kwehr·dohs
– for the restroom [toilet]	**– para ir al servicio** pah·rah eer ahl sehr·bee· theeyoh
Is it handicapped [disabled]-accessible?	**¿Tiene acceso para discapacitados?** teeyeh·neh ahk·theh·soh pah·rah dees·kah·pah·thee·tah·dohs

▶ For ticketing, see page 20.

Sights

Where *is/are*…?	**¿Dónde *está/están*…?** dohn·deh *ehs·tah/ehs·tahn*…
– the battleground	**– el campo de batalla** ehl kahm·poh deh bah·tah·yah
– the botanical garden	**– el jardín botánico** ehl khar·deen boh·tah·nee·koh

120

– the castle	– **el castillo** ehl kahs·tee·yoh
– the downtown area	– **el centro** ehl thehn·troh
– the fountain	– **la fuente** lah fwehn·teh
– the library	– **la biblioteca** lah bee·bleeyoh·teh·kah
– the market	– **el mercado** ehl mehr·kah·doh
– the museum	– **el museo** ehl moo·seh·oh
– the old town	– **el casco antiguo** ehl kahs·koh ahn·tee·gwoh
– the palace	– **el palacio** ehl pah·lah·thccyoh
– the park	– **el parque** ehl pahr·keh
– the ruins	– **las ruinas** lahs rwee·nahs
– the shopping area	– **la zona comercial** lahs thoh·nah koh·mehr·theeyahl
– the town square	– **la plaza** lah plah·thah
Can you show me on the map?	**¿Puede indicármelo en el mapa?** pweh·deh een·dee·kahr·meh·loh ehn ehl mah·pah

▶ For directions, see page 35.

Impressions

It's...	**Es...** ehs...
– amazing	**– increíble** een·kreh·<u>ee</u>·bleh
– beautiful	**– precioso** preh·<u>theeyoh</u>·soh
– boring	**– aburrido** ah·boo·<u>rree</u>·don
– interesting	**– interesante** een·teh·reh·<u>sahn</u>·teh
– magnificent	**– magnífico** mahg·<u>nee</u>·fee·koh
– romantic	**– romántico** roh·<u>mahn</u>·tee·koh
– strange	**– extraño** ex·<u>trah</u>·nyon
– stunning	**– impresionante** eem·preh·seeyoh·<u>nahn</u>·teh
– terrible	**– horrible** oh·<u>rree</u>·bleh
– ugly	**– feo** <u>feh</u>·oh
I (don't) like it.	**(No) Me gusta.** (noh) meh <u>goo</u>·stah

Religion

Where is...?	**¿Dónde está...?** <u>dohn</u>·deh ehs·<u>tah</u>...
– the cathedral	**– la catedral** lah kah·teh·<u>drahl</u>
– the *Catholic/Protestant* church	**– la iglesia *católica/protestante*** lah ee·<u>gleh</u>·seeyah *kah·<u>toh</u>·lee·kah/ proh·tehs·<u>tahn</u>·teh*
– the mosque	**– la mezquita** lah mehth·<u>kee</u>·tah
– the shrine	**– el santuario** ehl sahn·<u>twah</u>·reeyoh
– the synagogue	**– la sinagoga** lah see·nah·<u>goh</u>·gah
– the temple	**– el templo** ehl <u>tehm</u>·ploh
What time is *mass/the service*?	**¿A qué hora es *la misa/el culto*?** ah keh <u>oh</u>·rah ehs *lah <u>mee</u>·sah/ehl <u>kool</u>·toh*

Shopping

Essential

Where's the *market/mall [shopping centre]*?	**¿Dónde está el *mercado/centro comercial?* dohn·deh ehs·tah ehl mehr·kah·doh/then·troh koh·mehr·theeyahl**
I'm just looking.	**Sólo estoy mirando.** soh·loh ehs·toy mee·rahn·doh
Can you help me?	**¿Puede ayudarme?** pweh·deh ah·yoo·dahr·meh
I'm being helped.	**Ya me atienden.** yah meh ah·teeyehn·dehn
How much?	**¿Cuánto es?** kwahn·toh ehs
That one, please.	**Ése ♂/Ésa ♀, por favor.** eh·seh ♂/eh·sah ♀ pohr fah·bohr
That's all.	**Eso es todo.** eh·soh ehs toh·doh
Where can I pay?	**¿Dónde se paga?** dohn·deh seh pah·gah
I'll pay *in cash/by credit card.*	**Voy a pagar *en efectivo/con tarjeta de crédito.* boy ah pah·gahr ehn eh·fehk·tee·boh/kohn tahr·kheh·tah deh kreh·doo·toh**
A receipt, please.	**Un recibo, por favor.** oon reh·thee·boh pohr fah·bohr

There are many types of markets in the towns of Spain. You can find a wide variety of goods at these markets, including fruit and vegetables, antiques, souvenirs, regional specialty items and so on. Your hotel or local tourist office will have information on the markets for your area. Most permanent markets are open daily from early morning till early afternoon; travelling market times vary by location. Inclement weather may cause a market to close early or not open at all.

Stores

Where *is/are*...?	**¿Dónde *está/están*...?** <u>dohn</u>·deh *ehs·<u>tah</u>/ ehs·<u>tahn</u>...*
– the antiques store	**la tienda de antigüedades** lah <u>teeyehn</u>·dah deh ahn·tee·gweh·<u>dah</u>·dehs
– the bakery	**la panadería** lah pah·nah·deh·<u>ree</u>·ah
– the bank	**el banco** ehl <u>bahn</u>·koh
– the bookstore	**la librería** lah lee·breh·<u>ree</u>·ah
– the clothing store	**la tienda de ropa** lah <u>teeyehn</u>·dah deh <u>roh</u>·pah
– the delicatessen	**la charcutería** lah chahr·koo·teh·<u>ree</u>·ah
– the department stores	**los grandes almacenes** lohs <u>grahn</u>·dehs ahl·mah·<u>theh</u>·nehs
– the gift shop	**la tienda de regalos** lah <u>teeyehn</u>·dah deh reh·<u>gah</u>·lohs
– the health food store	**la tienda de alimentos naturales** lah <u>teeyehn</u>·dah deh ah·lee·<u>mehn</u>·tohs nah·too·<u>rahl</u>·ehs
– the jeweler	**la joyería** lah khoh·yeh·<u>ree</u>·ah
– the liquor store [off-licence]	**la tienda de bebidas alcohólicas** lah <u>teeyehn</u>·dah deh beh·<u>bee</u>·dahs ahl·koh·<u>oh</u>·lee·kahs

– the market	**– el mercado** chl mehr·kah·doh
– the pastry shop	**– la pastelería** lah pahs·teh·leh·ree·ah
– the pharmacy [chemist]	**– la farmacia** lah fahr·mah·theeyah
– the produce [grocery] store	**– la tienda de frutas y verduras** lah teeyehn·dah deh froo·tahs ee behr·doo·rahs
– the shoe store	**– la zapatería** lah thah·pah·teh·ree·ah
– the shopping mall [shopping centre]	**– el centro comercial** ehl then·troh koh mchr·theeyahl
– the souvenir store	**– la tienda de recuerdos** lah teeyehn·dah dch reh·kwehr·dohs
– the supermarket	**– el supermercado** ehl soo·pehr·mehr·kah·doh
– the tobacconist	**– el estanco** ehl ehs·tahn·koh
– the toy store	**– la juguetería** luh khoo·geh·tch·ree·ah

Services

Can you recommend...?	**¿Puede recomendarme...?** pweh·deh reh·koh·mehn·dahr·meh
– a barber	**– una peluquería de caballeros** oo·nah peh·loo·keh·ree·ah deh kah·bah·yeh·rohs
– a dry cleaner	**– una tintorería** oo·nah teen·toh·reh·ree·ah
– a hairstylist	**– una peluquería de señoras** oo·nah pch·loo·keh·ree·ah deh seh·nyoh·rahs
– a laundromat [launderette]	**– una lavandería** oo·nah lah·bahn·deh·ree·ah
– a nail salon	**– un salón de manicura** sah·lohn deh mah·nee·koo·rah
– a spa	**– un centro de salud y belleza** oon then·troh deh sah·lood ee beh·yeh·thah
– a travel agency	**– una agencia de viajes** oo·nah ah·khehn·theeyah deh beeyah·khehs

Can you…this?	¿Puede…esto? pweh·deh…ehs·toh
– alter	– hacerle un arreglo a ah·thehr·leh oon ah·rreh·gloh ah
– clean	– limpiar leem·peeyahr
– fix [mend]	– zurcir thoor·theer
– press	– planchar plahn·chahr
When will it be ready?	¿Cuándo estará listo? kwahn·doh ehs·tah·rah lees·toh

Spa

I'd like…	Quiero… keeyeh·roh…
– an *eyebrow/bikini* wax	– depilarme las *cejas/ingles* deh·pee·lahr·meh lahs *theh·khahs/een·glehs*
– a facial	– hacerme una limpieza de cutis ah·thehr·meh oo·nah leem·peeyeh·thah deh koo·tees
– a *manicure/ pedicure*	– hacerme la *manicura/pedicura* ah·thehr·meh lah *mah·nee·koo·rah/ peh·dee·koo·rah*
– a (sports) massage	– un masaje (deportivo) oon mah·sah·kheh (deh·pohr·tee·boh)
Do you do…?	¿Hacen…? ah·thehn…
– acupuncture	– acupuntura ah·koo·poon·too·rah
– aromatherapy	– aromaterapia ah·roh·mah·teh·rah·peeyah
– oxygen treatment	– oxígenoterapia oh·xee·kheh·noh·teh·rah·peeyah
Do you have a sauna?	¿Tienen una sauna? teeyehn·ehn oo·nah sawoo·nah

With its varied landscapes and more than 2,000 registered springs (mineral and other), Spain is a prime location for spas, wellness centers and health-based resorts. These facilities offer a variety of treatments, including relaxation therapies and herbal remedies. Day spas can be found throughout the country, especially in the larger cities, and resort and overnight spas often offer individual services to those not staying there. Many of these also offer a wide variety of other relaxing activities such as horseback riding, guided tours, golf and swimming. Some spas and resorts do not allow children, so check before booking if you are traveling with kids.

Hair Salon

I'd like…	**Quiero…** keeyeh·roh…
an appointment for *today/tomorrow*	**– pedir hora para *hoy/mañana*** peh·<u>deer</u> oh·rah <u>pah</u>·rah oy/mah·<u>nyah</u>·nah
– some color	**– teñirme el pelo** teh·<u>nyeer</u>·meh ehl peh·loh
– some highlights	**– hacerme mechas** ah·<u>thehr</u>·mch <u>meh</u>·chahs
– my hair styled	**– hacerme un peinado** ah·<u>thchr</u>·meh oon peyee·<u>nah</u>·doh
– a haircut	**– cortarme el pelo** kohr·<u>tahr</u> mch chl <u>peh</u>·loh
– a trim	**– cortarme las puntas** kohr·<u>tahr</u>·meh lahs <u>poon</u>·tahs
Not too short.	**No me lo corte demasiado.** noh meh loh <u>kohr</u>·teh deh·mah·<u>seeyah</u>·doh
Shorter here.	**Quíteme más de aquí.** <u>kee</u>·teh·meh mahs deh ah·<u>kee</u>

Sales Help

When do you *open/close*?	**¿A qué hora *abren/cierran*?** ah keh <u>oh</u>·rah <u>ah</u>·brehn/<u>theeyeh</u>·rrahn
Where *is/are*…?	**¿Dónde *está/están*…?** <u>dohn</u>·deh ehs·<u>tah</u>/ ehs·<u>tahn</u>…
– the cashier	**– la caja** lah <u>kah</u>·khah
– the escalators	**– las escaleras mecánicas** lahs ehs·kah·<u>leh</u>·rahs meh·<u>kah</u>·nee·kahs
– the elevator [lift]	**– el ascensor** ehl ahs·<u>thehn</u>·sohr
– the fitting room	**– el probador** ehl proh·bah·<u>dohr</u>
– the store directory	**– la guía de tiendas** lah <u>gee</u>·ah deh <u>teeyehn</u>·dahs
Can you help me?	**¿Puede ayudarme?** <u>pweh</u>·deh ah·yoo·<u>dahr</u>·meh
I'm just looking.	**Sólo estoy mirando.** <u>soh</u>·loh ehs·<u>toy</u> mee·<u>rahn</u>·doh
I'm being helped.	**Ya me atienden.** yah meh ah·<u>teeyehn</u>·dehn
Do you have…?	**¿Tienen…?** <u>teeyeh</u>·nehn…
Can you show me…?	**¿Podría enseñarme…?** poh·<u>dree</u>·ah ehn·seh·<u>nyahr</u>·meh…
Can you *ship/ wrap* it?	**¿Pueden *hacer un envío/envolverlo*?** <u>pweh</u>·dehn ah·<u>thehr</u> oon ehn·<u>bee</u>·oh/ ehn·bohl·<u>behr</u>·loh
How much?	**¿Cuánto es?** <u>kwahn</u>·toh ehs
That's all.	**Eso es todo.** <u>eh</u>·soh ehs <u>toh</u>·doh

▶ For clothing items, see page 134.

▶ For food items, see page 91.

▶ For souvenirs, see page 131.

You May Hear...

¿Necesita ayuda? neh·theh·<u>see</u>·tah
ah·<u>yoo</u>·dah

Can I help you?

Un momento. oon moh·<u>mehn</u>·toh

One moment.

¿Qué desea? keh deh·<u>seh</u>·ah

What would you like?

¿Algo más? <u>ahl</u>·goh mahs

Anything else?

Preferences ———————————

I'd like something…	**Quiero algo…** <u>keeyeh</u>·roh <u>ahl</u>·goh…
– cheap/expensive	**– barato/caro** bah·<u>rah</u>·toh/<u>kah</u>·roh
– larger/smaller	**– más grande/más pequeño** mahs <u>grahn</u>·doh/mahs peh·<u>keh</u>·nyoh
– from this region	**– de esta región** deh <u>ehs</u>·tah reh·<u>kheeyohn</u>
Around…euros.	**Alrededor de los…euros.** ahl·reh·deh·<u>dohr</u> deh lohs…<u>ew</u>·rohs
Is it real?	**¿Es auténtico♂/auténtica♀?** ehs awoo·<u>tehn</u>·tee·koh♂/awoo·<u>tehn</u>·tee·kah♀
Can you show me *this/that*?	**¿Puede enseñarme *esto/eso*?** <u>pweh</u>·deh ehn·seh·<u>nyahr</u>·meh *<u>ehs</u>·toh/<u>eh</u>·soh*

Decisions ———————————

That's not quite what I want.	**Eso no es realmente lo que busco.** <u>eh</u>·soh noh ehs reh·ahl·<u>mehn</u>·teh loh keh <u>boos</u>·koh
No, I don't like it.	**No, no me gusta.** noh noh meh <u>goos</u>·tah
It's too expensive.	**Es demasiado caro.** ehs deh·mah·<u>seeyah</u>·doh <u>kah</u>·roh
I have to think about it.	**Quiero pensármelo.** <u>keeyeh</u>·roh pehn·<u>sahr</u>·meh·loh
I'll take it.	**Me lo llevo.** meh loh <u>yeh</u>·boh

Bargaining

That's too much.	**Eso es demasiado.** eh·soh ehs deh·mah·<u>seeyah</u>·doh	
I'll give you…	**Le doy…** leh doy…	
I have only… euros.	**Sólo tengo…euros.** <u>soh</u>·loh <u>tehn</u>·goh…<u>ew</u>·rohs	
Is that your best price?	**¿Es el mejor precio que me puede hacer?** ehs ehl meh·<u>khohr</u> <u>preh</u>·theeyoh keh meh <u>pweh</u>·deh ah·<u>thehr</u>	
Can you give me a discount?	**¿Puede hacerme un descuento?** pweh·deh ah·<u>thehr</u>·meh oon dehs·<u>kwehn</u>·toh	

▶For numbers, see page 178.

Paying

How much?	**¿Cuánto es?** <u>kwahn</u>·toh ehs
I'll pay…	**Voy a pagar…** boy ah pah·<u>gahr</u>…
– in cash	**– en efectivo** ehn eh·fehk·<u>tee</u>·boh
– by credit card	**– con tarjeta de crédito** kohn tahr·<u>kheh</u>·tah deh <u>kreh</u>·dee·toh
– by traveler's check [cheque]	**– con cheque de viaje** kohn <u>cheh</u>·keh deh <u>beeyah</u>·kheh
A receipt, please.	**Un recibo, por favor.** oon reh·<u>thee</u>·boh pohr fah·<u>bohr</u>

> **i** Credit cards are widely accepted throughout Spain; you will need to show ID when using a credit card. Mastercard™ and Visa™ are the most commonly used; American Express® is accepted in most places. Debit cards are common in Spain and throughout Europe; these are usually accepted if backed by Visa™ or Mastercard™. Traveler's checks are not accepted everywhere; always have an alternate form of payment available. Cash is always accepted—some places, such as newsstands, tobacconists, flower shops and market or street stands, take cash only.

You May Hear...

¿Cómo va a pagar? koh·moh bah ah pah·gahr — How are you paying?

Su tarjeta ha sido rechazada. soo tahr·kheh·tah ah see·doh reh·chah·thah·dah — Your credit card has been declined.

Su documento de identidad, por favor. soo doh·koo·mehn·toh deh ee·dehn·tee·dahd pohr fah·bohr — ID, please.

No aceptamos tarjetas de crédito. noh ah·thehp·tah·mohs tahr·kheh·tahs deh kreh·dee·toh — We don't accept credit cards.

Sólo en efectivo, por favor. soh·loh ehn eh·fehk·tee·boh pohr fah·bohr — Cash only, please.

¿Tiene *cambio/billetes más pequeños*? teeyeh·neh *kahm·beeyoh/bee·yeh·tehs mahs peh·keh·nyohs* — Do you have *change/ small bills [notes]*?

Complaints

I'd like... — **Quiero...** keeyeh·roh...

– to exchange this — **– cambiar esto por otro** kahm·beeyahr ehs·toh pohr oh·troh

– to return this — **– devolver esto** deh·bohl·behr ehs·toh

– a refund — **– que me devuelvan el dinero** keh meh deh·bwehl·bahn ehl dee·neh·roh

– to speak to the manager — **– hablar con el encargado** ah·blahr kohn ehl ehn·kahr·gah·doh

Souvenirs

bottle of wine — **la botella de vino** lah boh·teh·yah deh bee·noh

box of chocolates — **la caja de bombones** lah kah·khah deh bohm·boh·nehs

castanets — **las castañuelas** lahs kahs·tah·nyweh·lahs

doll	**la muñeca** lah moo·<u>nyeh</u>·kah
fan (wooden, flamenco)	**el abanico de madera** ehl ah·bah·<u>nee</u>·koh deh mah·<u>deh</u>·rah
key ring	**el llavero** ehl yah·<u>beh</u>·roh
postcard	**la postal** lah pohs·<u>tahl</u>
pottery	**la cerámica** lah theh·<u>rah</u>·mee·kah
serrano ham	**el jamón serrano** ehl khah·<u>mohn</u> seh·<u>rrah</u>·noh
T-shirt	**la camiseta** lah kah·mee·<u>seh</u>·tah
terracotta bowl	**la cazuela de barro** lah kah·<u>thweh</u>·lah deh <u>bah</u>·rroh
toy	**el juguete** ehl khoo·<u>geh</u>·teh
wine	**el vino** ehl <u>bee</u>·noh
Can I see *this/that*?	**¿Puedo ver *esto/eso*?** <u>pweh</u>·doh behr <u>ehs</u>·toh/<u>eh</u>·soh
It's in the *window/display case*.	**Está en *el escaparate/la vitrina*.** ehs·<u>tah</u> ehn ehl ehs·kah·pah·<u>rah</u>·teh/lah bee·<u>tree</u>·nah
I'd like...	**Quiero...** <u>keeyeh</u>·roh...
– a battery	**– una pila** <u>oo</u>·nah <u>pee</u>·lah
– a bracelet	**– una pulsera** <u>oo</u>·nah pool·<u>seh</u>·rah
– a brooch	**– un broche** oon <u>broh</u>·cheh

– earrings	– **unos pendientes** <u>oo</u>·nohs pehn·<u>deeyehn</u>·tehs
– a necklace	– **un collar** oon <u>koh</u>·yahr
– a ring	– **un anillo** oon ah·<u>nee</u>·yoh
– a watch	– **un reloj de pulsera** oon reh·<u>lohkh</u> deh pool·<u>seh</u>·rah
I'd like…	**Quiero…** <u>keeyeh</u>·roh…
– copper	– **cobre** <u>koh</u>·breh
– crystal	– **cristal** krees·<u>tahl</u>
– diamonds	– **diamantes** deeyah·<u>mahn</u>·tehs
– *white/yellow* gold	– **oro *blanoo/amarillo*** oh·roh <u>blahn</u>·koh/ ah·mah·<u>ree</u>·yoh
– pearls	– **perlas** <u>pehr</u>·lahs
– pewter	– **peltre** <u>pehl</u>·treh
– platinum	– **platino** plah·<u>tee</u>·noh
– sterling silver	– **plata esterlina** plah·tah ehs·tehr·<u>lee</u>·nah
Is this real?	**¿Es auténtico?** chs awoo·<u>tehn</u>·tee·koh
Can you engrave it?	**¿Puede grabármelo?** <u>pweh</u>·deh grah·<u>bahr</u>·meh·loh

Spain produces a wide range of souvenirs, from typical tourist T-shirts to high-quality regional crafts. Spanish wine is popular and quality examples, such as sherry from Jerez and red wine from Rioja, can be found all over. Olive oil is also a popular gift. Classic Spanish souvenirs include bullfighting mementos, such as figurines, posters or capes, castanets, hand-painted flamenco fans and guitars. Reproduction paintings by Spain's most famous artists, such as Picasso, Dalí, Miró, Goya, El Greco or Velázquez, are also popular. Specialty regional goods include copperware, earthenware, leather goods, jewelry, lace, porcelain and wood carvings. Spanish swords and other metal work from Toledo are unique gifts, and Lladro® porcelain figurines are very popular. To find a good representation of each region's specialty goods at reasonable prices, visit the markets in each town.

> Throughout Spain you can find quality gold and silver jewelry. Córdoba is especially well-known for its silver filigree jewelry. Mallorca and Menorca, in the Balearic Islands, are known for their artificial pearls and artful costume jewelry. Look for tasteful items made from gold and Mallorca pearls. Quality jewelry can be purchased in jewelry stores, but for a more personal approach, visit the local markets. These, along with small specialty stores in rural villages and towns, are a great source for handmade jewelry.

Antiques

How old is it?	**¿Qué antigüedad tiene?** keh ahn·tee·gweh·<u>dahd</u> <u>teeyeh</u>·neh
Do you have anything from the…period?	**¿Tiene algo de la época…?** <u>teeyeh</u>·neh <u>ahl</u>·goh deh lah <u>eh</u>·poh·kah…
Do I have to fill out any forms?	**¿Tengo que rellenar algún impreso?** <u>tehn</u>·goh keh reh·yeh·<u>nahr</u> ahl·<u>goon</u> eem·<u>preh</u>·soh
Is there a certificate of authenticity?	**¿Tiene el certificado de autenticidad?** <u>teeyeh</u>·neh ehl thehr·tee·fee·<u>kah</u>·doh deh awoo·tehn·tee·thee·<u>dahd</u>

Clothing

I'd like…	**Quiero…** <u>keeyeh</u>·roh…
Can I try this on?	**¿Puedo probarme esto?** <u>pweh</u>·doh proh·<u>bahr</u>·meh <u>ehs</u>·toh
It doesn't fit.	**No me queda bien.** noh meh <u>keh</u>·dah beeyehn
It's too…	**Me queda demasiado…** meh <u>keh</u>·dah deh·mah·<u>seeyah</u>·doh…
– big	**– grande** <u>grahn</u>·deh
– small	**– pequeño** ♂ **/pequeña** ♀ peh·<u>keh</u>·nyoh ♂ / peh·<u>keh</u>·nyah ♀

– short	**corto** ♂ **/corta** ♀ kohr·toh ♂ /kohr·lah ♀
– long	**largo** ♂ **/larga** ♀ lahr·goh ♂ /lahr·gah ♀
Do you have this in size…?	**¿Tiene esto en la talla…?** teeyeh·neh ehs·toh ehn lah tah·yah…
Do you have this in a *bigger/ smaller* size?	**¿Tiene esto en una talla más *grande/ pequeña*?** teeyeh·neh ehs·toh chn oo·nah tah·yah mahs *grahn·deh/peh·keh·nyah*

▶ For numbers, see page 178.

You May See…

ROPA DE CABALLERO	men's clothing
ROPA DE SEÑORA	women's clothing
ROPA DE NIÑOS	children's clothing

Color

I'd like something…	**Busco algo…** boos·koh ahl·goh…
– beige	– **beis** behyees
– black	– **negro** neh·groh
– blue	– **azul** ah·thool
– brown	– **marrón** mah·rrohn
– green	– **verde** behr·deh
– gray	– **gris** grees
– orange	– **naranja** nah·rahn·khah
– pink	– **rosa** roh·sah
– purple	– **morado** moh·rah·doh
– red	– **rojo** roh·khoh
– white	– **blanco** blahn·koh
yellow	– **amarillo** ah·mah·ree·yoh

Clothes and Accessories

backpack	**la mochila**	lah moh-<u>chee</u>-lah
belt	**el cinturón**	ehl theen-too-<u>rohn</u>
bikini	**el bikini**	ehl bee-<u>kee</u>-nee
blouse	**la blusa**	lah <u>bloo</u>-sah
bra	**el sujetador**	ehl soo-kheh-tah-<u>dohr</u>
briefs [underpants]	**los calzoncillos**	lohs kahl-thohn-<u>thee</u>-yohs
coat	**el abrigo**	ehl ah-<u>bree</u>-goh
dress	**el vestido**	ehl behs-<u>tee</u>-doh
hat	**el sombrero**	ehl sohm-<u>breh</u>-roh
jacket	**la chaqueta**	lah chah-<u>keh</u>-tah
jeans	**los vaqueros**	lohs bah-<u>keh</u>-rohs
pajamas	**el pijama**	ehl pee-<u>khah</u>-mah
pants [trousers]	**los pantalones**	lohs pahn-tah-<u>loh</u>-nehs
pantyhose [tights]	**las medias**	lahs <u>meh</u>-deeyahs
purse [handbag]	**el bolso**	ehl <u>bohl</u>-soh
raincoat	**el impermeable**	ehl eem-pehr-meh-<u>ah</u>-bleh
scarf	**la bufanda**	lah boo-<u>fahn</u>-dah
shirt	**la camisa**	lah kah-<u>mee</u>-sah
shorts	**los pantalones cortos**	lohs pahn-tah-<u>loh</u>-nehs <u>kohr</u>-tohs
skirt	**la falda**	lah <u>fahl</u>-dah
socks	**los calcetines**	lohs kahl-theh-<u>tee</u>-nehs
suit	**el traje de chaqueta**	ehl <u>trah</u>-kheh deh chah-<u>keh</u>-tah
sunglasses	**las gafas de sol**	lahs <u>gah</u>-fahs deh sohl
sweater	**el jersey**	ehl khehr-<u>seyee</u>
sweatshirt	**la sudadera**	lah soo-dah-<u>deh</u>-rah

swimsuit	**el bañador** ehl bah·nyah·<u>dohr</u>
T-shirt	**la camiseta** lah kah·mee·<u>seh</u>·tah
tie	**la corbata** lah kohr·<u>bah</u>·tah
underwear	**la ropa interior** lah <u>roh</u>·pah een·teh·<u>reeyohr</u>

Fabric

I'd like…	**Quiero…** <u>keeyeh</u>·roh…
– cotton	**– algodón** ahl·goh·<u>dohn</u>
denim	**– tela vaquera** <u>teh</u>·lah bah·<u>keh</u>·rah
– lace	**– encaje** ehn·<u>kah</u>·kheh
– leather	**– cuero** <u>kweh</u>·roh
– linen	**– lino** <u>lee</u>·noh
– silk	**– seda** <u>seh</u>·dah
– wool	**– lana** <u>lah</u>·nah
Is it machine washable?	**¿Se puede lavar a máquina?** seh <u>pweh</u>·deh lah·<u>bahr</u> ah <u>mah</u>·kee·nah

Shoes

I'd like…	**Quiero…** <u>keeyeh</u>·roh…
– *high-heeled/flat* shoes	**– zapatos** *de taoón/planos* thah·<u>pah</u>·tohs *deh tah·<u>kohn</u>/plah·nohs*
– boots	**– botas** <u>boh</u>·tahs
– loafers	**– mocasines** moh·kah·<u>see</u>·nehs
– sandals	**– sandalias** sahn·<u>dah</u>·leeyahs
– shoes	**– zapatos** thah·<u>pah</u>·tohs
– slippers	**– zapatillas** thah·pah·<u>tee</u>·yahs
– sneakers	**– zapatillas de deporte** thah·pah·<u>tee</u>·yahs deh deh·<u>pohr</u>·teh
In size…	**En la talla…** ehn lah <u>tah</u>·yah…

▶For numbers, see page 178.

Sizes

small (S)	**pequeña (P)** peh·<u>keh</u>·nyah (peh)
medium (M)	**mediana (M)** meh·<u>deeyah</u>·nah (ehm)
large (L)	**grande (G)** <u>grahn</u>·deh (kheh)
extra large (XL)	**XL** ehkees·ehleh
petite	**tallas pequeñas** <u>tah</u>·yahs peh·<u>keh</u>·nyahs
plus size	**tallas grandes** <u>tah</u>·yahs <u>grahn</u>·dehs

Newsstand and Tobacconist ———————

Do you sell English-language newspapers?	**¿Venden periódicos en inglés?** <u>behn</u>·dehn peh·<u>reeyoh</u>·dee·kohs ehn een·<u>glehs</u>
I'd like…	**Quiero…** <u>keeyeh</u>·roh…
– candy [sweets]	**– caramelos** kah·rah·<u>meh</u>·lohs
– chewing gum	**– chicle** <u>chee</u>·kleh
– a chocolate bar	**– una chocolatina** <u>oo</u>·nah choh·koh·lah·<u>tee</u>·nah
– a cigar	**– un puro** oon <u>poo</u>·roh
– a *pack/carton* of cigarettes	**– un *paquete/cartón* de tabaco** oon pah·<u>keh</u>·teh/kahr·<u>tohn</u> deh tah·<u>bah</u>·koh
– a lighter	**– un mechero** oon meh·<u>cheh</u>·roh
– a magazine	**– una revista** <u>oo</u>·nah reh·<u>bees</u>·tah
– matches	**– cerillas** theh·<u>ree</u>·yahs
– a newspaper	**– un periódico** oon peh·<u>reeyoh</u>·dee·koh
– a pen	**– un bolígrafo** oon boh·<u>lee</u>·grah·foh
– a postcard	**– una postal** <u>oo</u>·nah pohs·tahl
– a *road/town* map of…	**– un *mapa de las carreteras/plano* de…** oon <u>mah</u>·pah deh lahs kah·rreh·<u>teh</u>·rahs/ <u>plah</u>·noh deh…
– stamps	**– sellos** <u>seh</u>·yohs

Photography

I'd like a/an... camera.	**Quiero una cámara...** <u>keeyeh</u>·roh oo·nah <u>kah</u>·mah·rah...
– automatic	**– automática** awoo·toh·<u>mah</u>·tee·kah
– digital	**– digital** dee·khee·<u>tahl</u>
– disposable	**– desechable** deh·seh·<u>chah</u>·bleh
I'd like...	**Quiero...** <u>keeyeh</u>·roh...
– a battery	**– una pila** <u>oo</u>·nah <u>pee</u>·lah
– digital prints	**– fotos digitales** <u>foh</u>·tohs dee·khee·<u>tah</u>·lehs
– a memory card	**– una tarjeta de memoria** <u>oo</u>·nah tahr·<u>kheh</u>·tah deh meh·<u>moh</u>·reeyah
Can I print digital photos here?	**¿Puedo imprimir aquí fotos digitales?** <u>pweh</u>·doh eem·pree·meer ah·<u>kee</u> <u>foh</u>·tohs dee·khee·<u>tah</u>·lehs

Sports and Leisure

Essential

When's the game?	**¿Cuándo empieza el partido?** <u>kwahn</u>·doh ehm·<u>peeyeh</u>·thah ehl pahr·<u>tee</u>·doh
Where's...?	**¿Dónde está...?** <u>dohn</u>·deh ehs·<u>tah</u>...
– the beach	**– la playa** lah <u>plah</u>·yah
– the park	**– el parque** ehl <u>pahr</u>·keh
– the pool	**– la piscina** lah pees·<u>thee</u>·nah
Is it safe to swim here?	**¿Es seguro nadar aquí?** ehs seh·<u>goo</u>·roh nah·<u>dahr</u> ah·<u>kee</u>
Can I rent [hire] golf clubs?	**¿Puedo alquilar palos de golf?** <u>pweh</u>·doh ahl·kee·<u>lahr</u> <u>pah</u>·lohs deh golf
How much per hour?	**¿Cuánto cuesta por hora?** <u>kwahn</u>·toh <u>kwehs</u>·tah pohr <u>oh</u>·rah

How far is it to…?	**¿A qué distancia está…?** ah keh dees·tahn·theeyah ehs·tah…
Can you show me on the map, please?	**¿Puede indicármelo en el mapa, por favor?** pweh·deh een·dee·kahr·meh·loh ehn ehl mah·pah pohr fah·bohr

Spectator Sports

When's…?	**¿Cuándo empieza…?** kwahn·doh ehm·peeyeh·thah…
– the basketball game	– **el partido de baloncesto** ehl pahr·tee·doh deh bah·lohn·thehs·toh
– the boxing match	– **la pelea de boxeo** lah peh·leh·ah deh bohks·eh·oh
– the cycling race	– **la vuelta ciclista** lah bwehl·tah thee·klees·tah
– the golf tournament	– **el torneo de golf** ehl tohr·neh·oh deh golf
– the soccer [football] game	– **el partido de fútbol** ehl pahr·tee·doh deh foot·bohl
– the tennis match	– **el partido de tenis** ehl pahr·tee·doh deh teh·nees
– the volleyball game	– **el partido de voleibol** ehl pahr·tee·doh deh boh·leyeh·bohl
Who's playing?	**¿Quienes juegan?** keeyeh·nehs khweh·gahn
Where is…?	**¿Dónde está…?** dohn·deh ehs·tah…
– the horsetrack	– **el hipódromo** ehl ee·poh·droh·moh
– the racetrack	– **el circuito de carreras** ehl theer·kwee·toh de kah·rreh·rahs
– the stadium	– **el estadio** ehl ehs·tah·deeyoh
Where can I place a bet?	**¿Dónde puedo hacer una apuesta?** dohn·deh pweh·doh ah·thehr oo·nah ah·pwehs·tah

i **Fútbol** (soccer) is the most popular sport in Spain; most cities in Spain have their own professional teams with a large fan base. Note that fans are extremely dedicated, so be sure not to insult the team. Almost all activity in Spain stops when there is an important soccer game on.

Golf is also popular and the golf courses on the Costa del Sol are worth a round. Other popular sports include basketball, tennis, auto racing, horse racing, hiking and climbing. **Jai alai** is a popular fast-paced game involving balls and curved wicker-basket gloves.

There are many casinos throughout Spain. Minimum entrance and gaming age is 18; ID is required and the dress code is business casual.

Participating

Where *is/are*…?	¿**Dónde *está/están*…?** dohn·deh *ehs·tah/ ehs·tahn*…
– the golf course	– **el campo de golf** ehl kahm·poh deh golf
– the gym	– **el gimnasio** ehl kheem·nah·seeyoh
– the park	– **el parque** ehl pahr·keh
– the tennis courts	– **las canchas de tenis** lahs kahn·chahs deh teh·nees
How much per…?	¿**Cuánto cuesta por…?** kwahn·toh kwehs·tah pohr…
– day	– **día** dee·ah
– hour	– **hora** oh·rah
– game	– **partido** pahr·tee·doh
– round	– **juego** khweh·goh

Can I rent [hire]…?	**¿Puedo alquilar…?** <u>pweh</u>·doh ahl·kee·<u>lahr</u>…
– golf clubs	**– palos de golf** <u>pah</u>·lohs deh golf
– equipment	**– equipo** eh·<u>kee</u>·poh
– a racket	**– una raqueta** <u>oo</u>·nah rah·<u>keh</u>·tah

At the Beach/Pool

Where's the *beach/pool*?	**¿Dónde está la *playa/piscina*?** <u>dohn</u>·deh ehs·<u>tah</u> lah *plah·yah/pees·<u>thee</u>·nah*
Is there…?	**¿Hay…?** aye…
– a kiddie pool	**– una piscina infantil** <u>oo</u>·nah pees·<u>thee</u>·nah een·fahn·<u>teel</u>
– an *indoor/outdoor* pool	**– una piscina *cubierta/exterior*** <u>oo</u>·nah pees·<u>thee</u>·nah *koo·<u>beeyehr</u>·tah/ehx·teh·<u>reeyohr</u>*
– a lifeguard	**– un socorrista** oon soh·koh·<u>rrees</u>·tah
Is it safe…?	**¿Es seguro…?** ehs seh·<u>goo</u>·roh…
– to swim	**– nadar** nah·<u>dahr</u>
– to dive	**– tirarse de cabeza** tee·<u>rahr</u>·seh deh kah·<u>beh</u>·thah
– for children	**– para los niños** <u>pah</u>·rah lohs <u>nee</u>·nyohs

▶ For travel with children, see page 155.

I'd like to rent [hire]…	**Quiero alquilar…** keeyeh·roh ahl·kee·<u>lahr</u>…
– a deck chair	**– una tumbona** <u>oo</u>·nah toom·<u>boh</u>·nah
– diving equipment	**– equipo de buceo** eh·<u>kee</u>·poh deh boo·<u>theh</u>·oh
– a jet ski	**– una moto acuática** <u>oo</u>·nah <u>moh</u>·toh ah·<u>kwah</u>·tee·kah
– a motorboat	**– una lancha motora** <u>oo</u>·nah <u>lahn</u>·chah moh·<u>toh</u>·rah
– a rowboat	**– una barca de remos** <u>oo</u>·nah <u>bahr</u>·kah deh <u>reh</u>·mohs
– snorkeling equipment	**– equipo de esnórquel** eh·<u>kee</u>·poh deh ehs·<u>nohr</u>·kehl
– a surfboard	**– una tabla de surf** <u>oo</u>·nah <u>tah</u>·blah deh soorf
– a towel	**– una toalla** <u>oo</u>·nah toh·<u>ah</u>·yah
– an umbrella	**– una sombrilla** <u>oo</u>·nah sohm·<u>bree</u>·yah
– water skis	**– unos esquís acuáticos** <u>oo</u>·nohs ehs·<u>kees</u> ah·<u>kwah</u>·tee·kohs
– a windsurfer	**– una tabla de windsurf** <u>oo</u>·nah <u>tah</u>·blah deh <u>weend</u>·soorf
For…hours.	**Por…horas.** pohr… <u>oh</u>·rahs

i Spain has more than 2,400 miles (4,000 km) of coastline and more than 1,700 beaches, with 16 different **Costas** (coastal regions). Two of the more famous coastal regions are **Costa del Sol** and **Costa Blanca**. Spain's Balearic and Canary Islands boast some of the most beautiful beaches in the world. If you decide to go for a swim, check the safety flags at each beach. Green flags indicate the water is safe, yellow flags indicate that you should use caution and red flags indicate that the water is unsafe for swimming.

Winter Sports

A lift pass for a day/five days, please.	**Un pase de *un día/cinco días* de acceso a los remontes.** oon *pah*-seh deh *oon dee*-ah/ *theen*-koh *dee*-ahs deh ahk-*theh*-soh ah lohs reh-*mohn*-tehs
I'd like to rent [hire]...	**Quiero alquilar...** *keeyeh*-roh ahl-kee-*lahr*...
– boots	**– botas** *boh*-tahs
– a helmet	**– un casco** oon *kahs*-koh
– poles	**– bastones** bahs-*toh*-nehs
– skis	**– esquís** ehs-kees
– a snowboard	**– una tabla de snowboard** *oo*-nah *tah*-blah deh *snoh*-bohrd
– snowshoes	**– raquetas de nieve** rah-*keh*-tahs deh *neeyeh*-beh
These are too big/small.	**Me quedan demasiado *grandes/ pequeños*.** meh *keh*-dahn deh-mah-*seeyah*-doh *grahn*-dehs/peh-*keh*-nyohs
Are there lessons?	**¿Dan clases?** dahn *klah*-sehs
I'm a beginner.	**Soy principiante.** soy preen-thee-*peeyahn*-teh
I'm experienced.	**Tengo experiencia.** *tehn*-goh ehx-peh-*reeyehn*-theeyah
A trail [piste] map, please.	**Un mapa de las pistas, por favor.** oon *mah*-pah deh lahs *pees*-tahs pohr fah-*bohr*

---

i Spain has three mountain ranges, the Pyrenees, the Sierra Nevada and the Cantabrian, with an average altitude of 2,000 feet (600 m). There are more than 30 ski resorts throughout Spain with more than 620 miles (1,000 km) of ski runs combined. In addition to skiing, most resorts and ski areas offer other winter activities such as snowboarding, snowmobiling, sledding and dog-sledding.

You May See...

TELESQUÍ	drag lift
TELEFÉRICO	cable car
TELESILLA	chair lift
PRINCIPIANTE	novice
NIVEL INTERMEDIO	intermediate
EXPERTO	expert
PISTA CERRADA	trail [piste] closed

In the Countryside

A map of…, please.	**Un mapa de…, por favor.** oon mah·pah deh… pohr fah·bohr
– this region	– **esta región** ehs·tah reh·kheeyohn
– the walking routes	– **las rutas de senderismo** lahs roo·tahs deh sehn·deh·rees·moh
– the bike routes	– **los senderos para bicicletas** lohs sehn·deh·rohs pah·rah bee·thee·kleh·tahs
– the trails	– **los senderos** lohs sehn·deh·rohs
Is It *easy/difficult*?	**¿Es *fácil/difícil*?** ehs *fah·theel/dee·fee·theel*
Is it *far/steep*?	**¿Está *lejos/empinado*?** ehs·tah *leh·khohs/ ehm·pee·nah·doh*
How far is it to…?	**¿A qué distancia está…?** ah koh dees·tahn·theeyah ehs·tah…
Can you show me on the map, please?	**¿Puede indicármelo en el mapa, por favor?** pweh·deh een·dee·kahr·meh·loh ehn ehl mah·pah pohr fah·bohr
I'm lost.	**Me he perdido.** meh eh pehr·dee·doh

Where is…?	¿Dónde está…? dohn·deh ehs·tah…
– the bridge	**– el puente** ehl pwehn·teh
– the cave	**– la cueva** lah kweh·bah
– the cliff	**– el acantilado** ehl ah·kahn·tee·lah·doh
– the desert	**– el desierto** ehl deh·seeyehr·toh
– the farm	**– la granja** lah grahn·khah
– the field	**– el campo** ehl kahm·poh
– the forest	**– el bosque** ehl bohs·keh
– the hill	**– la colina** lah koh·lee·nah
– the lake	**– el lago** ehl lah·goh
– the mountain	**– la montaña** lah mohn·tah·nyah
– the nature preserve	**– la reserva natural** lah reh·sehr·bah nah·too·rahl
– the overlook [viewpoint]	**– el mirador** ehl mee·rah·dohr
– the park	**– el parque** ehl pahr·keh
– the path	**– el camino** ehl kah·mee·noh
– the peak	**– el pico** ehl pee·koh
– the picnic area	**– la zona de picnic** lah thoh·nah deh peek·neek
– the pond	**– el estanque** ehl ehs·tahn·keh
– the river	**– el río** ehl ree·oh
– the sea	**– el mar** ehl mahr
– the (thermal) spring	**– el manantial (de aguas termales)** ehl mah·nahn·teeyahl (deh ah·gwahs tehr·mah·lehs)
– the stream	**– el arroyo** ehl ah·rroh·yoh
– the valley	**– el valle** ehl bah·yeh
– the vineyard	**– la viña** lah bee·nyah
– the waterfall	**– la cascada** lah kahs·kah·dah

146

Culture and Nightlife

Essential

What's there to do at night?	**¿Qué se puede hacer por las noches?** keh seh <u>pweh</u>·deh ah·<u>thehr</u> pohr lahs <u>noh</u>·chehs
Do you have a program of events?	**¿Tiene un programa de espectáculos?** teeyeh·neh oon proh·<u>grah</u>·mah deh ehs·pehk·<u>tah</u>·koo·lohs
What's playing tonight?	**¿Qué hay en cartelera esta noche?** koh ayc chn kahr·teh·<u>leh</u>·rah ehs·tah <u>noh</u>·cheh
Where's...?	**¿Dónde está...?** dohn·deh ehs·<u>tah</u>...
– the downtown area	**– el centro** ehl <u>thehn</u>·troh
– the bar	**– el bar** ehl bahr
– the dance club	**– la discoteca** lah dees·koh·<u>teh</u>·kah
Is there a cover charge?	**¿Hay que pagar entrada?** aye keh pah·<u>gahr</u> ehn·<u>trah</u>·dah

---

i Spain is famous for its centuries-old tradition of bullfighting. Known as **tauromaquia** or **corrida de toros**, bullfighting is seen as an art and tradition by many, and as a cruel and violent act against animals by others. Whether you find it fascinating or appalling, the bullfight is a unique experience in Spain. The bullfighting season runs from March to October; many towns have a vibrant festival in March to open the season.

Entertainment

Can you recommend…?	**¿Puede recomendarme…?** <u>pweh</u>·deh reh·koh·mehn·<u>dahr</u>·meh…
– a concert	**– un concierto** oon kohn·<u>theeyehr</u>·toh
– a movie	**– una película** <u>oo</u>·nah peh·<u>lee</u>·koo·lah
– an opera	**– una ópera** <u>oo</u>·nah <u>oh</u>·peh·rah
– a play	**– una obra de teatro** <u>oo</u>·nah <u>oh</u>·brah deh teh·<u>ah</u>·troh
When does it *start/end*?	**¿A qué hora *empieza/termina*?** ah keh <u>oh</u>·rah *ehm·<u>peeyeh</u>·thah/tehr·<u>mee</u>·nah*
What's the dress code?	**¿Cómo hay que ir vestido♂/vestida♀?** <u>koh</u>·moh aye keh eer behs·<u>tee</u>·doh♂/ behs·<u>tee</u>·dah♀
I like…	**Me gusta…** meh <u>goos</u>·tah…
– classical music	**– la música clásica** lah <u>moo</u>·see·kah <u>klah</u>·see·kah
– folk music	**– la música folk** lah <u>moo</u>·see·kah folk
– jazz	**– el jazz** ehl jazz
– pop music	**– la música pop** lah <u>moo</u>·see·kah pop
– rap	**– el rap** ehl rap

▶ For ticketing, see page 20.

148

i Tourist offices, travel agencies and guidebooks have extensive information regarding events throughout Spain. Dates of some annual events change each year, so check before you go. For listings of local events, check the daily newspapers or ask at your hotel or the local tourist office. Larger cities in Spain have many entertainment magazines and publications that are a good source for information. A few of the most popular annual events are listed below.

Carnaval is the festival that takes place the week before Lent. It's the Spanish equivalent of Mardi Gras.

Traditional Holy Week festivities are centered around Catholicism. Seville has some of the most spectacular and elaborate processional re-enactments of the religious events of Easter. Valencia is famous for building, then torching, giant papier-mâché figures.

The **Fiesta de San Fermín** is one of Spain's most famous events. The running of the bulls is an annual event that draws thousands of people to Pamplona and is televised worldwide.

You May Hear…

Por favor apaguen sus teléfonos móviles.
pohr fah·<u>bohr</u> ah·<u>pah</u>·gehn soos teh·<u>leh</u>·foh·nohs <u>moh</u>·bee·lehs

Turn off your cell [mobile] phones, please.

Nightlife

What's there to do at night?

¿Qué se puede hacer por las noches?
keh seh <u>pweh</u>·deh ah·<u>thehr</u> pohr lahs <u>noh</u>·chehs

Can you recommend…?	¿Puede recomendarme…? pweh·deh reh·koh·mehn·dahr·meh…
– a bar	– un bar oon bahr
– a casino	– un casino oon kah·see·noh
– a dance club	– una discoteca oo·nah dees·koh·teh·kah
– a flamenco performance	– un espectáculo de flamenco oon ehs·pehk·tah·koo·loh deh flah·mehn·koh
– a gay club	– una discoteca gay oo·nah dees·koh·teh·kah gay
– a jazz club	– un club de jazz oon kloob deh jazz
– a club with Spanish music	– un bar con música española oon bahr kohn moo·see·kah ehs·pah·nyoh·lah
Is there live music?	¿Hay música en vivo? aye moo·see·kah ehn bee·boh
How do I get there?	¿Cómo se llega allí? koh·moh seh yeh·gah ah·yee
Is there a cover charge?	¿Hay que pagar entrada? aye keh pah·gahr ehn·trah·dah
Let's go dancing.	Vamos a bailar. bah·mohs ah bayee·lahr

> **i**
>
> One of Spain's greatest cultural achievements is the
> **flamenco**. A combination of music, song and dance, the
> **flamenco** is an emotional performance that should not
> be missed when you are in Spain. Major cities such as
> Madrid, Seville and other Andalucian towns have **flamenco**
> performances year round. A **peña** is a small, intimate
> membership club (some allow guests) where you can view
> **flamenco** performed. **Tablaos** are typical public venues for
> **flamenco**. Seeing **flamenco** at a **tablao** can be an expensive
> night out, but well worth the money.

▼ Special Needs

▶ Business Travel   152
▶ Travel with Children   155
▶ For the Disabled   158

Business Travel

Essential

I'm here on business.	**Estoy aquí en viaje de negocios.** ehs-<u>toy</u> ah-<u>kee</u> ehn <u>beeyah</u>-kheh deh neh-<u>goh</u>-theeyohs
Here's my business card.	**Aquí tiene mi tarjeta.** ah-<u>kee</u> <u>teeyeh</u>-neh mee tahr-<u>kheh</u>-tah
Can I have your card?	**¿Puede darme su tarjeta?** <u>pweh</u>-deh <u>dahr</u>-meh soo tahr-<u>kheh</u>-tah
I have a meeting with…	**Tengo una reunión con…** <u>tehn</u>-goh <u>oo</u>-nah rewoo-<u>neeyohn</u> kohn…
Where's…?	**¿Dónde está…?** <u>dohn</u>-deh ehs-<u>tah</u>…
– the business center	**– el centro de negocios** ehl <u>thehn</u>-troh deh neh-<u>goh</u>-theeyohs
– the convention hall	**– el salón de congresos** ehl sah-<u>lohn</u> deh kohn-<u>greh</u>-sohs
– the meeting room	**– la sala de reuniones** lah <u>sah</u>-lah deh rewoo-<u>neeyohn</u>-ehs

Business Communication

I'm here to attend…	**Estoy aquí para asistir…** ehs-<u>toy</u> ah-<u>kee</u> <u>pah</u>-rah ah-sees-<u>teer</u>…
– a seminar	**– a un seminario** ah oon seh-mee-<u>nah</u>-reeyoh
– a conference	**– a una conferencia** ah <u>oo</u>-nah kohn-feh-<u>rehn</u>-theeyah
– a meeting	**– a una reunión** ah <u>oo</u>-nah rewoo-<u>neeyohn</u>
My name is…	**Me llamo…** meh <u>yah</u>-moh…
May I introduce my colleague…	**Le presento a mi compañero♂ / compañera♀ de trabajo…** leh preh-<u>sehn</u>-toh ah mee kohm-pah-<u>nyeh</u>-roh♂ / kohm-pah-<u>nyeh</u>-rah♀ deh trah-<u>bah</u>-khoh…

I have *a meeting/an appointment* with…	**Tengo una *reunión/cita* con…** tehn·goh oo·nah *rewoo·neeyohn/thee·tah* kohn…
I'm sorry I'm late.	**Perdone que haya llegado tarde.** pehr·doh·neh keh ah·yah yeh·gah·doh tahr·deh
I need an interpreter.	**Necesito un intérprete.** neh·theh·coo·toh oon een·tehr·preh·teh
You can reach me at the…Hotel.	**Puede contactarme en el Hotel…** pweh·deh kohn·tahk·tahr·meh ehn ehl oh·tehl…
I'm here until…	**Estaré aquí hasta…** ehs·tah·reh ah·kee ahs·tah…

It is common to greet colleagues with **buenos días** (good day). Shake hands if it is the first time you are meeting someone in a professional setting, or if it is someone you haven't seen in a while. When leaving, simply say **adiós, gracias** (goodbye, thank you).

I need to…	**Necesito…** neh·theh·<u>see</u>·toh…
– make a call	**– hacer una llamada** ah·<u>thehr</u> <u>oo</u>·nah yah·<u>mah</u>·dah
– make a photocopy	**– hacer una fotocopia** ah·<u>thehr</u> <u>oo</u>·nah foh·toh·<u>koh</u>·peeyah
– send an e-mail	**– enviar un correo electrónico** ehn·<u>beeyahr</u> oon koh·<u>rreh</u>·oh ee·lehk·<u>troh</u>·nee·koh
– send a fax	**– enviar un fax** ehn·<u>beeyahr</u> oon fahx
– send a package (overnight)	**– enviar un paquete (para entrega el día siguiente)** ehn·<u>beeyahr</u> oon pah·<u>keh</u>·teh (<u>pah</u>·rah ehn·<u>treh</u>·gah ehl <u>dee</u>·ah see·<u>geeyehn</u>·teh)
It was a pleasure to meet you.	**Ha sido un placer conocerle♂ / conocerla♀.** ah <u>see</u>·doh oon plah·<u>thehr</u> koh·noh·<u>thehr</u>·leh♂ / koh·noh·<u>thehr</u>·lah♀

▶For internet and communications, see page 50.

You May Hear…

¿Tiene cita? <u>teeyeh</u>·neh <u>thee</u>·tah	Do you have an appointment?
¿Con quién? kohn keeyehn	With whom?
Está en una reunión. ehs·<u>tah</u> ehn <u>oo</u>·nah rewoo·<u>neeyohn</u>	He/She is in a meeting.
Un momento, por favor. oon moh·<u>mehn</u>·toh pohr fah·<u>bohr</u>	One moment, please.
Siéntese. <u>theeyehn</u>·teh·seh	Have a seat.
¿Quiere algo de beber? <u>keeyeh</u>·reh <u>ahl</u>·goh deh beh·<u>behr</u>	Would you like something to drink?
Gracias por su visita. <u>grah</u>·theeyahs pohr soo bee·<u>see</u>·tah	Thank you for coming.

Travel with Children

Essential

Is there a discount for kids?	**¿Hacen descuento a niños?** ah·then dehs·<u>kwehn</u>·toh ah <u>nee</u>·nyohs
Can you recommend a babysitter?	**¿Puede recomendarme una canguro?** <u>pweh</u>·deh reh·koh·mehn·<u>dahr</u>·meh <u>oo</u>·nah kahn·<u>goo</u>·roh
Do you have a *child's seat/highchair*?	**¿Tienen una *silla para niños/trona*?** <u>teeyeh</u>·nehn <u>oo</u>·nah *<u>see</u>·yah <u>pah</u>·rah <u>nee</u>·nyohs/<u>troh</u>·nah*
Where can I change the baby?	**¿Dónde puedo cambiar al bebé?** <u>dohn</u>·deh <u>pweh</u>·doh kahm·<u>beeyahr</u> ahl beh·<u>beh</u>

Fun with Kids

Can you recommend something for kids?	**¿Puede recomendarme algo para los niños?** <u>pweh</u>·deh reh·koh·mehn·<u>dahr</u>·meh <u>ahl</u>·goh <u>pah</u>·rah lohs <u>nee</u>·nyohs
Where's...?	**¿Dónde está...?** <u>dohn</u>·deh ehs·<u>tah</u>...
– the amusement park	**– el parque de atracciones** ehl <u>pahr</u>·keh deh ah·trahk·<u>theeyoh</u>·nehs
– the arcade	**– el salón de juegos recreativos** ehl sah·<u>lohn</u> deh <u>khweh</u>·gohs reh·kreh·ah·<u>tee</u>·bohs
– the kiddie [paddling] pool	**– la piscina infantil** lah pees·<u>thee</u>·nah een·fahn·<u>teel</u>
– the park	**– el parque** ehl <u>pahr</u>·keh
– the playground	**– el parque infantil** ehl <u>pahr</u>·keh een·fahn·<u>teel</u>
– the zoo	**– el zoológico** ohl thoh·oh·<u>loh</u>·khee·koh
Are kids allowed?	**¿Se permite la entrada a niños?** seh pehr·<u>mee</u>·teh lah ehn·<u>trah</u>·dah ah <u>nee</u>·nyohs

| Is it safe for kids? | **¿Es seguro para niños?** ehs seh·<u>goo</u>·roh <u>pah</u>·rah <u>nee</u>·nyohs |
| Is it suitable for... year olds? | **¿Es apto para niños de...años?** ehs <u>ahp</u>·toh <u>pah</u>·rah <u>nee</u>·nyohs deh...<u>ah</u>·nyohs |

▶ For numbers, see page 178.

You May Hear...

¡Qué mono♂/mona♀! keh <u>moh</u>·noh♂/ <u>moh</u>·nah♀	How cute!
¿Cómo se llama? <u>koh</u>·moh seh <u>yah</u>·mah	What's his/her name?
¿Qué edad tiene? keh eh·<u>dahth</u> <u>teeyeh</u>·neh	How old is he/she?

Basic Needs for Kids

Do you have...?	**¿Tiene...?** <u>teeyeh</u>·neh...
– a baby bottle	**– un biberón** oon bee·beh·<u>rohn</u>
– baby wipes	**– toallitas** toh·ah·<u>yee</u>·tahs
– a car seat	**– un asiento para niños** oon ah·<u>seeyehn</u> toh <u>pah</u>·rah <u>nee</u>·nyohs
– a children's menu/portion	***– un menú/una ración* para niños** *oon meh·<u>noo</u>/<u>oo</u>·nah rah·<u>theeyohn</u> <u>pah</u>·rah <u>nee</u>·nyohs*

– a child's seat/ highchair	– una **silla para niños/trona** oo·nah _see·yah_ _pah_·rah _nee_·nyohs/_troh_·nah
– a crib/cot	– una **cuna/un catre** oo·nah koo·nah/oon kah·treh
– diapers [nappies]	– **pañales** pah·nyah·lehs
– formula	– **fórmula infantil** fohr·moo·lah een·fahn·teel
– a pacifier [soother]	– **un chupete** oon choo·peh·teh
– a playpen	– **un parque** oon pahr·keh
– a stroller [pushchair]	– **un cochecito** oon koh·cheh·thee·toh

Can I breastfeed the baby here? **¿Puedo darle el pecho al bebé aquí?** pweh·doh dahr·leh ehl peh·choh ahl beh·beh ah·kee

Where can I change the baby? **¿Dónde puedo cambiar al bebé?** dohn·deh pweh·doh kahm·beeyahr ahl beh·beh

▶For dining with kids, see page 65.

Babysitting

Can you recommend a babysitter? **¿Puede recomendarme una canguro?** pweh·deh reh·koh·mehn·dahr·meh oo·nah kahn·goo·roh

What's the charge? **¿Cuánto cuesta?** kwahn·toh kwehs·tah

I'll be back by... **Vuelvo a la/las...** bwehl·boh ah lah/lahs...

▶For when to use **la** or **las**, see page 175.

▶For time, see page 180.

I can be reached at... **Puede contactarme en el...** pweh·deh kohn·tahk·tahr·meh ehn ehl...

Health and Emergency

Can you recommend a pediatrician? **¿Puede recomendarme un pediatra?** pweh·deh reh·koh·mehn·dahr·meh oon peh·deeyah·trah

My child is allergic to...	**Mi hijo ♂/hija ♀ es alérgico ♂/alérgica ♀ a...** mee <u>ee</u>·khoh ♂/<u>ee</u>·khah ♀ ehs ah·<u>lehr</u>·khee·koh ♂/ah·<u>lehr</u>·khee·kah ♀ ah...
My child is missing.	**Mi hijo ♂/hija ♀ ha desaparecido.** mee <u>ee</u>·khoh ♂/<u>ee</u>·khah ♀ ah deh·sah·pah·reh·<u>thee</u>·doh
Have you seen a boy/girl?	**¿Ha visto a un niño ♂/una niña ♀?** ah <u>bees</u>·toh ah oon <u>nee</u>·nyoh ♂/<u>oo</u>·nah <u>nee</u>·nyah ♀

▶ For food items, see page 91.

▶ For health, see page 164.

▶ For police, see page 161.

For the Disabled

Essential

Is there...?	**¿Hay...?** aye...
– access for the disabled	**– acceso para los discapacitados** ahk·<u>theh</u>·soh <u>pah</u>·rah lohs dees·kah·pah·thee·<u>tah</u>·dohs
– a wheelchair ramp	**– una rampa para sillas de ruedas** <u>oo</u>·nah <u>rahm</u>·pah <u>pah</u>·rah <u>see</u>·yahs deh <u>rweh</u>·dahs
– a handicapped-[disabled-] accessible toilet	**– un baño con acceso para discapacitados** oon <u>bah</u>·nyoh kohn ahk·<u>theh</u>·soh <u>pah</u>·rah dees·kah·pah·thee·<u>tah</u>·dohs
I need...	**Necesito...** neh·theh·<u>see</u>·toh...
– assistance	**– ayuda** ah·<u>yoo</u>·dah
– an elevator [a lift]	**– un ascensor** oon ahs·thehn·<u>sohr</u>
– a ground-floor room	**– una habitación en la planta baja** <u>oo</u>·nah ah·bee·tah·<u>theeyohn</u> ehn lah <u>plahn</u>·tah <u>bah</u>·khah

Getting Help

I'm disabled.	**Soy discapacitado♂/discapacitada♀.** soy dees·kah·pah·thee·<u>tah</u>·doh♂/ dees·kah·pah·thee·<u>tah</u>·dah♀
I'm deaf.	**Soy sordo♂/sorda♀.** soy <u>sohr</u>·doh♂/ <u>sohr</u>·dah♀
I'm *visually/hearing* impaired.	**Tengo discapacidad *visual/auditiva.*** <u>tehn</u>·goh dees·kah·pah·thee·<u>dahd</u> bee·<u>swahl</u>/ awoo·dee·<u>tee</u>·bah
I'm unable to *walk far/use the stairs.*	**No puedo *caminar muy lejos/subir las escaleras.*** noh <u>pweh</u>·doh kah·mee·<u>nahr</u> mooy <u>leh</u>·khohs/soo·<u>beer</u> lahs ehs·kah·<u>leh</u>·rahs
Can I bring my wheelchair?	**¿Puedo traer la silla de ruedas?** <u>pweh</u>·doh trah·<u>ehr</u> lah <u>see</u>·yah deh <u>rweh</u>·dahs
Are guide dogs permitted?	**¿Permiten a perros guía?** pehr·mee·tehn ah <u>peh</u>·rrohs <u>gee</u>·ah
Can you help me?	**¿Puede ayudarme?** <u>pweh</u>·deh ah·yoo·<u>dahr</u>·meh
Please *open/hold* the door.	**Por favor, *abra/aguante* la puerta.** pohr tah·<u>bohr</u> <u>ah</u>·brah/ah·<u>gwahn</u>·teh lah <u>pwehr</u>·tah

159

▼ Resources

▶ **Emergencies**   *161*

▶ **Police**   *161*

▶ **Health**   *164*

▶ **Reference**   *172*

Emergencies

Essential

Help!	**¡Socorro!** soh-<u>koh</u>-rroh
Go away!	**¡Lárguese!** <u>lahr</u>-geh-seh
Stop, thief!	**¡Deténgase, ladrón!** deh-<u>tehn</u>-gah-seh lah-<u>drohn</u>
Get a doctor!	**¡Llame a un médico!** <u>yah</u>-meh ah oon <u>meh</u>-dee-koh
Fire!	**¡Fuego!** <u>fwuh</u>-goh
I'm lost.	**Me he perdido.** meh eh pehr-<u>dee</u>-doh
Can you help me?	**¿Puede ayudarme?** <u>pweh</u>-deh ah-yoo-<u>dahr</u>-meh

Police

Essential

Call the police!	**¡Llame a la policía!** <u>yah</u>-meh ah lah poh-lee-<u>thee</u>-ah
Where's the police station?	**¿Dónde está la comisaría?** <u>dohn</u>-deh ehs-<u>tah</u> lah koh-mee-sah-<u>ree</u>-ah
There was an *accident/attack*.	**Ha habido un *accidente/asalto*.** ah ah-<u>bee</u>-doh oon *ahk-thee-<u>dehn</u>-teh/ah-<u>sahl</u>-toh*
My son/daughter is missing.	**Mi hijo♂/hija♀ ha desaparecido.** mee <u>ee</u>-khoh♂/<u>ee</u>-khah♀ ah deh-sah-pah-reh-<u>thee</u>-doh

I need…	**Necesito…** neh·theh·<u>see</u>·toh…
– an interpreter	**– un intérprete** oon een·<u>tehr</u>·preh·teh
– to contact my lawyer	**– ponerme en contacto con mi abogado** poh·<u>nehr</u>·meh ehn kohn·<u>tahk</u>·toh kohn mee ah·boh·<u>gah</u>·doh
– to make a phone call	**– hacer una llamada** ah·<u>thehr</u> <u>oo</u>·nah yah·<u>mah</u>·dah
I'm innocent.	**Soy inocente.** soy ee·noh·<u>thehn</u>·teh

You May Hear…

Rellene este impreso. reh·<u>yeh</u>·neh <u>ehs</u>·teh eem·<u>preh</u>·soh	Fill out this form.
Su documento de identidad, por favor. soo doh·koo·<u>mehn</u>·toh deh ee·dehn·tee·<u>dahd</u> pohr fah·<u>bohr</u>	Your identification, please.
¿*Cuándo/Dónde* ocurrió? <u>*kwahn*</u>·*doh*/ <u>*dohn*</u>·*deh* oh·koo·<u>rreeyoh</u>	*When/Where* did it happen?
¿Puede describirle♂/describirla♀? <u>pweh</u>·deh dehs·kree·<u>beer</u>·leh♂/ dehs·kree·<u>beer</u>·lah♀	What does he/she look like?

▶ For emergency numbers, see page 56.

Lost Property and Theft

I'd like to report…	**Quiero denunciar…** keeyeh·roh deh·noon·theeyahr…
– a mugging	**– un asalto** oon ah·sahl·toh
– a rape	**– una violaoión** oo·nah beeyol·lah·theeyonn
– a theft	**– un robo** oon roh·boh
I was *mugged/ robbed*.	**Me han *asaltado/atracado*.** meh ahn ah·sahl·tah·doh/ah·trah·kah·doh
I lost my…	**He perdido…** eh pehr·dee·doh…
My…was stolen.	**Me han robado…** meh ahn·roh·bah·doh…
– backpack	**– la mochila** lah moh·chee·lah
– bicycle	**– la bicicleta** lah bee·thee·kleh·tah
– camera	**– la cámara** lah kah·mah·rah
– (rental [hire]) car	**– el coche (de alquiler)** ehl koh·cheh (deh ahl·kee·lehr)
– computer	**– el ordenador** ehl ohr·deh·nah·dohr
– credit card	**– la tarjeta de crédito** lah tahr·kheh·tah deh kreh·dee·toh
– jewelry	**– las joyas** lahs khoh·yahs
– money	**– el dinero** ehl dee·neh·roh
– passport	**– el pasaporte** ehl pah·sah·pohr·teh
– purse [handbag]	**– el bolso** ehl bohl·soh
– traveler's checks [cheques]	**– los cheques de viaje** lohs cheh·kehs deh beeyah·kheh
– wallet	**– la cartera** lah kahr·teh·rah
I need a police report.	**Necesito un certificado de la policía.** neh·theh·see·toh oon thehr·tee·fee·kah·doh deh lah poh·lee·thee·ah

Health

I'm sick [ill].	**Me encuentro mal.** meh ehn·<u>kwehn</u>·troh mahl
I need an English-speaking doctor.	**Necesito un médico que hable inglés.** neh·theh·<u>see</u>·toh oon <u>meh</u>·dee·koh keh <u>ah</u>·bleh een·<u>glehs</u>
It hurts here.	**Me duele aquí.** meh <u>dweh</u>·leh ah·<u>kee</u>
I have a stomachache.	**Tengo dolor de estómago.** <u>tehn</u>·goh doh·<u>lohr</u> deh ehs·<u>toh</u>·mah·goh

Finding a Doctor

Can you recommend a *doctor/dentist*?	**¿Puede recomendarme un *médico/ dentista*?** <u>pweh</u>·deh reh·koh·mehn·<u>dahr</u>·meh oon <u>meh</u>·dee·koh/dehn·<u>tees</u>·tah
Can the doctor come here?	**¿Podría el médico venir aquí?** poh·<u>dree</u>·ah ehl <u>meh</u>·dee·koh beh·<u>neer</u> ah·<u>kee</u>
I need an English-speaking doctor.	**Necesito un médico que hable inglés.** neh·theh·<u>see</u>·toh oon <u>meh</u>·dee·koh keh <u>ah</u>·bleh een·<u>glehs</u>
What are the office hours?	**¿Cuáles son las horas de consulta?** <u>kwah</u>·lehs sohn lahs <u>oh</u>·rahs deh kohn·<u>sool</u>·tah
I'd like an appointment...	**Quiero una cita...** <u>keeyeh</u>·roh <u>oo</u>·nah <u>thee</u>·tah...
– for today	**– para hoy** <u>pah</u>·rah ohy
– for tomorrow	**– para mañana** <u>pah</u>·rah mah·<u>nyah</u>·nah
– as soon as possible	**– lo antes posible** loh <u>ahn</u>·tehs poh·<u>see</u>·bleh
It's urgent.	**Es urgente.** ehs oor·<u>khehn</u>·teh

Symptoms

I'm...	**Estoy...** ehs·<u>toy</u>...
– bleeding	– **sangrando** sahn·<u>grahn</u>·doh
– constipated	– **estreñido** ♂ **/estreñida** ♀ ehs·treh·<u>nyee</u>·doh ♂ / ehs·treh·<u>nyee</u>·dah ♀
– dizzy	– **mareado** ♂ **/mareada** ♀ mah·reh·<u>ah</u>·doh ♂ / mah·reh·<u>ah</u>·dah ♀
I'm *nauseous/ vomiting.*	**Tengo náuseas/*vómitos*.** <u>tehn</u>·goh naw·seh·ahs/<u>boh</u>·mee·tohs
It hurts here.	**Me duele aquí.** meh <u>dweh</u>·leh ah·<u>kee</u>
I have...	**Tengo...** <u>tehn</u>·goh...
– an allergic reaction	– **una reacción alérgica** <u>oo</u>·nah reh·ahk·<u>theeyohn</u> ah·<u>lehr</u>·khee·kah
– chest pain	– **dolor de pecho** doh·<u>lohr</u> deh <u>peh</u>·choh
– an earache	– **dolor de oído** doh·<u>lohr</u> deh oh·<u>ee</u>·doh
– a fever	– **fiebre** <u>feeyeh</u>·breh
– pain	– **dolor** doh·<u>lohr</u>
– a rash	– **una erupción cutánea** <u>oo</u>·nah eh·roop·<u>theeyohn</u> koo·<u>tah</u>·nee·ah
– a sprain	– **un esguince** oon ehs·<u>geen</u>·theh
– some swelling	– **una hinchazón** <u>oo</u>·nah een·chah·<u>thohn</u>
– a stomachache	– **dolor de estómago** doh·<u>lohr</u> deh ehs·<u>toh</u>·mah·goh
– sunstroke	– **una insolación** <u>oo</u>·nah een·soh·lah·<u>theeyohn</u>
I've been sick [ill] for...days.	**Llevo...días que me encuentro mal.** <u>yeh</u>·boh...<u>dee</u>·ahs keh meh ehn·<u>kwehn</u>·troh mahl

▶ For numbers, see page 178.

Health Conditions

I'm…   **Soy…** soy…

– anemic   – **anémico**♂ /**anémica**♀ ah·*neh*·mee·koh♂ /
                        ah·*neh*·mee·kah♀

– asthmatic   – **asmático**♂ /**asmática**♀
                        ahs·*mah*·tee·koh♂ /ahs·*mah*·tee·kah♀

– diabetic   – **diabético**♂ /**diabética**♀
                        deeyah·*beh*·tee·koh♂ /deeyah·*beh*·tee·kah♀

I'm allergic to   **Soy alérgico**♂ /**alérgica**♀ **a** *los*
antibiotics/penicillin. ***antibióticos/la penicilina.***
                        soy ah·*lehr*·khee·koh♂ /ah·*lehr*·khee·kah♀
                        ah *lohs ahn·tee·beeyoh·tee·kohs/lah*
                        peh·nee·thee·lee·nah

▶For food items, see page 91.

I have *arthritis/*   **Tengo *artritis/la tensión (alta/baja).***
(high/low) blood   tehn·goh *ahr·tree·tees/lah tehn·seeyohn*
pressure.   *(ahl·tah/bah·khah)*

I have a heart   **Padezco del corazón.** pah·*dehth*·koh dehl
condition.   koh·rah·*thon*

I'm on…   **Estoy tomando…** ehs·*toy* toh·*mahn*·doh…

You May Hear…

¿Qué le pasa? keh leh *pah*·sah   What's wrong?

¿Dónde le duele? *dohn*·deh leh *dweh*·leh   Where does it hurt?

¿Le duele aquí? leh *dweh*·leh ah·*kee*   Does it hurt here?

¿Esta tomando algún medicamento?   Are you on
ehs·tah toh·*mahn*·doh ahl·*goon*   medication?
meh·dee·kah·*mehn*·toh

¿Es alérgico♂/alérgica♀ a algo?
ehs ah·<u>lehr</u>·khee·koh♂/ah·<u>lehr</u>·khee·kah♀
ah <u>ulil</u>·goh

Are you allergic to anything?

Abra la boca. <u>ah</u>·brah lah boh·kah

Open your mouth.

Respire hondo. rehs·<u>pee</u>·reh <u>ohn</u>·doh

Breathe deeply.

Tiene que ir al hospital. teeyeh·neh keh
eer ahl ohs·pee·<u>tahl</u>

Go to the hospital.

Hospital

Notify my family, please.	**Por favor, avise a mi familia.** pohr fah·<u>bohr</u> ah·<u>bee</u>·seh ah mee fah·<u>mee</u>·leeyah
I'm in pain.	**Tengo dolor.** <u>tehn</u>·goh doh·<u>lohr</u>
I need a doctor/nurse.	**Necesito *un médico/una enfermera*.** neh·thee·<u>see</u>·toh *oon meh·dee·koh/<u>oo</u>·nah ehn·fehr·<u>meh</u>·rah*
When are visiting hours?	**¿Qué horas de visita tienen?** keh <u>oh</u>·rahs deh bee·<u>see</u>·tah <u>teeyeh</u>·nehn
I'm visiting…	**Vengo a hacer una visita a…** <u>behn</u>·goh ah ah·<u>thehr</u> <u>oo</u>·nah bee·<u>see</u>·tah ah…

Dentist

I've *broken a tooth/lost a filling*.	**Se me ha *roto un diente/caído un empaste*.** seh meh ah *<u>roh</u>·toh oon <u>deeyehn</u>·teh/kah·<u>ee</u>·doh oon ehm·<u>pahs</u>·teh*
I have a toothache.	**Tengo dolor de muelas.** <u>tehn</u>·goh doh·<u>lohr</u> deh <u>mweh</u>·lahs
Can you fix this denture?	**¿Puede arreglarme la dentadura postiza?** <u>pweh</u>·deh ah·rreh·<u>glahr</u>·meh lah dehn·tah·<u>doo</u>·rah pohs·<u>tee</u>·thah

Gynecologist

I have *menstrual cramps/a vaginal infection*.	**Tengo *dolores menstruales/una infección vaginal*.** tehn·goh *doh·loh·rehs mehns·trwah·lehs/oo·nah een·fehk·theeyohn bah·khee·nahl*
I missed my period.	**No me ha venido la regla.** noh meh ah beh·nee·doh lah reh·glah
I'm on the Pill.	**Tomo la píldora.** toh·moh lah peel·doh·rah
I'm (not) pregnant.	**(No) Estoy embarazada.** (noh) ehs·toy ehm·bah·rah·thah·dah
My last period was…	**La última vez que me vino la regla fue…** lah ool·tee·mah behth keh meh bee·noh lah reh·glah fweh…

Optician

I lost…	**He perdido…** eh pehr·dee·doh…
– a contact lens	**– una lentilla** oo·nah lehn·tee·yah
– my glasses	**– las gafas** lahs gah·fahs
– a lens	**– una lente** oo·nah lehn·teh

Payment and Insurance

How much?	**¿Cuánto es?** kwahn·toh ehs
Can I pay by credit card?	**¿Puedo pagar con tarjeta de crédito?** pweh·doh pah·gahr kohn tahr·kheh·tah deh kreh·dee·toh
I have insurance.	**Tengo seguro médico.** tehn·goh seh·goo·roh meh·dee·koh
I need a receipt for my insurance.	**Necesito una factura para el seguro médico.** neh·theh·see·toh oo·nah fahk·too·rah pah·rah ehl seh·goo·roh meh·dee·koh

Pharmacy [Chemist]

Where's the pharmacy [chemist]?	**¿Dónde está la farmacia?** <u>dohn</u>·deh ehs·<u>tah</u> lah fahr·<u>mah</u>·theeyah
What time does it *open/close*?	**¿A qué hora *abre/cierra*?** ah keh <u>oh</u>·rah <u>ah</u>·breh/<u>theeyeh</u>·rrah
What would you recommend for...?	**¿Qué me recomienda para...?** keh meh roh·koh·<u>meeyehn</u>·dah <u>pah</u>·rah...
How much do I take?	**¿Qué dosis me tomo?** keh <u>doh</u>·sees meh <u>toh</u>·moh
Can you fill [make up] this prescription?	**¿Puede darme este medicamento?** <u>pweh</u>·deh <u>dahr</u>·meh <u>ehs</u>·teh meh·dee·kah·<u>mehn</u>·toh
I'm allergic to...	**Soy alérgico♂/alérgica♀ a...** soy ah·<u>lehr</u>·khee·koh♂/ah·<u>lehr</u>·khee·kah♀ ah...

169

i Pharmacies are easily identified by their green neon signs in the shape of a cross. Hours are generally from 9:00 a.m. until 1:30 p.m., closed for **siesta** and then open from 4:30 p.m. until 8:00 p.m. There are 24-hour pharmacies available in larger cities. A list of pharmacies that are open at night or on weekends can be found in the windows of all pharmacies, and the list is also published in local newspapers.

Dosage Instructions

How much do I take?	**¿Qué dosis me tomo?** keh <u>doh</u>·sees meh <u>toh</u>·moh
How often?	**¿Con qué frecuencia?** kohn keh freh·<u>kwehn</u>·theeyah
Is it safe for children?	**¿Está indicado para niños?** ehs·<u>tah</u> een·dee·<u>kah</u>·doh <u>pah</u>·rah <u>nee</u>·nyohs
I'm taking…	**Estoy tomando…** ehs·<u>toy</u> toh·<u>mahn</u>·doh…
Are there side effects?	**¿Tiene algún efecto secundario?** <u>teeyeh</u>·neh ahl·<u>goon</u> eh·<u>fehk</u>·toh seh·koon·<u>dah</u>·reeyoh

You May See…

UNA VEZ / TRES VECES AL DÍA	*once/three* times a day
COMPRIMIDO	tablet
GOTA	drop
CUCHARADITA	teaspoon
DESPUÉS DE / ANTES DE / CON LAS COMIDAS	*after/before/with* meals
CON EL ESTÓMAGO VACÍO	on an empty stomach
TRAGUE EL COMPRIMIDO ENTERO	swallow whole
PUEDE CAUSAR SOMNOLENCIA	may cause drowsiness
DE USO TÓPICO SOLAMENTE	for external use only

Health Problems

I need something for…	**Necesito algo para…** neh·theh·see·toh ahl·goh pah·rah…
– a cold	– **el catarro** ehl kah·tah·rroh
– a cough	– **la tos** lah tohs
– diarrhea	– **la diarrea** lah deeyah·rreh·ah
– insect bites	– **las picaduras de insecto** lahs pee·kah·doo·rahs deh een·sehk·toh
– motion [travel] sickness	– **la cinetosis** lah thee·neh·toh·sees
– a sore throat	– **las anginas** lahs ahn·khee·nahs
– sunburn	– **la quemadura solar** lah keh·mah·doo·rah soh·lahr
– an upset stomach	– **el malestar estomacal** ehl mah·lehs·tahr ehs·toh·mah·kahl

Basic Needs

I'd like…	**Quiero…** keeyeh·roh…
– acetaminophen [paracetamol]	– **paracetamol** pah·rah·thee·tah·mohl
– antiseptic cream	– **crema antiséptica** kreh·mah ahn·tee·sehp·tee·kah
– aspirin	– **aspirinas** ahs·pee·ree·nahs
– bandages	– **tiritas** tee·ree·tahs
– a comb	– **un peine** oon peyee·neh
– condoms	– **preservativos** preh·sehr·bah·tee·bohs
– contact lens solution	– **líquido de lentillas** lee·kee·doh deh lehn·tee·yahs
– deodorant	– **desodorante** deh·soh·doh·rahn·teh
– a hairbrush	– **un cepillo de pelo** oon theh·pee·yoh deh peh·loh

I'd like…	**Quiero…** <u>keeyeh</u>·roh…
– ibuprofen	– **ibuprofeno** ee·boo·proh·<u>feh</u>·noh
– insect repellent	– **repelente de insectos** reh·peh·<u>lehn</u>·teh deh een·<u>sehk</u>·tohs
– lotion	– **crema hidratante** <u>kreh</u>·mah ee·drah·<u>tahn</u>·teh
– a razor	– **una cuchilla** <u>oo</u>·nah koo·<u>chee</u>·yah
– razor blades	– **hojas de afeitar** <u>oh</u>·khahs deh ah·feyee·<u>tahr</u>
– sanitary napkins [pads]	– **compresas** kohm·<u>preh</u>·sahs
– shampoo/ conditioner	– **champú/suavizante** chahm·<u>poo</u>/ swah·bee·<u>thahn</u>·teh
– soap	– **jabón** khah·<u>bohn</u>
– sunscreen	– **protector solar** proh·tehk·<u>tohr</u> soh·<u>lahr</u>
– tampons	– **tampones** tahm·<u>poh</u>·nehs
– tissues	– **pañuelos de papel** pah·<u>nyweh</u>·lohs deh pah·<u>pehl</u>
– toilet paper	– **papel higiénico** pah·<u>pehl</u> ee·<u>kheeyeh</u>·nee·koh
– a toothbrush	– **un cepillo de dientes** oon theh·<u>pee</u>·yoh deh <u>deeyehn</u>·tehs
– toothpaste	– **pasta de dientes** <u>pahs</u>·tah deh <u>deeyehn</u>·tehs

▶ For basic needs for kids, see page 156.

Reference

Grammar

In Spanish, there are a number of forms for "you" (taking different verb forms): **tú** (singular) and **vosotros**♂/**vosotras**♀ (plural) are used when talking to relatives, close friends and children; **usted** (singular) and **ustedes** (plural) are used in all other cases. If in doubt, use **usted/ustedes**. The following abbreviations are used in this section: Ud. = Usted; Uds. = Ustedes; sing. = singular; pl. = plural; inf. = informal; for. = formal.

Regular Verbs

There are three verb types that follow a regular conjugation pattern. These verbs end in –ar, –er and –ir. Following are the present, past and future forms of the verbs **hablar** (to speak), **comer** (to eat) and **vivir** (to live). The different conjugation endings are in bold.

HABLAR		Present	Past	Future
I	**yo**	habl**o**	habl**é**	habl**aré**
you (sing.)	**tú**	habl**as**	habl**aste**	habl**arás**
he/she/you	**él/ella/Ud.**	habl**a**	habl**ó**	habl**ará**
we	**nosotros**	habl**amos**	habl**amos**	habl**aremos**
you (pl.)	**vosotros♂ / vosotras♀**	habl**áis**	habl**asteis**	habl**aréis**
they/you	**ellos/ellas/Uds.**	habl**an**	habl**aron**	habl**arán**
COMER		Present	Past	Future
I	**yo**	com**o**	com**í**	com**eré**
you (sing.)	**tú**	com**es**	com**iste**	com**erás**
he/she/you	**él/ella/Ud.**	com**e**	com**ió**	com**erá**
we	**nosotros**	com**emos**	com**imos**	com**eremos**
you (pl.)	**vosotros♂ / vosotras♀**	com**éis**	com**isteis**	com**eréis**
they/you	**ellos/ellas/Uds.**	com**en**	com**ieron**	com**erán**
VIVIR		Present	Past	Future
I	**yo**	viv**o**	viv**í**	viv**iré**
you (sing.)	**tú**	viv**es**	viv**iste**	viv**irás**
he/she/you	**él/ella/Ud.**	viv**e**	viv**ió**	viv**irá**
we	**nosotros**	viv**imos**	viv**imos**	viv**iremos**
you (pl.)	**vosotros♂ / vosotras♀**	viv**ís**	viv**isteis**	viv**iréis**
they/you	**ellos/ellas/Uds.**	viv**en**	viv**ieron**	viv**irán**

Irregular Verbs

In Spanish, there are many different irregular verbs; these aren't conjugated by following the normal rules. The two most commonly used, and confused, irregular verbs are **ser** and **estar**. Both verbs mean "to be". Following is the past, present and future tenses of **ser** and **estar** for easy reference.

SER	Present	Past	Future
yo	soy	fui	seré
tú (sing.)	eres	fuiste	serás
él/ella/Ud.	es	fue	será
nosotros	somos	fuimos	seremos
vosotros♂/ vosotras♀ (pl.)	sois	fuisteis	seréis
ellos/ellas/Uds.	son	fueron	serán

ESTAR	Present	Past	Future
yo	estoy	estuve	estaré
tú (sing.)	estás	estuviste	estarás
él/ella/Ud.	está	estuvo	estará
nosotros	estamos	estuvimos	estaremos
vosotros♂/ vosotras♀ (pl.)	estáis	estuvisteis	estaréis
ellos/ellas/Uds.	están	estuvieron	estarán

Ser is used to describe a fixed quality or characteristic. It is also used to tell time and dates. Example: **Yo soy estadounidense.** I am American.

Here **ser** is used because it is a permanent characteristic.

Estar is used when describing a physical location or a temporary condition. Example: **Estoy cansado.** I am tired.

Here **estar** is used because being tired is a temporary condition.

Nouns and Articles

Nouns are either masculine or feminine. Masculine nouns usually end in **–o**, and feminine nouns usually end in **–a**. Nouns become plural by adding an **–s**, or **–es** to nouns not ending in **–o** or **–a** (e.g. **tren** becomes **trenes**). Nouns in Spanish get an indefinite or definite article. An article must agree with the noun to which it refers in gender and number. Indefinite articles are the equivalent of "a", "an" or "some" in English, while definite articles are the equivalent of "the".

Indefinite examples; **un tren** ♂ (a train); **unos trenes** ♂ (some trains); **una mesa** ♀ (a table); **unas mesas** ♀ (some tables)

Definite examples: **el libro** ♂ (the book); **los libros** ♂ (the books); **la casa** ♀ (the house); **las casas** ♀ (the houses)

A possessive adjective relates to the gender of the noun that follows and must agree in number and gender.

	Singular	Plural
my	**mi**	**mis**
your (sing.)	**tu**	**tus**
his/her/its/your	**su**	**sus**
our	**nuestro** ♂ /**nuestra** ♀	**nuestros** ♂ /**nuestras** ♀
your (pl.)	**vuestro** ♂ /**vuestra** ♀	**vuestros** ♂ /**vuestras** ♀
their/your	**su**	**sus**

Examples: **¿Dónde está tu chaqueta?** Where is your jacket?

Vuestro vuelo sale a las ocho. Your flight leaves at eight.

Word Order

In Spanish, the conjugated verb comes after the subject.

Example: **Yo trabajo en Madrid.** I work in Madrid.

To ask a question, reverse the order of the subject and verb, change your intonation or use key question words such as **cuándo** (when).

Examples: **¿Cuándo cierra el banco?** When does the bank close?

Literally translates to: "When closes the bank?" Notice the order of the subject and verb is reversed; a question word also begins the sentence.

¿El hotel es viejo? Is the hotel old?

Literally: The hotel is old. This is a statement that becomes a question by raising the pitch of the last syllable of the sentence.

Negation

To form a negative sentence, add **no** (not) before the verb.

Example: **Fumamos.** We smoke.

No fumamos. We don't smoke.

Imperatives

Imperative sentences, or sentences that are a command, are formed by adding the appropriate ending to the stem of the verb (i.e. the verb in the infinitive without the **-ar**, **-er**, **-ir** ending). Example: Speak!

you (sing.) (inf.)	**tú**	**¡Habla!**
you (sing.) (for.)	**Ud.**	**¡Hable!**
we	**nosotros**	**¡Hablemos!**
you (inf.)	**vosotros**	**¡Hablad!**
you (pl.) (for.)	**Uds.**	**¡Hablen!**

Comparative and Superlative

The comparative is usually formed by adding **más** (more) or **menos** (less) before the adjective or noun. The superlative is formed by adding the appropriate definite article (**la/las**, **el/los**) and **más** (the most) **menos** (the least) before the adjective or noun. Example:

grande	**más grande**	**el ♂/la ♀ más grande**
big	bigger	biggest
caro ♂/cara ♀	**menos caro ♂/cara ♀**	**el ♂/la ♀ menos caro ♂/cara ♀**
expensive	less expensive	least expensive

Possessive Pronouns

Pronouns serve as substitutes for specific nouns and must agree with the noun in gender and number.

	Singular	Plural
mine	**mío**♂/**mía**♀	**míos**♂/**mías**♀
yours (inf.)	**tuyo**♂/**tuya**♀	**tuyos**♂/**tuyas**♀
yours	**suyo**♂/**suya**♀	**suyos**♂/**suyas**♀
his/her/its	**suyo**♂/**suya**♀	**suyos**♂/**suyas**♀
ours	**nuestro**♂/**nuestra**♀	**nuestros**♂/**nuestras**♀
yours (inf.)	**vuestro**♂/**vuestra**♀	**vuestros**♂/**vuestras**♀
theirs	**suyo**♂/**suya**♀	**suyos**♂/**suyas**♀

Example: **Ese asiento es mío.** That seat is mine.

Adjectives

Adjectives describe nouns and must agree with the noun in gender and number. In Spanish, adjectives usually come after the noun. Masculine adjectives generally end in –e, feminine adjectives in –a. If the masculine form ends in –e or with a consonant, the feminine form is generally the same. Most adjectives form their plurals the same way as nouns.

Examples: **Su hijo**♂/**hija**♀ **es simpático**♂/**simpática**♀. Your son/daughter is nice.

El mar♂/**La flor**♀ **es azul.** The ocean/The flower is blue.

Adverbs and Adverbial Expressions

Adverbs are used to describe verbs. Some adverbs are formed by adding –**mente** to the adjective.

Example: **Roberto conduce lentamente.** Robert drives slowly.

The following are some common adverbial time expressions:

actualmente presently

todavía no not yet

todavía still

ya no not anymore

Numbers

0	**cero** theh·roh	
1	**uno** oo·noh	
2	**dos** dohs	
3	**tres** trehs	
4	**cuatro** kwah·troh	
5	**cinco** theen·koh	
6	**seis** seyees	
7	**siete** seeyeh·teh	
8	**ocho** oh·choh	
9	**nueve** nweh·beh	
10	**diez** deeyehth	
11	**once** ohn·theh	
12	**doce** doh·theh	
13	**trece** treh·theh	
14	**catorce** kah·tohr·theh	
15	**quince** keen·theh	
16	**dieciséis** deeyeh·thee·seyees	
17	**diecisiete** deeyeh·thee·seeyeh·teh	
18	**dieciocho** deeyeh·thee·oh·choh	
19	**diecinueve** deeyeh·thee·nweh·beh	
20	**veinte** beyeen·teh	
21	**veintiuno** beyeen·tee·oo·noh	
22	**veintidós** beyeen·tee·dohs	
30	**treinta** treyeen·tah	

31	**treinta y uno** <u>treyeen</u>·tah ee <u>oo</u>·noh
40	**cuarenta** kwah·<u>rehn</u>·tah
50	**cincuenta** theen·<u>kwehn</u>·tah
60	**sesenta** seh·<u>sehn</u>·tah
70	**setenta** seh·<u>tehn</u>·tah
80	**ochenta** oh·<u>chehn</u>·tah
90	**noventa** noh·<u>behn</u>·tah
100	**cien** theeyehn
101	**ciento uno** the<u>eyehn</u>·toh <u>oo</u>·noh
200	**doscientos** dohs·the<u>eyehn</u>·tohs
500	**quinientos** kee·ne<u>eyehn</u>·tohs
1,000	**mil** meel
10,000	**diez mil** deeyehth meel
1,000,000	**un millón** oon mee·<u>yohn</u>

Ordinal Numbers

first	**primero** ♂ **/primera** ♀ pree·<u>meh</u>·roh ♂ /pree·<u>meh</u>·rah ♀
second	**segundo** ♂ **/segunda** ♀ seh·<u>goon</u>·doh ♂ /seh·<u>goon</u>·dah ♀
third	**tercero** ♂ **/tercera** ♀ tehr·<u>theh</u>·roh ♂ /tehr·<u>theh</u>·rah ♀
fourth	**cuarto** ♂ **/cuarta** ♀ <u>kwahr</u>·toh ♂ /<u>kwahr</u>·tah ♀
fifth	**quinto** ♂ **/quinta** ♀ <u>keen</u>·toh ♂ /<u>keen</u>·tah ♀
once	**una vez** <u>oo</u>·nah behth
twice	**dos veces** dohs <u>beh</u>·thes
three times	**tres veces** trehs <u>beh</u>·thes

Large numbers are read as in English. Example: 1,234,567 would be **un millón, doscientos treinta y cuatro mil, quinientos sesenta y siete** (one million, two hundred thirty-four thousand, five hundred sixty-seven). Notice the use of **y** (and) between tens and units for numbers between 31 (**treinta y uno**; literally, thirty and one) and 99 (**noventa y nueve**; literally, ninety and nine).

Time

What time is it?	**¿Qué hora es?** keh <u>oh</u>·rah ehs
It's noon [midday].	**Son las doce del mediodía.** sohn lahs <u>doh</u>·theh dehl meh·deeyoh·<u>dee</u>·ah
At midnight.	**A medianoche.** ah meh·deeyah·<u>noh</u>·cheh
From one o'clock to two o'clock.	**De una a dos en punto.** deh <u>oo</u>·nah ah dohs ehn <u>poon</u>·toh
Five after [past] three.	**Las tres y cinco.** lahs trehs ee <u>theen</u>·koh
A quarter to five.	**Las cinco menos cuarto.** lahs <u>theen</u>·koh <u>meh</u>·nohs <u>kwahr</u>·toh
5:30 a.m./p.m.	**Las cinco y media de la mañana/tarde.** lahs <u>theen</u>·koh ee <u>meh</u>·deeyah deh lah *mah·<u>nyah</u>·nah/<u>tahr</u>·deh*

Spaniards use the 24-hour clock when writing time, especially in schedules. The morning hours from 1:00 a.m. to noon are the same as in English. After that, just add 12 to the time: 1:00 p.m. would be 13:00, 5:00 p.m. would be 17:00 and so on.

Days

Essential

Monday	**lunes** <u>loo</u>·nehs
Tuesday	**martes** mahr·tehs
Wednesday	**miércoles** meeyehr·koh·lehs
Thursday	**jueves** <u>khweh</u>·behs
Friday	**viernes** <u>beeyehr</u>·nehs
Saturday	**sábado** <u>sah</u>·bah·doh
Sunday	**domingo** doh·<u>meen</u>·goh

 In Spain, the week begins with Monday and ends on Sunday. This distinction is especially apparent when looking at calendars—Monday will be the first column instead of Sunday.

Dates

yesterday	**ayer** ah·<u>yehr</u>
today	**hoy** oy
tomorrow	**mañana** mah·<u>nyah</u>·nah
day	**día** <u>dee</u>·ah
week	**semana** seh·<u>mah</u>·nah
month	**mes** mehs
year	**año** <u>ah</u>·nyoh

i Spain follows a day-month-year format:
Examples: **el 25 de agosto de 2007** = August 25, 2007
25.8.07 = 8/25/2007

Months

January	**enero** eh·<u>neh</u>·roh
February	**febrero** feh·<u>breh</u>·roh
March	**marzo** <u>mahr</u>·thoh
April	**abril** ah·<u>breel</u>
May	**mayo** <u>mah</u>·yoh
June	**junio** <u>khoo</u>·neeyoh
July	**julio** <u>khoo</u>·leeyoh
August	**agosto** ah·<u>gohs</u>·toh
September	**septiembre** sehp·<u>teeyehm</u>·breh
October	**octubre** ohk·<u>too</u>·breh
November	**noviembre** noh·<u>beeyehm</u>·breh
December	**diciembre** dee·<u>theeyehm</u>·breh

Seasons

the spring	**la primavera**	lah pree·mah·<u>beh</u>·rah
the summer	**el verano**	ehl beh·<u>rah</u>·noh
the fall [autumn]	**el otoño**	ehl oh·<u>toh</u>·nyoh
the winter	**el invierno**	ehl een·<u>beeyehr</u>·noh

Holidays

January 1: New Year's Day, **Año Nuevo**

January 6: Epiphany, **Epifanía**

February 8: Carnaval, **Carnaval**

March 19: Feast of St. Joseph, **San José**

May 1: Labor Day, **Día del Trabajo**

July 25: Feast of St. James, **Santiago Apóstol**

August 15: Feast of the Assumption, **Asunción**

October 12: Spain's National Day, **Día de la Hispanidad**

November 1: All Saint's Day, **Todos los Santos**

December 6: Constitution Day, **Día de la Constitución**

December 8: Feast of the Immaculate Conception, **Immaculada Concepción**

December 25: Christmas, **Navidad**

Easter festivities take place on different dates each year since this holiday is traditionally celebrated on the first Sunday after the first full moon on or after the spring equinox.

Conversion Tables

When you know	Multiply by	To find
ounces	28.3	grams
pounds	0.45	kilograms
inches	2.54	centimeters
feet	0.3	meters
miles	1.61	kilometers
square inches	6.45	sq. centimeters
square feet	0.09	sq. meters
square miles	2.59	sq. kilometers
pints (U.S./Brit)	0.47/0.56	liters
gallons (U.S./Brit)	3.8/4.5	liters
Fahrenheit	5/9, after −32	Centigrade
Centigrade	9/5, then +32	Fahrenheit

Mileage

1 km – 0.62 mi	20 km – 12.4 mi
5 km – 3.10 mi	50 km – 31.0 mi
10 km – 6.20 mi	100 km – 61.0 mi

Measurement

1 gram	**un gramo** oon <u>grah</u>·moh	= 0.035 oz.
1 kilogram (kg)	**un kilogramo** oon kee·loh·<u>grah</u>·moh	= 2.2 lb
1 liter (l)	**un litro** oon <u>lee</u>·troh	= 1.06 U.S/0.88 Brit. quarts
1 centimeter (cm)	**un centímetro** oon thehn·<u>tee</u>·meh·troh	= 0.4 inch
1 meter (m)	**un metro** oon <u>meh</u>·troh	= 3.28 ft.
1 kilometer (km)	**un kilómetro** oon kee·<u>loh</u>·meh·troh	= 0.62 mile

Temperature

-40° C – -40° F	-1° C – 30° F	20° C – 68° F
-30° C – -22° F	0° C – 32° F	25° C – 77° F
-20° C – -4° F	5° C – 41° F	30° C – 86° F
-10° C – 14° F	10° C – 50° F	35° C – 95° F
-5° C – 23° F	15° C – 59° F	

Oven Temperature

100° C – 212° F	177° C – 350° F
121° C – 250° F	204° C – 400° F
149° C – 300° F	260° C – 500° F

Related Websites

www.spain.info
*official website for
tourism in Spain*

www.tourspain.es
Spain's tourist board website

www.iberia.com
*Iberia's (the national airline of
Spain) website*

www.tsa.gov
*U.S. Transportation Security
Administration (TSA)*

www.caa.co.uk
*U.K. Civil Aviation Authority
(CAA)*

www.renfe.es
official railway website of Spain

www.metromadrid.es
*subway information for the Madrid
Metro*

www.tmb.net
*subway information for the
Barcelona **Metro** (in English)*

www.metrobilbao.net
*subway information for the Bilbao
Metro (in English)*

www.spain.ferries.org
*information on the different ferry
systems from Spain*

www.hihostels.com
Hostelling International website

www.correos.es
official post office website of Spain

English–Spanish Dictionary

A

abbey la abadía
accept v aceptar
access el acceso
accident el accidente
accommodation el alojamiento
account la cuenta
acupuncture la acupuntura
adapter el adaptador
address la dirección
admission la entrada
after después; **~noon** la tarde;
  ~shave el bálsamo para después
  del afeitado
age la edad
agency la agencia
AIDS el sida
air el aire; **~ conditioning**
  el aire acondicionado; **~ pump**
  el aire; **~line** la compañía aérea;
  ~mail el correo aéreo; **~plane**
  el avión; **~port** el aeropuerto
aisle el pasillo; **~ seat** el asiento
  de pasillo
allergic alérgico; **~ reaction**
  la reacción alérgica
allow v permitir
alone solo
alter v **(clothing)** hacer un arreglo
alternate route el otro camino
aluminum foil el papel de
  aluminio

amazing increíble
ambulance la ambulancia
American estadounidense
amusement park el parque de
  atracciones
anemic anémico
anesthesia la anestesia
animal el animal
ankle el tobillo
antibiotic el antibiótico
antiques store la tienda de
  antigüedades
antiseptic cream la crema
  antiséptica
anything algo
apartment el apartamento
appendix (body part) el apéndice
appetizer el aperitivo
appointment la cita
arcade el salón de juegos
  recreativos
area code el prefijo
arm el brazo
aromatherapy la aromaterapia
around (the corner) doblando (la
  esquina)
arrivals (airport) las llegadas
arrive v llegar
artery la arteria
arthritis la artritis
arts las letras
Asian asiático
aspirin la aspirina
asthmatic asmático
ATM el cajero automático
attack el asalto
attend v asistir

adj	adjective	**BE**	British English	**v**	verb
adv	adverb	**n**	noun		

attraction (place) el sitio de
interés
attractive guapo
Australia Australia
Australian australiano
automatic automático;
~ car coche automático
available disponible

B

baby el bebé; ~ bottle el biberón;
~ wipe la toallita; ~sitter el/la
canguro
back la espalda; ~ache el dolor
de espalda; ~pack la mochila
bag la maleta
baggage el equipaje;
~ claim la recogida de
equipajes; ~ ticket el talón de
equipaje
bakery la panadería
ballet el ballet
bandage la tirita
bank el banco
bar el bar
barbecue la barbacoa
barber la peluquería de caballeros
baseball el béisbol
basket (grocery store) la cesta
basketball el baloncesto
bathroom el baño
battery (car) la batería
battery la pila
battleground el campo de batalla
be v ser, estar
beach la playa
beautiful precioso
bed la cama; ~ and breakfast
la pensión
begin v empezar

before antes de
beginner principiante
behind detrás de
beige beis
belt el cinturón
berth la litera
best el/la mejor
better mejor
bicycle la bicicleta
big grande
bigger más grande
bike route el sendero para
bicicletas
bikini el biquini;
~ wax la depilación de las ingles
bill v (charge) cobrar;
~ n (money) el billete;
~ n (of sale) el recibo
bird el pájaro
birthday el cumpleaños
black negro
bladder la vejiga
bland soso
blanket la manta
bleed v sangrar
blood la sangre; ~ pressure
la tensión arterial
blouse la blusa
blue azul
board v embarcar
boarding pass la tarjeta de
embarque
boat el barco
bone el hueso
book el libro; ~store la librería
boots las botas
boring aburrido
botanical garden el jardín
botánico
bother v molestar

187

bottle la botella; **~ opener** el abrebotellas
bowl el cuenco
box la caja
boxing match la pelea de boxeo
boy el niño; **~friend** el novio
bra el sujetador
bracelet la pulsera
brakes (car) los frenos
break v romper
break-in (burglary) el allanamiento de morada
breakdown la avería
breakfast el desayuno
breast el seno; **~feed** dar el pecho
breathe v respirar
bridge el puente
briefs (clothing) los calzoncillos
bring v traer
British británico
broken roto
brooch el broche
broom la escoba
brother el hermano
brown marrón
bug el insecto
building el edificio
burn v **(CD)** grabar
bus el autobús; **~ station** la estación de autobuses;
~ stop la parada de autobús;
~ ticket el billete de autobús;
~ tour el recorrido en autobús
business los negocios;
~ card la tarjeta de negocios;
~ center el centro de negocios;
~ class la clase preferente;
~ hours el horario de atención al público
butcher el carnicero

buttocks las nalgas
buy v comprar
bye adiós

C

cabaret el cabaré
cabin (house) la cabaña;
~ (ship) el camarote
cable car el teleférico
cafe la cafetería
call v llamar; **~** n la llamada
calories las calorías
camera la cámara;
digital ~ la cámara digital;
~ case la funda para la cámara;
~ store la tienda de fotografía
camp v acampar; **~ stove** el hornillo; **~site** el cámping
can opener el abrelatas
Canada Canadá
Canadian canadiense
cancel v cancelar
candy el caramelo
canned goods las conservas
canyon el cañón
car el coche; **~ hire [BE]** el alquiler de coches;
~ park [BE] el aparcamiento;
~ rental el alquiler de coches;
~ seat el asiento de niño
carafe la garrafa
card la tarjeta; **ATM ~** la tarjeta de cajero automático;
credit ~ la tarjeta de crédito;
debit ~ la tarjeta de débito;
phone ~ la tarjeta telefónica
carry-on (piece of hand luggage) el equipaje de mano
cart (grocery store) el carrito;
~ (luggage) el carrito para el equipaje

carton el cartón; ~ **of cigarettes** el cartón de tabaco

case (amount) la caja

cash v cobrar; ~ n el efectivo; ~ **advance** sacar dinero de la tarjeta

cashier el cajero

casino el casino

castle el castillo

cathedral la catedral

cave la cueva

CD el CD

cell phone el teléfono móvil

Celsius el grado centígrado

centimeter el centímetro

certificate el certificado

chair la silla; ~ **lift** la telesilla

change v (buses) cambiar; ~ n (money) el cambio

charcoal el carbón

charge v (credit card) cobrar; ~ n (cost) el precio

cheap barato

cheaper más barato

check v (on something) revisar; ~ v (luggage) facturar; ~ n (payment) el cheque; ~-in (airport) la facturación; ~-in (hotel) el registro; ~ing account la cuenta corriente; ~-out (hotel) la salida

Cheers! ¡Salud!

chemical toilet el váter químico

chemist [BE] la farmacia

cheque [BE] el cheque

chest (body part) el pecho; ~ **pain** el dolor de pecho

chewing gum el chicle

child el niño; ~ **seat** la silla para niños

children's menu el menú para niños

children's portion la ración para niños

Chinese chino

chopsticks los palillos chinos

church la iglesia

cigar el puro

cigarette el cigarrillo

class la clase; **business** ~ la clase preferente; **economy** ~ la clase económica; **first** ~ la primera clase

classical music la música clásica

clean v limpiar; ~ adj limpio; ~ing **product** el producto de limpieza; ~ing **supplies** los productos de limpieza

clear v (on an ATM) borrar

cliff el acantilado

cling film [BE] el film transparente

close v (a shop) cerrar

closed cerrado

clothing la ropa; ~ **store** la tienda de ropa

club la discoteca

coat el abrigo

coffee shop la cafetería

coin la moneda

colander el escurridor

cold n (sickness) el catarro; ~ adj (temperature) frío

colleague el compañero de trabajo

cologne la colonia

color el color

comb el peine

come v venir

complaint la queja

computer el ordenador

concert el concierto; ~ **hall** la sala de conciertos

condition (medical) el estado de salud

conditioner el suavizante

condom el preservativo

conference la conferencia

confirm v confirmar

congestion la congestión

connect v (internet) conectarse

connection (internet) la conexión; ~ (flight) la conexión de vuelo

constipated estreñido

consulate el consulado

consultant el consultor

contact v ponerse en contacto con

contact lens la lentilla de contacto; ~ solution el líquido de lentillas de contacto

contagious contagioso

convention hall el salón de congresos

conveyor belt la cinta transportadora

cook v cocinar

cooking gas el gas butano

cool (temperature) frío

copper el cobre

corkscrew el sacacorchos

cost v costar

cot el catre

cotton el algodón

cough v toser; ~ n la tos

country code el código de país

cover charge la entrada

crash v (car) estrellarse

cream (ointment) la pomada

credit card la tarjeta de crédito

crew neck el cuello redondo

crib la cuna

crystal el cristal

cup la taza

currency la moneda; ~ exchange el cambio de divisas; ~ exchange office la casa de cambio

current account [BE] la cuenta corriente

customs las aduanas

cut v (hair) cortar; ~ n (injury) el corte

cute mono

cycling el ciclismo

D

damage v causar daño

damaged ha sufrido daños

dance v bailar; ~ club la discoteca

dangerous peligroso

dark oscuro

date (calendar) la fecha

day el día

deaf sordo

debit card la tarjeta de débito

deck chair la tumbona

declare v declarar

decline v (credit card) rechazar

deeply hondo

degrees (temperature) los grados

delay v retrasarse

delete v (computer) borrar

delicatessen la charcutería

delicious delicioso

denim tela vaquero

dentist el dentista

denture la dentadura

deodorant el desodorante

department store los grandes almacenes

departures (airport) las salidas

deposit *v* depositar; ~ *n* **(bank)** el depósito bancario; ~ *v* **(reserve a room)** la fianza
desert el desierto
dessert el postre
detergent el detergente
develop *v* **(film)** revelar
diabetic diabético
dial *v* marcar
diamond el diamante
diaper el pañal
diarrhea la diarrea
diesel el diesel
difficult difícil
digital digital; ~ **camera** la cámara digital; ~ **photos** las fotos digitales; ~ **prints** las fotos digitales
dining room el comedor
dinner la cena
direction la dirección
dirty sucio
disabled discapacitado; ~ **accessible [BE]** el acceso para discapacitados
discharge (bodily fluid) la secreción
disconnect (computer) desconectar
discount el descuento
dish (kitchen) el plato; ~**washer** el lavavajillas; ~**washing liquid** el líquido lavavajillas
display *v* mostrar; ~ **case** la vitrina
disposable desechable; ~ **razor** la cuchilla desechable
dive *v* bucear
diving equipment el equipo de buceo
divorce *v* divorciar
dizzy mareado

doctor el médico
doll la muñeca
dollar (U.S.) el dólar
domestic nacional; ~ **flight** el vuelo nacional
door la puerta
dormitory el dormitorio
double bed la cama de matrimonio
downtown el centro
dozen la docena
drag lift el telesquí
dress (piece of clothing) el vestido; ~ **code** las normas de vestuario
drink *v* beber; ~ *n* la bebida; ~ **menu** la carta de bebidas; ~**ing water** el agua potable
drive *v* conducir
driver's license number el número de permiso de conducir
drop (medicine) la gota
drowsiness la somnolencia
dry cleaner la tintorería
dubbed doblada
during durante
duty (tax) el impuesto; ~**-free** libre de impuestos
DVD el DVD

E

ear la oreja; ~**ache** el dolor de oído
earlier más temprano
early temprano
earrings los pendientes
east el este
easy fácil
eat *v* comer
economy class la clase económica
elbow el codo
electric outlet el enchufe eléctrico

elevator el ascensor

e-mail *v* enviar un correo electrónico; ~ *n* el correo electrónico; ~ **address** la dirección de correo electrónico

emergency la emergencia; ~ **exit** la salida de urgencia

empty *v* vaciar

enamel (jewelry) el esmalte

end *v* terminar

English el inglés

engrave *v* grabar

enjoy *v* disfrutar

enter *v* entrar

entertainment el entretenimiento

entrance la entrada

envelope el sobre

equipment el equipo

escalators las escaleras mecánicas

e-ticket el billete electrónico

EU resident el/la residente de la UE

euro el euro

evening la noche

excess el exceso

exchange *v* (money) cambiar; ~ *v* (goods) devolver; ~ *n* (place) la casa de cambio; ~ **rate** el tipo de cambio

excursion la excursión

excuse *v* (to get past) pedir perdón; ~ *v* (to get attention) disculparse

exhausted agotado

exit *v* salir; ~ *n* la salida

expensive caro

expert (skill level) experto

exposure (film) la foto

express rápido; ~ **bus** el autobús rápido; ~ **train** el tren rápido

extension (phone) la extensión

extra adicional; ~ **large** equis ele (XL)

extract *v* (tooth) extraer

eye el ojo

eyebrow wax la depilación de cejas

F

face la cara

facial la limpieza de cutis

family la familia

fan (appliance) el ventilador; ~ (souvenir) el abanico

far lejos; ~-sighted hipermétrope

farm la granja

fast rápido; ~ **food** la comida rápida

faster más rápido

fat free sin grasa

father el padre

fax *v* enviar un fax; ~ *n* el fax; ~ **number** el número de fax

fee la tasa

feed *v* alimentar

ferry el ferry

fever la fiebre

field (sports) el campo

fill *v* llenar ; ~ **out** *v* (form) rellenar

filling (tooth) el empaste

film (camera) el carrete

fine (fee for breaking law) la multa

finger el dedo; ~**nail** la uña del dedo

fire fuego; ~ **department** los bomberos; ~ **door** la puerta de incendios

first primero; ~ **class** la primera clase

fit (clothing) quedar bien

fitting room el probador

fix *v* (repair) reparar
flashlight la linterna
flight el vuelo
floor el suelo
flower la flor
folk music la música folk
food la comida
foot el pie
football [BE] el fútbol
for para/por
forecast el pronóstico
forest el bosque
fork el tenedor
form el formulario
formula (baby) la fórmula infantil
fort el fuerte
fountain la fuente
free gratuito
freezer el congelador
fresh fresco
friend el amigo
frying pan la sartén
full completo;
~-service el servicio completo;
~-time a tiempo completo

G

game el partido
garage (parking) el garaje;
~ (repair) el taller
garbage bag la bolsa de basura
gas la gasolina; ~ station la
gasolinera
gate (airport) la puerta
gay gay; ~ bar el bar gay;
~ club la discoteca gay
gel (hair) la gomina
get to *v* ir a
get off *v* (a train/bus/subway)
bajarse

gift el regalo; ~ shop la tienda
de regalos
girl la niña; ~friend la novia
give *v* dar
glass (drinking) el vaso;
~ (material) el vidrio
glasses las gafas
go *v* (somewhere) ir a
gold el oro
golf golf; ~ course el campo
de golf; ~ tournament el torneo
de golf
good *n* el producto; ~ *adj* bueno;
~ afternoon buenas tardes;
~ evening buenas noches;
~ morning buenos días;
~bye adiós
gram el gramo
grandchild el nieto
grandparent el abuelo
gray gris
green verde
grocery store el supermercado
ground la tierra; ~ floor la
planta baja; ~cloth la tela
impermeable
group el grupo
guide el guía; ~ book la guía;
~ dog el perro guía
gym el gimnasio
gynecologist el ginecólogo

H

hair el pelo; ~ dryer el secador
de pelo; ~ salon la peluquería;
~brush el cepillo de pelo;
~cut el corte de pelo; ~spray
la laca; ~style el peinado;
~stylist el estilista
half medio; ~ hour la media
hora; ~-kilo el medio kilo

hammer el martillo
hand la mano; ~ **luggage [BE]** el equipaje de mano; ~**bag [BE]** el bolso
handicapped discapacitado; ~-**accessible** el acceso para discapacitados
hangover la resaca
happy feliz
hat el sombrero
have v tener
head (body part) la cabeza; ~**ache** el dolor de cabeza; ~**phones** los cascos
health la salud; ~ **food store** la tienda de alimentos naturales
heart el corazón; ~ **condition** padecer del corazón
heat v calentar; ~ n el calor
heater [heating BE] la calefacción
hello hola
helmet el casco
help v ayudar; ~ n la ayuda
here aquí
hi hola
high alto; ~**chair** la trona; ~**way** la autopista
hiking boots las botas de montaña
hill la colina
hire v **[BE]** alquilar; ~ **car [BE]** el coche de alquiler
hitchhike v hacer autostop
hockey el hockey
holiday [BE] las vacaciones
horse track el hipódromo
hospital el hospital
hostel el albergue
hot (temperature) caliente; ~ **(spicy)** picante; ~ **spring**

el agua termale; ~ **water** el agua caliente
hotel el hotel
hour la hora
house la casa; ~**hold goods** los artículos para el hogar; ~**keeping services** el servicio de limpieza de habitaciones
how (question) cómo; ~ **much (question)** cuánto cuesta
hug v abrazar
hungry hambriento
hurt v **(have pain)** tener dolor
husband el marido

I

ibuprofen el ibuprofeno
ice el hielo; ~ **hockey** el hockey sobre hielo
icy helado
identification el documento de identidad
ill v **(to feel)** encontrarse mal
in dentro
include v incluir
indoor pool la piscina cubierta
inexpensive barato
infected infectado
information (phone) el número de teléfono de información; ~ **desk** el mostrador de información
insect el insecto; ~ **bite** la picadura de insecto; ~ **repellent** el repelente de insectos
insert v introducir
insomnia el insomnio
instant message el mensaje instantáneo
insulin la insulina

insurance el seguro; **~ card**
la tarjeta de seguro; **~ company**
la compañía de seguros
interesting interesante
intermediate el nivel intermedio
international (airport area)
internacional; **~ flight** el vuelo
internacional; **~ student card**
la tarjeta internacional de
estudiante
internet la internet; **~ cafe**
el cibercafé; **~ service**
el servicio de internet; **wireless ~**
el acceso inalámbrico
interpreter el/la intérprete
intersection el cruce
intestine el intestino
introduce v presentar
invoice [BE] la factura
Ireland Irlanda
Irish irlandés
iron v planchar; **~** n (clothes)
la plancha
Italian italiano

J

jacket la chaqueta
jar el bote
jaw la mandíbula
jazz el jazz; **~ club** el club de jazz
jeans los vaqueros
jet ski la moto acuática
jeweler la joyería
jewelry las joyas
join v acompañar a
joint (body part) la articulación

K

key la llave; **~ card** la llave
electrónica; **~ ring** el llavero

kiddie pool la piscina infantil
kidney (body part) el riñón
kilo el kilo; **~gram** el kilogramo;
~meter el kilómetro
kiss v besar
kitchen la cocina; **~ foil [BE]**
el papel de aluminio
knee la rodilla
knife el cuchillo

L

lace el encaje
lactose intolerant alérgico a la
lactosa
lake el lago
large grande; **~er** más grande
last último
late (time) tarde; **~er** más tarde
launderette [BE] la lavandería
laundromat la lavandería
laundry la colada; **~ facility**
la lavandería; **~ service**
el servicio de lavandería
lawyer el abogado
leather el cuero
to leave v salir
left (direction) la izquierda
leg la pierna
lens la lente
less menos
lesson la lección
letter la carta
library la biblioteca
life la vida; **~ jacket** el chaleco
salvavidas; **~guard** el socorrista
lift n [BE] el ascensor;
~ v (to give a ride) llevar en
coche; **~ pass** el pase de acceso
a los remontes

light *n* (overhead) la luz;
~ *v* (cigarette) dar fuego;
~bulb la bombilla
lighter el mechero
like *v* gustar; I like me gusta
line (train) la línea
linen el lino
lip el labio
liquor store la tienda de bebidas
alcohólicas
liter el litro
little pequeño
live *v* vivir
liver (body part) el hígado
loafers los mocasines
local de la zona
lock *v* cerrar; ~ *n* el cerrojo
locker la taquilla
log on *v* (computer) iniciar
sesión
log off *v* (computer) cerrar
sesión
long largo; ~ sleeves
las mangas largas;
~-sighted [BE] hipermétrope
look *v* mirar
lose *v* (something) perder
lost perdido; ~ and found
la oficina de objetos perdidos
lotion la crema hidratante
louder más alto
love *v* querer; ~ *n* el amor
low bajo; ~er más bajo
luggage el equipaje; ~ cart
el carrito de equipaje; ~ locker
la consigna automática; ~ ticket
el talón de equipaje; hand ~ [BE]
el equipaje de mano
lunch la comida
lung el pulmón

M

magazine la revista
magnificent magnífico
mail *v* enviar por correo;
~ *n* el correo; ~box el buzón de
correo
main principal; ~ attractions
los principales sitios de interés;
~ course el plato principal
make up a prescription *v* [BE]
despachar medicamentos
mall el centro comercial
man el hombre
manager el gerente
manicure la manicura
manual car el coche con
transmisión manual
map el mapa
market el mercado
married casado
marry *v* casarse
mass (church service) la misa
massage el masaje
match la cerilla
meal la comida
measure *v* (someone) medir
measuring cup la taza medidora
measuring spoon la cuchara
medidora
mechanic el mecánico
medicine el medicamento
medium (size) mediano
meet *v* (someone) conocer
meeting la reunión; ~ room
la sala de reuniones
membership card la tarjeta de
socio
memorial (place) el monumento
conmemorativo
memory card la tarjeta de memoria

mend v zurcir
menstrual cramps los dolores menstruales
menu la carta
message el mensaje
meter (parking) el parquímetro
microwave el microondas
midday [BE] el mediodía
midnight la medianoche
mileage el kilometraje
mini-bar el minibar
minute el minuto
missing desaparecido
mistake el error
mobile móvil; ~ **home** la caravana; ~ **phone [BE]** el teléfono móvil
mobility la movilidad
money el dinero
month el mes
mop la fregona
moped el ciclomotor
more más
morning la mañana
mosque la mezquita
mother la madre
motion sickness el mareo
motor el motor; ~ **boat** la lancha motora; ~ **cycle** la motocicleta; ~ **way [BE]** la autopista
mountain la montaña; ~ **bike** la bicicleta de montaña
mousse (hair) la espuma para el pelo
mouth la boca
movie la película; ~ **theater** el cine
mug v asaltar
muscle (body part) el músculo
museum el museo
music la música; ~ **store** la tienda de música

N

nail la uña; ~ **file** la lima de uñas; ~ **salon** el salon de manicura
name el nombre
napkin la servilleta
nappy [BE] el pañale
nationality la nacionalidad
nature preserve la reserva natural
(be) nauseous v tener náuseas
near cerca; ~**-sighted** miope; ~**by** cerca de aquí
neck el cuello
necklace el collar
need v necesitar
newspaper el periódico
newsstand el quiosco
next próximo
nice amable
night la noche; ~**club** la discoteca
no no
non sin; ~**-alcoholic** sin alcohol; ~**-smoking** para no fumadores
noon el mediodía
north el norte
nose la nariz
note [BE] el billete
nothing nada
notify v avisar
novice (skill level) principiante
now ahora
number el número
nurse el enfermero/la enfermera

O

office la oficina; ~ **hours (doctor's)** las horas de consulta; ~ **hours (other offices)** el horario de oficina

off-licence [BE] la tienda de bebidas alcohólicas

oil el aceite

OK de acuerdo

old viejo

on the corner en la esquina

once una vez

one uno; **~-way ticket** el billete de ida; **~-way street** la calle de sentido único

only solamente

open v abrir; **~** adj abierto

opera la ópera; **~ house** el teatro de la ópera

opposite frente a

optician el oculista

orange (color) naranja

orchestra la orquesta

order v pedir

outdoor pool la piscina exterior

outside fuera

over sobre; **~ the counter (medication)** sin receta; **~look (scenic place)** el mirador; **~night** por la noche

oxygen treatment la oxígenoterapia

P

p.m. de la tarde

pacifier el chupete

pack v hacer las maletas

package el paquete

paddling pool [BE] la piscina infantil

pad [BE] la compresa

pain el dolor

pajamas los pijamas

palace el palacio

pants los pantalones

pantyhose las medias

paper el papel; **~ towel** el papel de cocina

paracetamol [BE] el paracetamol

park v aparcar; **~** n el parque; **~ing garage** el párking; **~ing lot** el aparcamiento

parliament building el palacio de las cortes

part (for car) la pieza; **~-time** a tiempo parcial

pass through v estar de paso

passenger el pasajero

passport el pasaporte; **~ control** el control de pasaportes

password la contraseña

pastry shop la pastelería

path el camino

pay v pagar; **~ phone** el teléfono público

peak (of a mountain) la cima

pearl la perla

pedestrian el peatón

pediatrician el pediatra

pedicure la pedicura

pen el bolígrafo

penicillin la penicilina

penis el pene

per por; **~ day** por día; **~ hour** por hora; **~ night** por noche; **~ week** por semana

perfume el perfume

period (menstrual) la regla; **~ (of time)** la época

permit v permitir

petite las tallas pequeñas

petrol la gasolina; **~ station** la gasolinera

pewter el peltre

pharmacy la farmacia

phone v hacer una llamada;
~ n el teléfono; ~ **call** la llamada
de teléfono; ~ **card** la tarjeta
telefónica; ~ **number** el número de
teléfono

photo la foto; ~**copy** la fotocopia;
~**graphy** la fotografía

pick up v (something) recoger

picnic area la zona para picnic

piece el trozo

Pill (birth control) la píldora

pillow la almohada

**personal identification number
(PIN)** la clave

pink rosa

piste [BE] la pista; ~ **map [BE]**
el mapa de pistas

pizzeria la pizzería

place v (a bet) hacer una apuesta

plane el avión

plastic wrap el film transparente

plate el plato

platform [BE] (train) el andén

platinum el platino

play v jugar; ~ n (theater) la obra
de teatro; ~**ground** el patio de
recreo; ~**pen** el parque

please por favor

pleasure el placer

plunger el desatascador

plus size la talla grande

pocket el bolsillo

poison el veneno

poles (skiing) los bastones

police la policía; ~ **report** el
certificado de la policía;
~ **station** la comisaría

pond el estanque

pool la piscina

pop music la música pop

portion la ración

post [BE] el correo;
~ **office** la oficina de correos;
~**box [BE]** el buzón de correos;
~**card** la tarjeta postal

pot la olla

pottery la cerámica

pounds (British sterling)
las libras esterlinas

pregnant embarazada

prescribe v recetar

prescription la receta

press v (clothing) planchar

price el precio

print v imprimir

problem el problema

produce las frutas y verduras;
~ **store** la frutería y verdulería

prohibit v prohibir

pronounce v pronunciar

public el público

pull v (door sign) tirar

purple morado

purse el bolso

push v (door sign) empujar;
~**chair [BE]** el cochecito de niño

Q

quality la calidad

question la pregunta

quiet tranquilo

R

racetrack el circuito de carreras

racket (sports) la raqueta

railway station [BE] la estación
de trenes

rain la lluvia; ~**coat** el chubasquero;
~**forest** el bosque pluvial;
~**y** lluvioso

rap (music) el rap
rape v violar; ~ n la violación
rash la erupción cutánea
razor blade la hoja de afeitar
reach v localizar
ready listo
real auténtico
receipt el recibo
receive v recibir
reception la recepción
recharge v recargar
recommend v recomendar
recommendation la recomendación
recycle v reciclar
red rojo
refrigerator la nevera
region la región
registered mail el correo
  certificado
regular normal
relationship la relación
rent v alquilar
rental car el coche de alquiler
repair v arreglar
repeat v repetir
reservation la reserva;
  ~ desk la taquilla
reserve v reservar
restaurant el restaurante
restroom el servicio
retired jubilado
return v (something) devolver;
  ~ n [BE] la ida y vuelta
rib (body part) la costilla
right (direction) derecha;
  ~ of way prioridad de paso
ring el anillo
river el río
road map el mapa de carreteras
rob v atracar

robbed atracado
romantic romántico
room la habitación; ~ key la llave
  de habitación; ~ service el servicio
  de habitaciones
round-trip ida y vuelta
route la ruta
rowboat la barca de remos
rubbish [BE] la basura; ~ bag
  [BE]
  la bolsa de basura
rugby el rubgy
ruins las ruinas
rush la prisa

S

sad triste
safe n la caja fuerte; ~ adj seguro
sales tax el IVA
same mismo
sandals las sandalias
sanitary napkin la compresa
saucepan el cazo
sauna la sauna
save v (computer) guardar
savings (account) la cuenta de
  ahorro
scanner el escáner
scarf la bufanda
schedule v programar;
  ~ n el horario
school el colegio
science la ciencia
scissors las tijeras
sea el mar
seat el asiento
security la seguridad
see v ver
self-service el autoservicio

sell *v* vender
seminar el seminario
send *v* enviar
senior citizen jubilado
separated (marriage) separado
serious serio
service (in a restaurant) el servicio
sexually transmitted disease (STD) la enfermedad de transmisión sexual
shampoo el champú
sharp afilado
shaving cream la crema de afeitar
sheet la sábana
ship *v* enviar
shirt la camisa
shoe store la zapatería
shoes los zapatos
shop *v* comprar
shopping ir de compras;
~ area la zona de compras;
~ centre [BE] el centro comercial;
~ mall el centro comercial
short corto; ~ sleeves las mangas cortas;
~s los pantalones cortos;
~-sighted [BE] miope
shoulder el hombro
show *v* enseñar
shower la ducha
shrine el santuario
sick enfermo
side el lado;
~ dish la guarnición;
~ effect el efecto secundario;
~ order la guarnición
sightsee *v* hacer turismo
sightseeing tour el recorrido turístico
sign *v* (name) firmar

silk la seda
silver la plata
single (unmarried) soltero; ~ bed la cama; ~ prints una copia;
~ room una habitación individual
sink el lavabo
sister la hermana
sit *v* sentarse
size la talla
skin la piel
skirt la falda
ski *v* esquiar; ~ *n* el esquí;
~ lift el telesquí
sleep *v* dormir; ~er car el coche cama; ~ing bag el saco de dormir
slice *v* cortar en rodajas
slippers las zapatillas
slower más despacio
slowly despacio
small pequeño
smaller más pequeño
smoke *v* fumar
smoking (area) la zona de fumadores
snack bar la cafetería
sneakers las zapatillas de deporte
snorkeling equipment el equipo de esnórquel
snow la nieve; ~board la tabla de snowboard; ~shoe la raqueta de nieve; ~y nevado
soap el jabón
soccer el fútbol
sock el calcetín
some alguno
soother [BE] el chupete
sore throat las anginas
sorry lo siento
south el sur

souvenir el recuerdo; **~ store** la tienda de recuerdos
spa el centro de salud y belleza
Spain España
Spanish el español
spatula la espátula
speak v hablar
special (food) la especialidad de la casa
specialist (doctor) el especialista
specimen el ejemplar
speeding el exceso de velocidad
spell v deletrear
spicy picante
spine (body part) la columna vertebral
spoon la cuchara
sports los deportes; **~ massage** el masaje deportivo
sporting goods store la tienda de deportes
sprain el esguince
square cuadrado; **~ kilometer** el kilómetro cuadrado; **~ meter** el metro cuadrado
stadium el estadio
stairs las escaleras
stamp v (a ticket) picar; **~ n (postage)** el sello
start v empezar
starter [BE] el aperitivo
station la estación; **bus ~** la estación de autobuses; **gas ~** la gasolinera; **muster ~ [BE]** el punto de reunión; **petrol ~ [BE]** la gasolinera; **subway ~** el metro; **train ~** la estación de tren
statue la estatua
stay v quedarse
steal v robar
steep empinado

sterling silver la plata esterlina
sting el escozor
stolen robado
stomach el estómago; **~ache** el dolor de estómago
stop v pararse; **~ n** la parada
store directory la guía de tiendas
storey [BE] la planta
stove el horno
straight recto
strange extraño
stream el arroyo
stroller el cochecito
student el estudiante
study v estudiar
studying estudiando
stunning impresionante
subtitle el subtítulo
subway el metro; **~ station** la estación de metro
suit el traje
suitcase la maleta
sun el sol; **~block** el protector solar total; **~burn** la quemadura solar; **~glasses** las gafas de sol; **~ny** soleado; **~screen** el protector solar; **~stroke** la insolación
super (fuel) súper; **~market** el supermercado
surfboard la tabla de surf
surgical spirit [BE] el alcohol etílico
swallow v tragar
sweater el jersey
sweatshirt la sudadera
sweet (taste) dulce; **~s [BE]** los caramelos
swelling la hinchazón
swim v nadar; **~suit** el bañador

symbol (keyboard) el símbolo
synagogue la sinagoga

T

table la mesa
tablet (medicine)
  el comprimido
take v llevar; ~ away [BE] para
  llevar
tampon el tampón
tapas bar el bar de tapas
taste v probar
taxi el taxi
team el equipo
teaspoon la cucharadita
telephone el teléfono
temple (religious) el templo
temporary provisional
tennis el tenis
tent la tienda de campaña;
  ~ peg la estaca; ~ pole
  el mástil
terminal (airport) la terminal
terracotta la terracotta
terrible terrible
text v (send a message) enviar
  un mensaje de texto;
  ~ n (message) el texto
thank v dar las gracias a;
  ~ you gracias
that eso
theater el teatro
theft el robo
there ahí
thief el ladrón
thigh el muslo
thirsty sediento
this esto
throat la garganta

ticket el billete; ~ office
  el despacho de billetes; ~ed
  passenger el pasajero con billete
tie (clothing) la corbata
time el tiempo; ~table [BE]
  el horario
tire la rueda
tired cansado
tissue el pañuelo de paper
tobacconist el estanco
today hoy
toe el dedo del pie; ~nail la uña
  del pie
toilet [BE] el servicio;
  ~ paper el papel higiénico
tomorrow mañana
tongue la lengua
tonight esta noche
too demasiado
tooth el diente; ~brush el cepillo
  de dientes; ~paste la pasta de
  dientes
total (amount) el total
tough (food) duro
tourist el turista; ~ information
  office la oficina de turismo
tour el recorrido turístico
tow truck la grúa
towel la toalla
tower la torre
town la ciudad; ~ hall
  el ayuntamiento; ~ map el mapa
  de ciudad; ~ square la plaza
toy el juguete; ~ store la tienda
  de juguetes
track (train) el andén
traditional tradicional
traffic light el semáforo
trail la pista; ~ map el mapa de
  la pista

trailer el remolque
train el tren; ~ station
la estación de tren
transfer v cambiar
translate v traducir
trash la basura
travel v viajar; ~ agency
la agencia de viajes;
~ sickness el mareo;
~er's check [cheque BE]
el cheque de viaje
tree el árbol
trim (hair cut) cortarse las
puntas
trip el viaje
trolley [BE] el carrito
trousers [BE] los pantalones
T-shirt la camiseta
turn off v apagar
turn on v encender
TV la televisión
type v escribir a máquina
tyre [BE] la rueda

United Kingdom (U.K.) el Reino
Unido
United States (U.S.) los Estados
Unidos
ugly feo
umbrella el paraguas
unattended desatendido
unbranded medication [BE]
el fármaco genérico
unconscious inconsciente
underground [BE] el metro;
~ station [BE] la estación de
metro
underpants [BE] los calzoncillos
understand v entender

underwear la ropa interior
university la universidad
unleaded (gas) la gasolina sin
plomo
upper superior
urgent urgente
use v usar
username el nombre de usuario
utensil el cubierto

vacancy la habitación libre
vacation las vacaciones
vaccination la vacuna
vacuum cleaner la aspiradora
vagina la vagina
vaginal infection la infección
vaginal
valid validez
valley el valle
valuable valioso
value el valor
VAT [BE] el IVA
vegetarian vegetariano
vehicle registration el registro
del coche
viewpoint [BE] el mirador
village el pueblo
vineyard la viña
visa (passport document)
el visado
visit v visitar; ~ing hours
el horario de visita
visually impaired la persona con
discapacidad visual
vitamin la vitamina
V-neck el cuello de pico
volleyball game el partido de
voleibol
vomit v vomitar

W

wait v esperar; ~ n la espera;
~**ing room** la sala de espera
waiter el camarero
waitress la camarera
wake v despertarse; ~**-up call**
la llamada despertador
walk v caminar; ~ n la caminata;
~**ing route** la ruta de senderismo
wall clock el reloj de pared
wallet la cartera
warm v (something) calentar;
~ *adj* (temperature) calor
washing machine la lavadora
watch el reloj
water skis los esquís acuáticos
waterfall la cascada
weather el tiempo
week la semana; ~**end** el fin de
semana; ~**ly** semanal
welcome v acoger
well bien; ~**-rested** descansado
west el oeste
what (question) qué
wheelchair la silla de ruedas;
~ **ramp** la rampa para silla de
ruedas
when (question) cuándo
where (question) dónde
white blanco; ~ **gold** el oro blanco
who (question) quién
widowed viudo

wife la mujer
window la ventana; ~ **case**
el escaparate
windsurfer el surfista
wine list la carta de vinos
wireless inalámbrico; ~ **internet**
el acceso inalámbrico a internet;
~ **internet service** el servicio
inalámbrico a internet; ~ **phone**
el teléfono móvil
with con
withdraw v retirar;
~**al** (bank) retirar fondos
without sin
woman la mujer
wool la lana
work v trabajar
wrap v envolver
wrist la muñeca
write v escribir

Y

year el año
yellow amarillo; ~ **gold** el oro
amarillo
yes sí
yesterday ayer
young joven
youth hostel el albergue juvenil

Z

zoo el zoológico

Spanish–English Dictionary

A

a tiempo completo full-time
a tiempo parcial part-time
la abadía abbey
el abanico fan (souvenir)
abierto *adj* open
el abogado lawyer
abrazar *v* hug
el abrebotellas bottle opener
el abrelatas can opener
el abrigo coat
abrir *v* open
el abuelo grandparent
aburrido boring
acampar *v* camp
el acantilado cliff
el acceso access;
  ~ inalámbrico a internet
  wireless internet; **~ para
  discapacitados** handicapped-
  [disabled- BE] accessible
el accidente accident
el aceite oil
aceptar *v* accept
acoger *v* welcome
acompañar a *v* join
la acupuntura acupuncture
el adaptador adapter
adicional extra
adiós goodbye
las aduanas customs
el aeropuerto airport
afilado sharp
la agencia agency; **~ de
  viajes** travel agency
agotado exhausted

el agua water; **~ caliente** hot
  water; **~ potable** drinking water
las aguas termales hot spring
ahí there
ahora now
el aire air, air pump;
  ~ acondicionado air conditioning
el albergue hostel;
  ~ juvenil youth hostel
alérgico allergic;
  ~ a la lactosa lactose intolerant
algo anything
el algodón cotton
alguno some
alimentar *v* feed
el allanamiento de morada
  break-in (burglary)
la almohada pillow
el alojamiento accommodation
alquilar *v* rent [hire BE];
  el ~ de coches car rental
  [hire BE]
alto high
amable nice
amarillo yellow
la ambulancia ambulance
el amigo friend
el amor *n* love
el andén track [platform BE]
  (train)
anémico anemic
la anestesia anesthesia
las anginas sore throat
el anillo ring
el animal animal
antes de before
el antibiótico antibiotic
el año year
apagar *v* turn off
el aparcamiento parking lot
  [car park BE]

aparcar *v* park
el apartamento apartment
el apéndice appendix (body part)
el aperitivo appetizer [starter BE]
aquí here
el árbol tree
la aromaterapia aromatherapy
arreglar *v* repair
el arroyo stream
la arteria artery
la articulación joint (body part)
los artículos goods; **~ para el hogar** household good
la artritis arthritis
asaltar *v* mug
el asalto attack
el ascensor elevator [lift BE]
asiático Asian
el asiento seat; **~ de niño** car seat; **~ de pasillo** aisle seat
asistir *v* attend
asmático asthmatic
la aspiradora vacuum cleaner
la aspirina aspirin
atracado robbed
atracar *v* rob
Australia Australia
australiano Australian
auténtico real
el autobús bus; **~ rápido** express bus
automático automatic
la autopista highway [motorway BE]
el autoservicio self-service
la avería breakdown
el avión airplane, plane
avisar *v* notify
ayer yesterday
la ayuda *n* help
ayudar *v* help

el ayuntamiento town hall
azul blue

B

bailar *v* dance
bajarse *v* get off (a train, bus, subway)
bajo low
el ballet ballet
el baloncesto basketball
el bálsamo para después del afeitado aftershave
el banco bank
el bañador swimsuit
el baño bathroom
el bar bar; **~ de tapas** tapas bar; **~ gay** gay bar
barato cheap, inexpensive
la barbacoa barbecue
la barca de remos rowboat
el barco boat
los bastones poles (skiing)
la basura trash [rubbish BE]
la batería battery (car)
el bebé baby
beber *v* drink
la bebida *n* drink
beis beige
el béisbol baseball
besar *v* kiss
el biberón baby bottle
la biblioteca library
la bicicleta bicycle; **~ de montaña** mountain bike
el billete *n* bill (money); **~** ticket; **~ de autobús** bus ticket; **~ de ida** one-way (ticket); **~ de ida y vuelta** round trip [return BE]; **~ electrónico** e-ticket
el biquini bikini
blanco white

la blusa blouse
la boca mouth
el bolígrafo pen
la bolsa de basura garbage [rubbish BE] bag
el bolsillo pocket
el bolso purse [handbag BE]
los bomberos fire department
la bombilla lightbulb
borrar v clear (on an ATM); ~ v delete (computer)
el bosque forest; ~ pluvial rainforest
las botas boots; ~ de montaña hiking boots
el bote jar
la botella bottle
el brazo arm
británico British
el broche brooch
bucear to dive
bueno *adj* good
buenas noches good evening
buenas tardes good afternoon
buenos días good morning
la bufanda scarf
el buzón de correo mailbox [postbox BE]

C

la cabaña cabin (house)
el cabaré cabaret
la cabeza head (body part)
la cafetería cafe, coffee shop, snack bar
la caja case (amount); ~ fuerte *n* safe
el cajero cashier; ~ automático ATM
el calcetín sock
la calefacción heater [heating BE]

calentar *v* heat, warm
la calidad quality
la calle de sentido único one-way street
calor hot, warm (temperature)
las calorías calories
los calzoncillos briefs [underpants BE] (clothing)
la cama single bed; ~ de matrimonio double bed
la cámara camera; ~ digital digital camera
la camarera waitress
el camarero waiter
el camarote cabin (ship)
cambiar *v* change, exchange, transfer
el cambio *n* change (money); ~ de divisas currency exchange
caminar *v* walk
la caminata *n* walk
el camino path
la camisa shirt
la camiseta T-shirt
el cámping campsite
el campo field (sports); ~ de batalla battleground; ~ de golf golf course
Canadá Canada
canadiense Canadian
cancelar *v* cancel
el/la canguro babysitter
cansado tired
el cañón canyon
la cara face
los caramelos candy [sweets BE]
la caravana mobile home
el carbón charcoal
el carnicero butcher
caro expensive
el carrete film (camera)

el carrito cart [trolley BE] (grocery store); ~ de equipaje luggage cart

la carta letter

la carta menu; ~ de bebidas drink menu; ~ para niños children's menu; ~ de vinos wine list

la cartera wallet

el cartón carton; ~ de tabaco carton of cigarettes

la casa house; ~ de cambio currency exchange office

casado married

casarse v marry

la cascada waterfall

el casco helmet

los cascos headphones

el casino casino

el castillo castle

el catarro cold (sickness)

la catedral cathedral

el catre cot

causar daño v damage

el cazo saucepan

el CD CD

la cena dinner

el centímetro centimeter

el centro downtown area; ~ comercial shopping mall [centre BE]; ~ de negocios business center; ~ de salud y belleza spa

el cepillo de pelo hair brush

la cerámica pottery

cerca near; ~ de aquí nearby

la cerilla n match

cerrado closed

cerrar v close, lock; ~ sesión v log off (computer)

el cerrojo n lock

el certificado certificate; ~ de la policía police report

la cesta basket (grocery store)

el chaleco salvavidas life jacket

el champú shampoo

la chaqueta jacket

la charcutería delicatessen

el cheque n check [cheque BE] (payment); ~ de viaje traveler's check [cheque BE]

el chicle chewing gum

chino Chinese

el chubasquero raincoat

el chupete pacifier [soother BE]

el cibercafé internet cafe

el ciclismo cycling

el ciclomotor moped

la ciencia science

el cigarrillo cigarette

la cima peak (of a mountain)

el cine movie theater

la cinta transportadora conveyor belt

el cinturón belt

el circuito de carreras racetrack

la cita appointment

la ciudad town

la clase class; ~ económica economy class; ~ preferente business class

la clave personal identification number (PIN)

el club de jazz jazz club

cobrar v bill (charge); ~ v cash; ~ v charge (credit card)

el cobre copper

el coche car; ~ de alquiler rental [hire BE] car; ~ automático automatic car; ~ cama sleeper [sleeping BE] car; ~ con transmisión manual manual car

el cochecito stroller [pushchair BE]

la cocina kitchen
cocinar v cook
el código de país country code
el codo elbow
la colada laundry
el colegio school
la colina hill
el collar necklace
la colonia cologne
el color color
la columna vertebral spine (body part)
el comedor dining room
comer v eat
la comida food, lunch, meal; **~ rápida** fast food
la comisaría police station
cómo how
el compañero de trabajo colleague
la compañía company; **~ aérea** airline; **~ de seguros** insurance company
comprar v buy, shop
la compresa sanitary napkin [pad BE]
el comprimido tablet (medicine)
con with; **~ plomo** leaded (gas)
el concierto concert
conducir v drive
conectarse v connect (internet)
la conexión connection (internet); **~ de vuelo** connection (flight)
la conferencia conference
confirmar v confirm
el congelador freezer
la congestión congestion
conocer v meet (someone)
la consigna automática luggage locker

el consulado Consulate
el consultor consultant
contagioso contagious
la contraseña password
el control de pasaportes passport control
el corazón heart
la corbata tie (clothing)
el correo n mail [post BE]; **~ aéreo** airmail; **~ certificado** registered mail; **~ electrónico** n e-mail
cortar v cut (hair); **~ en rodajas** to slice
cortarse las puntas v trim (hair cut)
el corte n cut (injury); **~ de pelo** haircut
corto short
costar v cost
la costilla rib (body part)
la crema cream; **~ antiséptica** antiseptic cream; **~ de afeitar** shaving cream; **~ hidratante** lotion
el cristal crystal
el cruce intersection
cuándo when (question)
cuánto cuesta how much
el cubierto utensil
la cuchara spoon; **~ medidora** measuring spoon
la cucharadita teaspoon
la cuchilla desechable disposable razor
el cuchillo knife
el cuello neck; **~ de pico** V-neck; **~ redondo** crew neck
el cuenco bowl
la cuenta account; **~ de ahorro** savings account; **~ corriente** checking [current BE] account
cuero leather
la cueva cave

el cumpleaños birthday
la cuna crib

D

dar to give; **~ el pecho** breastfeed;
~ fuego light (cigarette);
~ las gracias a v thank
de from, of; **~ acuerdo** OK;
~ la mañana a.m.; **~ la tarde**
p.m.; **~ la zona** local
declarar v declare
el dedo finger; **~ del pie** toe
dolotroor v opoll
delicioso delicious
la dentadura denture
el dentista dentist
dentro in
la duplluolon wax;
~ de cejas eyebrow wax;
~ de las ingles bikini wax
deportes sports
depositar v deposit
el depósito bancario deposit (bank)
la derecha right (direction)
desaparecido missing
el desatascador plunger
desatendido unattended
el desayuno breakfast
descansado well-rested
desconectar v disconnect
(computer)
el descuento discount
desechable disposable
el desierto desert
el desodorante deodorant
despachar medicamentos
v fill [make up BE] a prescription
el despacho de billetes ticket office
despacio slowly
despertarse v wake

después after
el detergente detergent
detrás de behind (direction)
devolver v exchange, return
(goods)
el día day
diabético diabetic
el diamante diamond
la diarrea diarrhea
el diente tooth
el diesel diesel
difícil difficult
digital digital
el dinero money
la dirección direction
la dirección address;
~ de correo electrónico
e-mail address
discapacitado handicapped
[disabled BE]
la discoteca club (dance, night);
~ gay gay club
disculparse v excuse (to get
attention)
disfrutar v enjoy
disponible available
divorciar v divorce
doblada dubbed
doblando (la esquina) around
(the corner)
la docena dozen
**el documento de
Identidad** Identification
el dólar dollar (U.S.)
el dolor pain; **~ de
cabeza** headache; **~ de
espalda** backache; **~ de
estómago** stomachache;
~ de oído earache; **~ de pecho**
chest pain

los dolores menstruales menstrual cramps

dónde where (question)

dormir *v* sleep

el dormitorio dormitory

la ducha shower

dulce sweet (taste)

durante during

el DVD DVD

E

la edad age

el edificio building

el efectivo cash

el efecto secundario side effect

el ejemplar specimen

embarazada pregnant

embarcar *v* board

la emergencia emergency

el empaste filling (tooth)

empezar *v* begin, start

empinado steep

empujar *v* push (door sign)

en la esquina on the corner

el encaje lace

encender *v* turn on

el enchufe eléctrico electric outlet

encontrarse mal *v* be ill

la enfermedad de transmisión sexual sexually transmitted disease (STD)

el enfermero/la enfermera nurse

enfermo sick

enseñar *v* show

entender *v* understand

la entrada admission/cover charge; ~ entrance

entrar *v* enter

el entretenimiento entertainment

enviar *v* send, ship; ~ **por correo** *v* mail; ~ **un correo electrónico** *v* e-mail; ~ **un fax** *v* fax ; ~ **un mensaje de texto** *v* text (send a message)

envolver *v* wrap

la época period (of time)

el equipaje luggage [baggage BE]; ~ **de mano** carry-on (piece of hand luggage)

el equipo team

el equipo equipment; ~ **de buceo** diving equipment; ~ **de esnórquel** snorkeling equipment

equis ele (XL) extra large

el error mistake

la erupción cutánea rash

las escaleras stairs; ~ **mecánicas** escalators

el escáner scanner

el escaparate window case

la escoba broom

el escozor sting

escribir *v* write; ~ **a máquina** *v* type

el escurridor colander

el esguince sprain

el esmalte enamel (jewelry)

eso that

la espalda back

España Spain

el español Spanish

la espátula spatula

la especialidad de la casa special (food)

el especialista specialist (doctor)

la espera *n* wait

esperar *v* wait

la espuma para el pelo mousse (hair)

el esquí *n* ski

esquiar *v* ski

los esquís acuáticos water skis

esta noche tonight

la estaca tent peg

la estación station;
~ de autobuses bus station;
~ de metro subway [underground BE] station; ~ de tren train [railway BE] station

el estadio stadium

el estado de salud condition (medical)

los Estados Unidos United States (U.S.)

estadounidense American

el estanco tobacconist

el estanque pond

estar *v* be; ~ de paso *v* pass through

la estatua statue

el este east

el estilista hairstylist

esto this

el estómago stomach

estrellarse *v* crash (car)

estreñido constipated

estudiando studying

el estudiante student

estudiar *v* study

el euro euro

el exceso excess; ~ de velocidad speeding

la excursión excursion

experto expert (skill level)

la extensión extension (phone)

extraer *v* extract (tooth)

extraño strange

F

fácil easy

la factura bill [invoice BE]

la facturación check-in (airport)

facturar check (luggage)

la falda skirt

la familia family

la farmacia pharmacy [chemist BE]

el fax *n* fax

la fecha date (calendar)

feliz happy

feo ugly

el ferry ferry

la fianza deposit (to reserve a room)

la fiebre fever

el film transparente plastic wrap [cling film BE]

el fin de semana weekend

firmar *v* sign (name)

la flor flower

la fórmula infantil formula (baby)

el formulario form

la foto exposure (film); ~ photo;
~copia photocopy;
~grafía photography;
~ digital digital photo

la fregona mop

los frenos brakes (car)

frente a opposite

fresco fresh

frío cold (temperature)

las frutas y verduras produce

la frutería y verdulería produce store

el fuego fire

la fuente fountain

fuera outside

el fuerte fort

fumar *v* smoke

la funda para la cámara camera case

el fútbol soccer [football BE]

las gafas glasses;
~ **de sol** sunglasses

el garaje garage (parking)

la garganta throat

la garrafa carafe

el gas butano cooking gas

la gasolina gas [petrol BE];
~ **sin plomo** unleaded gas

la gasolinera gas [petrol BE] station

gay gay

el gerente manager

el gimnasio gym

el ginecólogo gynecologist

la gomina gel (hair)

la gota drop (medicine)

grabar v burn (CD); ~ v engrave

gracias thank you

los grados degrees (temperature);
~ **centígrado** Celsius

el gramo gram

grande large

los grandes almacenes department store

la granja farm

gratuito free

gris gray

la grúa tow truck

el grupo group

guapo attractive

guardar v save (computer)

la guarnición side dish, order

el guía guide

la guía guide book; ~ **de tiendas** store directory

gustar v like; **me gusta** I like

ha sufrido daños damaged

la habitación room;
~ **individual** single room;
~ **libre** vacancy

hablar v speak

hacer v have; ~ **una apuesta** v place (a bet); ~ **un arreglo** v alter; ~ **una llamada** v phone; ~ **las maletas** v pack; ~ **turismo** sightseeing

hambriento hungry

helado icy

la hermana sister

el hermano brother

el hielo ice

el hígado liver (body part)

la hinchazón swelling

hipermétrope far-sighted [long-sighted BE]

el hipódromo horsetrack

el hockey hockey; ~ **sobre hielo** ice hockey

la hoja de afeitar razor blade

hola hello

el hombre man

el hombro shoulder

hondo deeply

la hora hour

el horario n schedule [timetable BE]

los horarios hours; ~ **de atención al público** business hours; ~ **de oficina** office hours; ~ **de visita** visiting hours

las horas de consulta office hours (doctor's)

el hornillo camp stove

el horno stove

el hospital hospital

el hotel hotel

hoy today
el hueso bone

I

el ibuprofeno ibuprofen
la ida y vuelta round-trip [return BE]
la iglesia church
impresionante stunning
imprimir v print
el impuesto duty (tax)
incluir v include
inconsciente unconscious
increíble amazing
la infección vaginal vaginal infection
infectado infected
el inglés English
iniciar sesión v log on (computer)
el insecto bug
la insolación sunstroke
el insomnio insomnia
la insulina insulin
interesante interesting
internacional international (airport area)
la internet internet
el/la intérprete interpreter
el intestino intestine
introducir v insert
ir a v go (somewhere)
ir de compras v go shopping
Irlanda Ireland
irlandés Irish
el IVA sales tax [VAT BE]
la izquierda left (direction)

J

el jabón soap
el jardín botánico botanical garden
el jazz jazz

el jersey sweater
joven young
las joyas jewelry
la joyería jeweler
jubilado retired
jugar v play
el juguete toy

K

el kilo kilo; ~**gramo** kilogram; ~**metraje** mileage
el kilómetro kilometer; ~ **cuadrado** square kilometer

L

el labio lip
la laca hairspray
el ladrón thief
el lago lake
la lana wool
la lancha motora motor boat
largo long
el lavabo sink
la lavadora washing machine
la lavandería laundromat [launderette BE]
lavar v wash
el lavavajillas dishwasher
la lección lesson
lejos far
la lengua tongue
la lente lens
las lentillas de contacto contact lens
las letras arts
las libras esterlinas pounds (British sterling)
libre de impuestos duty-free
la librería bookstore
el libro book

la lima de uñas nail file
limpiar *v* clean
la limpieza de cutis facial
limpio *adj* clean
la línea line (train)
el lino linen
la linterna flashlight
el líquido liquid; **~ de lentillas de contacto** contact lens solution; **~ lavavajillas** dishwashing liquid
listo ready
la litera berth
el litro liter
la llamada *n* call; **~ de teléfono** phone call; **~ despertador** wake-up call
llamar *v* call
la llave key; **~ de habitación** room key; **~ electrónica** key card
el llavero key ring
las llegadas arrivals (airport)
llegar *v* arrive
llenar *v* fill
llevar *v* take; **~ en coche** lift (to give a ride)
la lluvia rain
lluvioso rainy
lo siento sorry
localizar *v* reach
la luz light (overhead)

M

la madre mother
magnífico magnificent
el malestar estomacal upset stomach
la maleta bag, suitcase
la mandíbula jaw
las mangas cortas short sleeves
las mangas largas long sleeves

la manicura manicure
la mano hand
la manta blanket
mañana tomorrow; **la ~** morning
el mapa map; **~ de carreteras** road map; **~ de ciudad** town map; **~ de la pista** trail [piste BE] map
el mar sea
marcar *v* dial
mareado dizzy
el mareo motion [travel BE] sickness
el marido husband
marrón brown
el martillo hammer
más more; **~ alto** louder; **~ bajo** lower; **~ barato** cheaper; **~ despacio** slower; **~ grande** larger; **~ pequeño** smaller; **~ rápido** faster; **~ tarde** later; **~ temprano** earlier
el masaje massage; **~ deportivo** sports massage
el mástil tent pole
el mecánico mechanic
el mechero lighter
la media hora half hour
mediano medium (size)
la medianoche midnight
el medicamento medicine
el médico doctor
medio half; **~ kilo** half-kilo; **~día** noon [midday BE]
medir *v* measure (someone)
mejor best
menos less
el mensaje message; **~ instantáneo** instant message
el mercado market
el mes month
la mesa table

el metro subway [underground BE]
el metro cuadrado square meter
la mezquita mosque
el microondas microwave
el minibar mini-bar
el minuto minute
el mirador overlook [viewpoint BE]
  (scenic place)
mirar v look
la misa mass (church service)
mismo same
los mocasines loafers
la mochila backpack
molestar v bother
la moneda coin, currency
mono cute
la montaña mountain
el monumento conmemorativo
  memorial (place)
morado purple
el mostrador de información
  information desk
mostrar v display
la moto acuática jet ski
la motocicleta motorcycle
movilidad mobility
la mujer wife, woman
la multa fine (fee for breaking law)
la muñeca doll; ~ wrist
el músculo muscle
el museo museum
la música music; ~ clásica
  classical music; ~ folk folk
  music; ~ pop pop music
el muslo thigh

N

nacional domestic
la nacionalidad nationality
nada nothing

nadar v swim
las nalgas buttocks
naranja orange (color)
la nariz nose
necesitar v need
los negocios business
negro black
nevado snowy
la nevera refrigerator
el nieto grandchild
la niña girl
el niño boy, child
el nivel intermedio intermediate
no no
la noche evening, night
el nombre name;
  ~ de usuario username
normal regular
las normas de vestuario dress code
el norte north
la novia girlfriend
el novio boyfriend
el número number; ~ de fax
  fax number; ~ de permiso
  de conducir driver's license
  number; ~ de teléfono phone
  number; ~ de teléfono de
  información information (phone)

O

la obra de teatro n play (theater)
el oculista optician
el oeste west
la oficina office; ~ de correos
  post office; ~ de objetos
  perdidos lost and found; ~ de
  turismo tourist information office
el ojo eye
la olla pot
la ópera opera
el ordenador computer

la oreja ear
la orina urine
el oro gold; ~ amarillo yellow gold; ~ blanco white gold
la orquesta orchestra
oscuro dark
el otro camino alternate route
la oxígenoterapia oxygen treatment

P

padecer del corazón heart condition
el padre father
pagar v pay
el pájaro bird
el palacio palace; ~ de las cortes parliament building
los palillos chinos chopsticks
la panadería bakery
los pantalones pants [trousers BE]; ~ cortos shorts
el pañal diaper [nappy BE]
el pañuelo de paper tissue
el papel paper; ~ de aluminio aluminum [kitchen BE] foil; ~ de cocina paper towel; ~ higiénico toilet paper
el paquete package
para for; ~ llevar to go [take away BE]; ~ no fumadores non-smoking
el paracetamol acetaminophen [paracetamol BE]
la parada n stop; ~ de autobús bus stop
el paraguas umbrella
pararse v stop
el párking parking garage
el parque playpen; ~ park; ~ de atracciones amusement park

el partido game; ~ de fútbol soccer [football BE]; ~ de voleibol volleyball game
el pasajero passenger; ~ con billete ticketed passenger
el pasaporte passport
el pase de acceso a los remontes lift pass
el pasillo aisle
la pasta de dientes toothpaste
la pastelería pastry shop
el patio de recreo playground
el peatón pedestrian
el pecho chest (body part)
el pediatra pediatrician
la pedicura pedicure
pedir v order
el peinado hairstyle
el peine comb
la película movie
peligroso dangerous
el pelo hair
el peltre pewter
la peluquería de caballeros barber
la peluquería hair salon
los pendientes earrings
el pene penis
la penicilina penicillin
la pensión bed and breakfast
pequeño small
perder v lose (something)
perdido lost
el perfume perfume
el periódico newspaper
la perla pearl
permitir v allow, permit
el perro guía guide dog
la persona con discapacidad visual visually impaired person

la **picadura de insecto** insect bite
picante spicy
picar *v* stamp (a ticket)
el **pie** foot
la **piel** skin
la **pierna** leg
la **pieza** part (for car)
los **pijamas** pajamas
la **pila** battery
la **píldora** Pill (birth control)
la **piscina** pool; ~ **cubierta** indoor
pool; ~ **exterior** outdoor pool;
~ **infantil** kiddie [paddling BE]
pool
la **pista** trail [piste BE]
la **pizzería** pizzeria
el **placer** pleasure
la **plancha** *n* iron (clothes)
planchar *v* iron
la **planta** floor [storey BE];
~ **baja** ground floor
la **plata** silver;
~ **esterlina** sterling silver
el **platino** platinum
el **plato** dish (kitchen);
~ **principal** main course
la **playa** beach
la **plaza** town square
la **policía** police
la **pomada** cream (ointment)
ponerse en contacto con
v contact
por for; ~ per; ~ **día** per day;
~ **favor** please; ~ **hora** per hour;
~ **la noche** overnight; ~ **noche**
per night; ~ **semana** per week
el **postre** dessert
el **precio** price
precioso beautiful
el **prefijo** area code
la **pregunta** question

presentar *v* introduce
el **preservativo** condom
la **primera clase** first class
primero first
los **principales sitios de**
interés main attraction
principiante beginner, novice
(skill level)
la **prioridad de paso** right of way
la **prisa** rush
el **probador** fitting room
probar *v* taste
el **problema** problem
el **producto** good;
~ **de limpieza** cleaning product
programar *v* schedule
prohibir *v* prohibit
el **pronóstico** forecast
pronunciar *v* pronounce
el **protector solar** sunscreen
provisional temporary
próximo next
el **público** public
el **pueblo** village
el **puente** bridge
la **puerta** gate (airport); ~ door;
~ **de incendios** fire door
el **pulmón** lung
la **pulsera** bracelet
el **puro** cigar

Q

qué what (question)
quedar bien *v* fit (clothing)
quedarse *v* stay
la **queja** complaint
la **quemadura solar** sunburn
querer *v* love (someone)
quién who (question)
el **quiosco** newsstand

R

la **ración** portion; ~ **para niños** children's portion
la **rampa para silla de ruedas** wheelchair ramp
el **rap** rap (music)
rápido express, fast
la **raqueta** racket (sports); ~ **de nieve** snowshoe
la **reacción alérgica** allergic reaction
recargar v recharge
la **recepción** reception
la **receta** prescription
recetar v prescribe
rechazar v decline (credit card)
recibir v receive
el **recibo** receipt
reciclar recycling
recoger v pick up (something)
la **recogida de equipajes** baggage claim
la **recomendación** recommendation
recomendar v recommend
el **recorrido** tour; ~ **en autobús** bus tour; ~ **turístico** sightseeing tour
recto straight
el **recuerdo** souvenir
el **regalo** gift
la **región** region
el **registro** check-in (hotel); ~ **del coche** vehicle registration
la **regla** period (menstrual)
el **Reino Unido** United Kingdom (U.K.)
la **relación** relationship
rellenar v fill out (form)
el **reloj** watch; ~ **de pared** wall clock

el **remolque** trailer
reparar v fix (repair)
el **repelente de insectos** insect repellent
repetir v repeat
la **resaca** hangover
la **reserva** reservation; ~ **natural** nature preserve
reservar v reserve
el/la **residente de la UE** EU resident
respirar v breathe
el **restaurante** restaurant
retirar v withdraw; ~ **fondos** withdrawal (bank)
retrasarse v delay
la **reunión** meeting
revelar v develop (film)
revisar v check (on something)
la **revista** magazine
el **riñón** kidney (body part)
el **río** river
robado stolen
robar v steal
el **robo** theft
la **rodilla** knee
rojo red
romántico romantic
romper v break
la **ropa** clothing; ~ **interior** underwear
rosa pink
roto broken
el **rubgy** rugby
la **rueda** tire [tyre BE]; ~ **pinchada** flat tire [tyre BE]
las **ruinas** ruins
la **ruta** route; ~ **de senderismo** walking route

la sábana sheet
el sacacorchos corkscrew
el saco de dormir sleeping bag
la sala room; **~ de conciertos** concert hall; **~ de espera** waiting room; **~ de reuniones** meeting room
la salida check-out (hotel)
la salida *n* exit; **~ de urgencia** emergency exit
las salidas departures (airport)
salir *v* exit, leave
el salón room; **~ de congresos** convention hall; **~ de juegos recreativos** arcade; **~ de manicura** nail salon
¡Salud! Cheers!
la salud health
las sandalias sandals
sangrar *v* bleed
la sangre blood
el santuario shrine
la sartén frying pan
la sauna sauna
el secador de pelo hair dryer
la secreción discharge (bodily fluid)
la seda silk
sediento thirsty
la seguridad security
el seguro insurance
seguro safe (protected)
el sello *n* stamp (postage)
el semáforo traffic light
la semana week
semanal weekly
el seminario seminar
el sendero trail; **~ para bicicletas** bike route
el seno breast

sentarse *v* sit
separado separated (marriage)
ser *v* be
serio serious
el servicio restroom [toilet BE]; **~** service (in a restaurant); **~ completo** full-service; **~ de habitaciones** room service; **~ inalámbrico a internet** wireless internet service; **~ de internet** internet service; **~ de lavandería** laundry service; **~ de limpieza de habitaciones** housekeeping service
la servilleta napkin
sí yes
el SIDA AIDS
la silla chair; **~ para niños** child seat; **~ de ruedas** wheelchair
el símbolo symbol (keyboard)
sin without; **~ alcohol** non-alcoholic; **~ grasa** fat free; **~ receta** over the counter (medication)
la sinagoga synagogue
el sitio de interés attraction (place)
el sobre envelope
el socorrista lifeguard
el sol sun
solamente only
soleado sunny
solo alone
soltero single (marriage)
el sombrero hat
la somnolencia drowsiness
sordo deaf
soso bland
el suavizante conditioner
el subtítulo subtitle
sucio dirty
la sudadera sweatshirt
el suelo floor

el sujetador bra

súper super (fuel)

superior upper

el supermercado grocery store, supermarket

la supervisión supervision

el sur south

el surfista windsurfer

T

la tabla board; **~ de snowboard** snowboard; **~ de surf** surfboard

la talla size; **~ grande** plus size; **~ pequeña** petite size

el taller garage (repair)

el talón de equipaje luggage [baggage BE] ticket

el tampón tampon

la taquilla locker; **~** reservation desk

tarde late (time)

la tarde afternoon

la tarjeta card; **~ de cajero automático** ATM card; **~ de crédito** credit card; **~ de débito** debit card; **~ de embarque** boarding pass; **~ internacional de estudiante** international student card; **~ de memoria** memory card; **~ de negocios** business card; **~ postal** postcard; **~ de seguro** insurance card; **~ de socio** membership card; **~ telefónica** phone card

la tasa fee

el taxi taxi

la taza cup; **~ medidora** measuring cup

el teatro theater; **~ de la ópera** opera house

la tela impermeable groundcloth [groundsheet BE]

el teleférico cable car

el teléfono telephone; **~ móvil** cell [mobile BE] phone; **~ público** pay phone

la telesilla chair lift

el telesquí ski/drag lift

la televisión TV

el templo temple (religious)

temprano early

el tenedor fork

tener v have; **~ dolor** v hurt (have pain); **~ náuseas** v be nauseous

el tenis tennis

la tensión arterial blood pressure

la terminal terminal (airport)

terminar v end

la terracotta terracotta

terrible terrible

el texto n text (message)

el tiempo time; **~** weather

la tienda store; **~ de alimentos naturales** health food store; **~ de antigüedades** antique store; **~ de bebidas alcohólicas** liquor store [off-licence BE]; **~ de campaña** tent; **~ de deportes** sporting goods store; **~ de fotografía** camera store; **~ de juguetes** toy store; **~ de música** music store; **~ de recuerdos** souvenir store; **~ de regalos** gift shop; **~ de ropa** clothing store

las tijeras scissors

la tintorería dry cleaner

el tipo de cambio exchange rate

tirar v pull (door sign)

la tirita bandage

la toalla towel

la toallita baby wipe

el tobillo ankle

el torneo de golf golf tournament